MOBILE HOME ENERGY AND REPAIR GUIDE

BY JOHN T. KRIGGER

WITH GRAPHICS
BY ROBERT C. STARKEY

Saturn Resource Management, Helena, Montana 1992

Sponsored By:
The U.S. Department of Energy
Weatherization Assistance Program
Western Area Power Administration
Pennsylvania Energy Office

DEDICATION: To my parents, Don and Ann Krigger and to 13 million Americans and Canadians living in manufactured homes.

ACKNOWLEDGEMENTS

Technical Contributors

Rob DeSoto, State of Colorado, Division of Housing, Denver CO
Rick Hanger, Sunpower Consumer Association, Wheatridge, CO
Butch Huizinga, BG's Mobile Home & RV Repair, Helena, MT
Ron Judkoff, Solar Energy Research Institute, Golden, CO
Jim Kleyman, Delray Beach, FL
Leon Neal, North Carolina Alternative Energy Corp., Research Triangle Park, NC
The Staff of the National Center for Appropriate Technology, Butte, MT
George Porter, Manufactured Housing Resources, Nassua, ME
Maureen Shaughnessy, Native Design, Helena, MT
Cal Steiner and the Weatherization Crew of Dickinson CAP, Dickinson, ND

Technical Consultants

Jim and Randy Annis, Lily Pond Manufactured Housing, Gilford, NH
Jim Cummings, Florida Solar Energy Center, Cape Canaveral, FL
Rudy Leatherman, Corporation for Ohio Appalachian Development, Athens, OH
Bob Marx, Nordyne Corporation, St. Louis, MO
Clint McKie, Manufactured Housing Services, Carlsbad, NM
Gary Nelson, The Energy Conservatory, Minneapolis, MN
John Tooley, Natural Florida Retrofit Inc., Montverde, FL

The author also thanks the following:

Energy Resource Center, University of Illinois at Chicago for permission to adapt and reprint graphics from: <u>Mobile Home Retrofit Handbook</u>, by Paul A. Knight, May 1985.

National Center for Appropriate Technology and Bonneville Power Administration for permission to adapt and reprint information from: <u>Mobile Home Weatherization: A Guidebook for Installers</u> including illustrations by Chester Hansen.

This book was edited and produced by:
Saturn Resource Management, 324 Fuller, Suite S-8, Helena, MT 59601.
Cover Design: Robert Starkey
Editing: Raelen Williard, Leonard Sander
Computer Support: Jerry Spencer
Photography: John Krigger
Printed by: Comstock Graphics, Helena, MT and Century Lithographers, Helena, MT
Copyright © 1992 John T. Krigger
All rights reserved.

CONTENTS

INTRODUCTION

HOW TO USE THIS GUIDE

GETTING STARTED 1

1.1 Introduction 1
    1.1.1 Selecting Repair Projects 1
    1.1.2 Selecting Weatherization Projects 1
    1.1.3 History of Mobile Homes 2
1.2 Codes and Standards 3
1.3 Mobile Home Research 5
1.4 Mobile Home Construction 7
    1.4.1 What Makes a Mobile Home Different 7
    1.4.2 Mobile Home Manufacturing 8
1.5 Foundations and Installation 8
    1.5.1 Introduction 9
    1.5.2 Drainage and Site Preparation 10
    1.5.3 Foundations 11
    1.5.4 Installing Anchors 13
    1.5.5 Installation Procedures 14
    1.5.6 Leveling a Mobile Home 14
    1.5.7 Installing a Ground Cover 15
    1.5.8 Skirting 15
1.6 Landscaping 17
    1.6.1 General Climatic Considerations 18
    1.6.2 Orientation 20
    1.6.3 How Plants Affect Microclimate and Energy 20
1.7 Moisture and Ventilation 22
1.8 Exhaust Fans and Dehumidifiers 24
1.9 Indoor Air Quality 25

ENVELOPES 130

2.1 Introduction to Mobile Home Envelopes 27
2.2 Air Leakage Control 27
    2.2.1 Blower Door Testing 28
2.3 Insulation Methods and Materials 30
    2.3.1 R-Values 30
    2.3.2 Natural Air Changes, Moisture, and Ventilation 31
    2.3.3 Fiberglass Insulation 31
    2.3.4 Polystyrene Beads 32
    2.3.5 Cellulose Blowing Material 33
    2.3.6 Rigid Foam Board 33

CONTENTS

    2.3.7 Blowing Insulation 33
    2.3.8 Radiant Barriers/Reflective Coatings 35
2.4 Floors 35
    2.4.1 Introduction To Floors 35
    2.4.2 What To Look For 36
    2.4.3 Design and Construction Characteristics 37
    2.4.4 Repairs to the Floor Area 38
    2.4.5 Insulating Floors 39
2.5 Walls 41
    2.5.1 Design and Construction Characteristics 41
    2.5.2 What To Look For 42
    2.5.3 Wall Insulation and Moisture 42
    2.5.4 Wall Repair and Renovation 43
    2.5.5 Wall Insulation 43
        2.5.5.1 Blowing Insulation Into Wall Cavities 44
        2.5.5.2 Stuffing Fiberglass Insulation 45
        2.5.5.3 Removing Exterior Siding 46
2.6 Roofs 48
    2.6.1 Design and Construction Characteristics 48
    2.6.2 Moisture and Roof Insulation 48
    2.6.3 Safety and Roof Insulation 49
    2.6.4 Rooftop Insulation 50
        2.6.4.1 Insulated Rubber Roof Cap 50
        2.6.4.2 Sprayed Urethane Roof Cap 52
        2.6.4.3 Metal Roof Caps 53
    2.6.5 Roof Cavity Insulation 53
    2.6.6 Sealing the Ceiling 54
    2.6.7 Roof Repair 55
2.7 Doors 57
    2.7.1 Design and Construction Characteristics 57
    2.7.2 Doors - What to Look For 57
    2.7.3 Weatherstripping Doors 58
    2.7.4 Replacing Doors 59
2.8 Windows 60
    2.8.1 Design and Construction Characteristics 60
    2.8.2 Prime Windows 61
    2.8.3 Storm Windows 61
    2.8.4 Windows - What to Look For 63
    2.8.5 Windows and Condensation 63
    2.8.6 Repairing Windows 64
    2.8.7 Replacing Windows 65

CONTENTS

HEATING SYSTEMS 67

3.1 Heating Systems 67
3.2 Fuel-Burning Furnaces 67
    3.2.1 Natural Gas and Propane Furnaces 68
    3.2.2 Oil Burning Furnaces 69
3.3 Heating Controls 71
    3.3.1 Burner Controls 72
    3.3.2 Fan Controls and Furnace Operating Temperatures 72
    3.3.3 Automatic Thermostats 73
3.4 Air Circulation and Distribution 74
    3.4.1 Improving Supply and Return Air Systems 76
    3.4.2 Cleaning the Blower and Heat Exchanger 78
3.5 Electric Furnaces 79
3.6 Heat Pumps 81
3.7 Zone Heating 82
3.8 Wood Heat Safety 83

SUMMER COOLING 87

4.1 Summer Cooling 87
4.2 Shading 87
    4.2.1 Window Films, Reflecting Glass, and Interior Window Treatments 88
    4.2.2 Sun Screens 89
    4.2.3 Awnings 89
4.3 Air Circulation and Ventilation 90
4.4 Air Conditioning 91
    4.4.1 Introduction to Air Conditioners 92
    4.4.2 Packaged Air Conditioners 93
    4.4.3 Split-System Air Conditioners 95
    4.4.4 Central Air Conditioning Controls 96
    4.4.5 Distribution Systems 97
    4.4.6 Room Air Conditioners 98
    4.4.7 Energy Ratings of Air Conditioners 100
4.5 Evaporative Coolers 100
    4.5.1 Installation 101
    4.5.2 Maintenance 101
4.6 Refrigerators 102

PLUMBING AND ELECTRICAL 103

5.1 Introduction 103
5.2 Water Heating Systems 103
    5.2.1 Water Heating - What to Look For 104

CONTENTS

    5.2.2 Setting Hot Water Temperature 105
    5.2.3 Maintenance 105
    5.2.4 Cleaning a Water Heater 106
    5.2.5 Tank/Closet Insulation 107
    5.2.6 Pipe Insulation 108
    5.2.7 Low-Flow Showerheads 108
    5.2.8 Purchasing a Water Heater 108
5.3 Plumbing Systems 109
    5.3.1 Supply Piping 109
    5.3.2 Drains, Traps, and Vents 110
    5.3.3 Plumbing Leaks 111
5.4 Electrical Systems 112
    5.4.1 Service Equipment and Feeder Wires 112
    5.4.2 Branch and Appliance Circuits 114
    5.4.3 Grounding 114
    5.4.4 Testing 115
    5.4.5 Special Safety Precautions 115
GLOSSARY 117
APPENDIX A, Businesses and Organizations 122
APPENDIX B, Fire Safety 123
APPENDIX C, Suggestions for Moving Mobile Homes 124
APPENDIX D, Maintenance Tips 125
APPENDIX E, Energy Cost Index Chart 126
APPENDIX F, Mobile Home Energy Rating 127
APPENDIX G, Estimated Costs for Labor and Materials for Improvements 128
APPENDIX H, Foundation Design Reference 130
APPENDIX I, Energy Project Summary 130
BIBLIOGRAPHY 134
INDEX 135

INTRODUCTION

Your Mobile Home Energy and Repair Guide presents energy conservation measures and repair procedures specifically adapted to mobile homes for all U.S. climates. This information is condensed from the collective experience of dozens of expert technicians in the fields of weatherization, mobile home repair, and mobile home heating and cooling. This guide also relies strongly on the research done by the United States Department of Energy (DOE) and others.

This manual is about manufactured homes which are designed to particular engineering standards, and built in long, narrow sections on steel trailers with wheels and axles. The term "mobile home" was coined in the fifties to distinguish larger manufactured houses, designed as permanent, stationary homes, from the smaller and more vehicular house trailer. The term, "mobile home" is used in this manual to mean a manufactured home built on a trailer (hereafter called a "chassis") and designed to be delivered over the road to a permanent location, either as a single- or multiple-section unit.

This guidebook is written for repair service technicians, weatherization technicians, park owners, and also for home owners who are interested in improving their mobile homes. It contains specific instructions for energy conservation and repair work along with general information about choosing and purchasing various improvements. There is also quite a bit of background and reference information on topics like: foundations, codes, costs of improvements, and plumbing and electrical matters, among others.

Of the approximately eight million mobile homes in service today, three million were built in the 1980s and 1990s and five million were built in the 1960s and 1970s. Mobile homes comprise about 10% of all the single family housing in the United States but in many rural areas they are more than 50% of single-family housing. Nearly 13 million people live in mobile homes in the United States and Canada.

Mobile homes, especially used ones, offer a great resource for affordable housing. Used homes are for sale at dealers and repossession lots for as little as $1000. Buyers should be cautious however, because these older units may require extensive repair and weatherization to bring them up to modern stands of comfort and energy efficiency. Still, the low purchase price may allow the buyer to invest in necessary repairs and weatherization. You should never invest money in a new or used home unless you will have enough money left to install the home properly, on a good foundation.

"Weatherization" consists of home improvement projects that reduce energy consumption and increase comfort. "Repair" means to put something that has deteriorated or been damaged back in good condition. Weatherization and repair projects in mobile homes are closely related to each other because many of the energy conservation problems of mobile homes relate to their parts being damaged or deteriorated.

In spite of their affordability and popularity, there has been a lack of accurate and clear information about how to repair and weatherize mobile homes. Most publications related to home repair, renovation, and energy conservation are written for site-built homes. Mobile homes are different from site-built homes in many ways including: foundations; construction details; windows and doors; plumbing; and their specialized heating systems and cooling systems that meet standards listed in the United States Department of Housing and Urban Development (HUD) mobile home construction code.

The author hopes that Your Mobile Home Energy and Repair Guide will help to fill the information gap on mobile/manufactured homes and will encourage improvements in the comfort, safety, energy efficiency, and physical repair of these homes.

HOW TO USE THIS GUIDE

This guidebook is divided into five sections: Getting Started; Envelopes; Heating Systems; Summer Cooling; and Plumbing and Electrical. The first section, Getting Started, covers topics such as: mobile home research, construction, foundations, setup, landscaping, moisture, and ventilation. The second section, Envelopes, discusses air leakage, repair procedures, and weatherization techniques related to walls, floors, and ceilings. The third section, Heating Systems, addresses the operation, repair, and maintenance of heating systems. The fourth section, titled Summer Cooling, discusses both mechanical and non-mechanical strategies for staying cool in the summer months. The last section, Plumbing and Electrical, gives general information about mobile home plumbing and electrical equipment including water heating.

Use the table of contents to familiarize yourself with the organization and to find sections relating to your particular interests. Use the index at the end of the manual to pinpoint information about very specific questions and interests. An extensive glossary is included to provide a quick reference to unfamiliar terms. The bibliography includes references, mentioned in the text, and books suggested for additional reading.

An appendix is a summary of information, or a piece of information that is too specific to fit comfortably in the body of the book. The appendixes include: Related Businesses and Organizations; Fire Safety; Suggestions for Moving Mobile Homes; Maintenance Tips for Mobile Homes; Foundation Design Reference; Energy Cost Index; Mobile Home Energy Rating; Estimated Costs of Selected Retrofits for Mobile Homes; and an Energy Project Summary.

Because information in one section may be related to another section there are numerous cross references in parentheses like this: (See Section #?). All illustrations are referenced in the text like this: (see figure #). **Important points that stand out as being essential are written in bold.** *Caution:* *Pay attention to the important safety information presented throughout the book in this format.*

The information presented here relates directly to energy conservation measures and repair procedures that are unique to mobile homes. This guidebook will not cover subjects like: using tools, understanding electricity, or general construction techniques because there are already many books available about these subjects available at libraries and bookstores.

Use this guidebook as a reference, a decision-making tool, instruction manual, and as a way to understand the operation, maintenance, and repair of your home. The book's special focus is, of course, on energy conservation.

The key to using this manual is to attempt only those tasks that you feel confident that you can perform. For example, you should not attempt to move a mobile home unless you are familiar with blocking, jacking, and hauling large loads. Electrical service work should only be done by technicians that have the understanding and confidence that come from training and experience.

However, even you home owners and park owners, who will not be performing any of your own service work, will find this guide as a valuable way to educate yourself as a consumer. If you know more about maintenance, repair, and energy conservation, you'll make better decisions about the service work you purchase.

NOTE: Additional copies of this guide can be ordered on the postage-paid reply form at the back of the book. We plan to reprint this book periodically and would like your opinion on how we can improve it and make it more useful for you. Please send us your comments or suggestions on the postage-paid reply form at the back of the book.

GETTING STARTED

1.1 Introduction

1.1.1 Selecting Repair Projects

The soundness of the foundation and of the structure of the walls, floor, and ceiling are the most important priorities to maintaining the value and livability of a home. Any weakness or damage to these areas should be the first repair priorities. Plumbing leaks, roof leaks, and site-related moisture problems share this top priority because they can severely damage the structure. Electrical and heating problems are urgent problems because they affect the health and safety of the residents. Repair priorities and procedures are discussed throughout this manual in the sections relating to particular parts of the home. For example, look for floor repairs in Section 2.4, Floors and look for plumbing repairs in Section 5.3, Plumbing Systems.

1.1.2 Selecting Weatherization Projects

If you live in a mobile home that has high energy costs, you should determine the most efficient and cost-effective ways to lower those costs. "Cost-effective" means that the predicted energy savings will pay back the expenses for an improvement within a reasonable period of time. The weatherization measures discussed in this book will generally pay for themselves in two to ten years if they are used under the proper circumstances. To decide what measures to perform, you should:

1. Identify your problem areas;
2. Identify possible repair and weatherization solutions to those problems;
3. Determine the cost of all of your project options;
4. Decide which projects to do; and
5. Decide which projects to do yourself and which ones require special skills and equipment.

Prioritize your weatherization project options and complete the most urgent and cost-effective projects first. This guidebook will help you develop the decision-making skills necessary to decide which projects are the most cost-effective based on the funds available. There are six major factors that should guide your choice of repair and weatherization measures and how much money you can cost-effectively spend on each measure.

1. Climate - If all other factors are identical, a homeowner in Duluth, Minnesota, can cost-effectively spend about twice as much on weatherization as a homeowner in St. Louis, Missouri. Duluth is approximately twice as cold as St. Louis, so measures that reduce heating consumption are twice as cost-effective. A homeowner in Miami can cost-effectively spend about double what a homeowner in St. Louis spends on cooling measures because Miami is approximately twice as warm.

2. Energy Cost - If energy costs are twice in one location what they are in another, then you could cost-effectively spend about twice as much money on an energy conservation measure in the more expensive location as you could where energy costs are less. (see Appendix F, Energy Cost Index Chart.)

3. Existing Conditions - The more severe the problem, the more it pays to tackle it. Adding insulation to an uninsulated wall is far more cost-effective than adding insulation to an already insulated wall. Patching a large hole in the belly of a mobile home is more cost-effective than caulking a small crack around a window.

GETTING STARTED

4. Energy Usage - The more energy a mobile home owner uses, the more money that can be cost-effectively spent to reduce the high consumption. (see Appendix F, Energy Rating for Mobile Homes.)

5. Project Cost - The cost of various energy conservation measures varies widely from place to place and situation to situation. The more a project costs, the longer it takes to return its initial cost. (see Appendix G, Estimated Costs of Selected Retrofits for Mobile Homes.)

6. Project Selection - A homeowner, technician, or human service agency cannot always afford to do all the repair or energy conservation projects possible. Select those projects that will produce the most energy savings, and do those projects first. (see Appendix I, Energy Project Summary.)

1.1.3 History of Mobile Homes

Camping trailers first appeared in the early 1920s when motoring Americans, who had already embraced car camping, conceived a more comfortable and convenient home on wheels. Early camping trailers were lightwieght homemade units which combined junk automotive chassis parts and the simple wood technology used in yauchts. Manufactured camping trailers dominated the highways in the 1930s as some families starting living year round in trailer parks. Larger trailers, which provided more space and comfort for permanent residents came to be known as "house trailers". These 8-foot-wide house trailers were home to tens of thousands of transient war workers and returning veterans after World War II.

In the early 1950s, manufacturers began producing house trailers that were 10 feet wide and calling them "mobile homes". The Trailer Coach Manufacturers' Association changed its name to the Mobile Home Manufacturers' Association (MHMA), signaling the birth of the new product that was more a permanent home and less a vehicle. Mobile homes evolved away from the rounded, aerodynamic features of an car or yaucht and toward toward the house-like features of today's mobile home. The mobile home with its drapes, movable furniture, and house-like architectural features has dominated the low-cost and rural housing market from the late 50s until today. In the late 1960s, double-section homes appeared and since then have become more popular every year. Today's double-section and

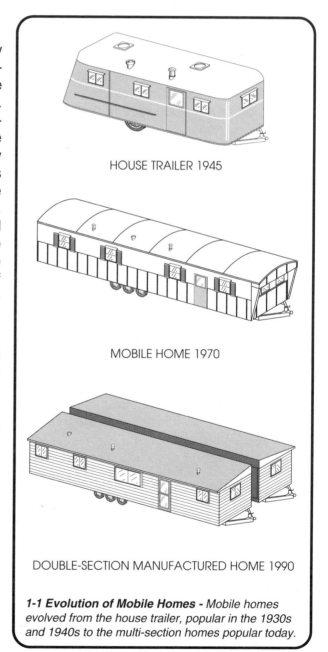

HOUSE TRAILER 1945

MOBILE HOME 1970

DOUBLE-SECTION MANUFACTURED HOME 1990

1-1 Evolution of Mobile Homes - Mobile homes evolved from the house trailer, popular in the 1930s and 1940s to the multi-section homes popular today.

GETTING STARTED

triple-section homes are almost indistinguishable from site-built homes.

In the 1960s competition was brisk, sales high, and quality sometimes poor. A report by the Center for Automotive Safety in the early 1970s prompted a Congressional investigation. In 1974, the Mobile Home Construction and Safety Standards Act passed Congress. This legislation ordered the Department of Housing and Urban Development (HUD) to establish and enforce a code for mobile home construction. In 1975, the MHMA changed its name to the Manufactured Housing Institute (MHI) and began calling its product a "manufactured home" instead of a "mobile home." In 1980 Congress recognized the name change to "manufactured home" but the term "mobile home" persists in common usage and is used in this manual to mean a single-section or multi-section home built on a steel chassis.

1.2 Codes and Standards

The American National Standards Institute (ANSI) developed construction standards for mobile homes in 1963 on behalf of the Mobile Home Manufacturers' Association (MHMA). By 1973, most mobile homes were designed and built by the ANSI Standard because 45 state governments had adopted it.

In 1976, the United States Department of Housing and Urban Development (HUD) adopted the "Manufactured Home Construction and Safety Standards," commonly called the "HUD Code" as the only applicable building code for mobile home construction. The HUD Code set minimum performance standards for roof support strength, mechanical equipment, thermal performance, safety, and other construction details that increased the quality of mobile homes nationwide as it came into force in the late 1970s.

The National Council of States on Building Codes and Standards (NCS/BCS) is HUD's code consultant and enforcer. State Approved Agencies (SAAs) under the direction of NCS/BCS inspect manufacturers and investigate complaints from consumers. You can obtain a list of SAAs from NCS/BCS (see Appendix A).

HUD and ANSI both publish standards describing acceptable practices for building foundations and installing mobile homes. The Manufactured Housing Institute (MHI) publishes the Model Manufactured Home Installation Manual which serves as a guide for installation manuals written by manufacturers (see Bibliography). A few states have adopted their own standards for installing mobile homes but many more have adopted the ANSI Standard for installation.

Mobile homes must usually meet specific code requirements for the connection of utilities like water, sewer, natural gas, and

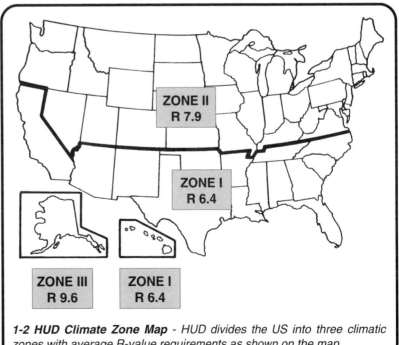

1-2 HUD Climate Zone Map - HUD divides the US into three climatic zones with average R-value requirements as shown on the map.

3

GETTING STARTED

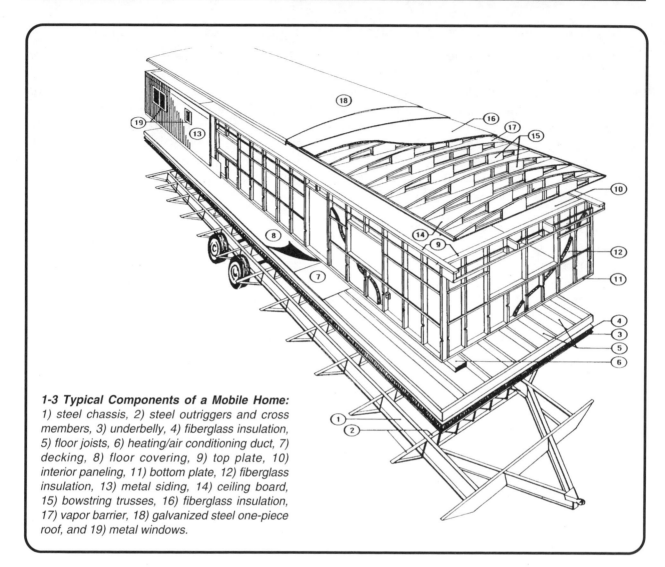

1-3 Typical Components of a Mobile Home:
1) steel chassis, 2) steel outriggers and cross members, 3) underbelly, 4) fiberglass insulation, 5) floor joists, 6) heating/air conditioning duct, 7) decking, 8) floor covering, 9) top plate, 10) interior paneling, 11) bottom plate, 12) fiberglass insulation, 13) metal siding, 14) ceiling board, 15) bowstring trusses, 16) fiberglass insulation, 17) vapor barrier, 18) galvanized steel one-piece roof, and 19) metal windows.

electricity. Some local building departments look to the HUD Code for guidance in regulating modifications to mobile homes. However, most local building authorities are not knowledgeable about or interested in how mobile homes in their communities are modified by their owners. Many state and local building departments simply exempt mobile homes from building codes.

The local codes are enforced by local building departments as part of the process of issuing building permits. The local or state building officials and fire marshals interpret the building codes and are responsible for enforcing them. Cities, counties, and states may adopt any of several common building codes covering construction practices, fire prevention, and safe procedures for the installation of plumbing, wiring, and mechanical devices in the home. If the city or county has not adopted building codes, then the building codes adopted by the state apply. Even if local codes apply to mobile homes, most repairs and weatherization measures are not considered to be major changes and will not usually require a building permit.

The 1976 HUD Code set the maximum allowable overall transmission heat loss coefficient for new mobile homes depending on their location. The HUD Code divides the country into three climate zones (see figure **1-2**). The average R-value requirement for mobile homes in Zone I is R-6.4; in Zone II, R-7.9; and in Zone 3, R-9.6. In 1985, sections were added to the HUD Code to control formaldehyde in building and to require mechanical ventilation in mobile homes. In 1991, HUD

GETTING STARTED

Code changes are pending that would raise minimum insulation requirements for mobile home envelopes set in 1976. Mobile homes built before 1976 are generally less energy efficient than those built after the HUD Code came into force, although some of these older homes are well-insulated.

Mobile homes built before 1976 may have some or all of the following characteristics (see figure **1-3**):
- Little or no insulation;
- No vapor barrier in the ceiling;
- One to two inches of fiberglass insulation wrapped around the outside of wall, floor, and roof framing;
- 2x2 or 2x3 wall studs;
- Uninsulated supply and return air ducts in the floor or ceiling; and
- Jalousie windows;

Mobile homes conforming to the 1976 HUD Code for climate zone 2 (see figure **1-2**) must have:
- Insulation of approximately R-8 in the walls, floor, and ceiling;
- A vapor barrier in the ceiling;
- A rodent barrier;
- 2x4 wall studs;
- Supply and return ducts for heating systems that are enclosed in the heated envelope, or insulated to R-4;
- Single-hung or slider windows with interior storms;

1.3 Mobile Home Research

From 1988 to 1991, the Solar Energy Research Institute (SERI) conducted mobile home energy conservation experiments that were funded by DOE. The experiments were designed to test the effectiveness of weatherization and energy conservation measures for mobile homes in cold climates. Many of the conservation methods tested by SERI are described in this manual. During the experiments, seven mobile homes were rolled into a warehouse and tested before and after the conservation measures listed below were installed.

1. Interior storm windows
2. General repairs including blower door-guided air sealing and duct repair
3. Blown-in belly insulation
4. Wall insulation
5. Roof cavity blown-in insulation
6. Roof cap
7. Belly wrap (wrapping fiberglass blanket under underbelly)
8. Insulated skirting

Scientists at SERI used an experimental

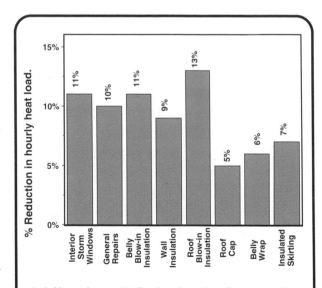

1-4 Heat Loss % Reduction for Conservation Projects - *The bar graph shows the average savings over original hourly heat loss after the energy conservation projects listed were completed on the mobile homes tested by SERI.*

GETTING STARTED

procedure called coheating to monitor changes in heat loss after conservation measures were installed in the mobile homes. This procedure used electric space heaters to heat the mobile homes and was a key element in obtaining the very high quality experimental results. Initially, electric resistance space heaters that are 100% efficient were used to heat the mobile homes. The electrical energy used by the space heaters was easy to measure, so it was relatively simple for the scientists at SERI to accurately measure the hourly heat loss. The hourly heat loss is equal to the heat provided to the mobile home by the space heaters each hour. Once they knew the existing heat loss of the mobile home, the scientists measured the reduction in heat loss that occurred after each of the above conservation measures was installed. They also measured overall heating efficiency and how efficiency changed as a result of weatherization and tune-up procedures.

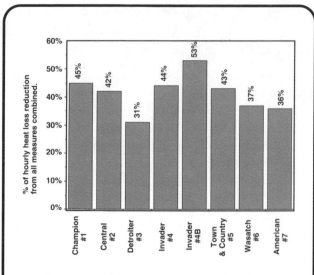

1-5 Heat Loss % Reduction for Mobile Homes - This bar graph shows the overall savings from all the conservation projects performed on the seven mobile homes tested by SERI.

The heat loss percentage reductions resulting from the energy conservation measures applied to the mobile homes are averaged on the bar graph in figure **1-4**. The overall heat loss percentage reductions for the mobile homes are shown in the bar graph in figure **1-5**.

The SERI scientists were able to accurately measure air infiltration using a tracer gas. Finally, they used 28 fans to simulate wind and measured the effect of wind on heat loss and on the effectiveness of the conservation measures. The most important general findings from this excellent two-year study on weatherization measures for cold climates are summarized below.

1. The most cost-effective measures for colder climates appear to be: blower door-directed air sealing and duct repair, furnace tune-up, belly blow, interior storm windows, and roof blow.

2. Furnace tune-ups, sealing duct leaks, and belly insulation directly increase the overall heating efficiency. The average increase in efficiency from these experiments was 15 percentage points.

3. Wall insulation can be a practical and cost-effective energy conservation measure on mobile homes built before 1976.

4. Blown-in belly insulation slightly outperforms insulated skirting in still-air conditions and significantly outperforms skirting in windy conditions. Savings from this method were 42% greater than skirting with a 3.5 mph wind.

5. Skirting, roof caps, and wrapping the belly with a fiberglass blanket seem to be less cost-effective than the other methods. Belly wraps are not very practical or durable.

6. The conservation measures listed above are more cost-effective in a 3.5 mph wind than in calm conditions.

The National Center for Appropriate Technology (NCAT) has done similar warehouse testing

GETTING STARTED

with similar results for PENELEC, a utility in Pennsylvania. This study has shown that large savings are possible using zone heating (see Section 3.7, Zone Heating).

The Florida Solar Energy Center (FSEC) has performed numerous studies of the cost-effectiveness of energy conservation projects in warm climates. In very warm climates like Florida, wall and floor insulation have been found not to be cost-effective, especially if the wall and floor already contain some insulation. Roof insulation is more cost-effective than wall or floor insulation. Air infiltration is a major problem in warm humid climates, particularly in forced air distribution systems. One recent study by FSEC found that effective duct repair can save 15-25% in mobile homes located in hot humid climates.

1.4 Mobile Home Construction

1.4.1 What Makes a Mobile Home Different

Mobile homes employ a number of unique features and construction practices to cut costs and produce a home that is portable. Because mobile homes are portable, they have to be lightweight and strong. Mobile homes use building materials more efficiently than conventional homes. They can enclose more usable space with less weight and material (see figures **1-3** and **1-6**).

1-6 Mobile Home Assembly - The chassis, floor, walls, and roof are assembled separately, then moved by cranes, and fastened together on the assembly line.

The following is a brief list of ways mobile homes differ from conventional homes.

1. The wooden frame of the mobile home is bolted to a steel chassis that usually remains with the mobile home throughout its service life.

2. Mobiles are constructed in long and narrow segments with shallow roof cavities to allow for highway travel.

3. Floors, roofs, and the outer side of exterior walls usually have only one layer of cladding. Many mobile homes don't have subflooring or exterior sheathing.

4. Windows and doors have lightweight metal frames which usually fit over the exterior

GETTING STARTED

siding.

5. Single framing rather than double framing around door and window openings is the industry standard.

6. The interior wall paneling on exterior walls provides the structural rigidity needed to keep metal-sided mobile home walls rectangular.

7. Sealed-combustion furnaces have been the industry standard since the early 1970s.

8. Mobile homes are built on an assembly line in a factory setting.

9. Steel strapping is used to reinforce joints between wall segments and between other components to prevent them from coming loose during transit.

1.4.2 Mobile Home Manufacturing

Mobile home manufacturing differs a lot from site-built house construction. An understanding of the ways mobile homes are built will aid in repairing and weatherizing them. Different parts of the home, such as the floors, walls, and roof, are built separately and then assembled on the production line to form the final product (see figure **1-6**).

The first part of the home to be built is the welded steel chassis. The standard chassis consists of two 10-inch steel I-beams to which crossmembers and outriggers are welded. The hitch and axle assembly are bolted to the I-beams, rather than welded, so they can be removed when the home is set up at the site, if desired. The floor assembly is constructed separately and then fastened to the chassis. Water lines, waste lines, ductwork, insulation, and the rodent barrier are all attached to the floor before it is attached to the chassis.

The home is then assembled from the inside out. The furnace and major plumbing fixtures are installed before any walls are attached to the floor. Walls are preassembled on tables, with interior paneling or drywall attached to the framing before the wall assembly is placed on the floor. Interior walls are installed first and then exterior walls are attached.

At this point in the assembly line the interior is nearly complete, but the exterior walls are not yet wired, insulated, or sided. With wall cavities open, all final electrical connections to the interior walls are completed and insulation, usually unfaced fiberglass batts, is installed. After the walls are completed, the exterior siding is attached, and the windows and doors are installed. Then the ceiling/roof assembly, which is built separately, is placed on top of the walls and fastened in place. Finally, the interior trim work is completed and the home is ready for transport.

Mobile homes are built in various sizes by about 200 manufacturers nationwide. Single-section homes dominate the market and most currently manufactured are at least 14 feet wide. However, older mobile homes still in service are largely between 10 and 14 feet wide. Double-section and triple-section mobile homes from 24 to 48 feet wide look like conventional homes and are assembled using sections 12 to 16 foot wide. They have steadily gained popularity. Standard lengths for mobile home sections range from 50 to 80 feet.

1.5 Foundations and Installation

Manufactured homes can last as long as site-built homes providing they are installed correctly using the manufacturer's instructions on a permanent foundation. The foundation must resist gravity, water, snow, ice, wind, and in some cases even earthquakes. The foundation must support the weight of the home and its contents plus the force of external loads like snow and wind. A poor

GETTING STARTED

foundation and/or a botched installation can cause premature deterioration of the home.

1.5.1 Introduction

This section on foundations is written to give the reader general knowledge of the materials and techniques for installing permanent and inexpensive foundations. Foundations are the key to installing a home on its site successfully and permanently. Inadequate foundations and site preparation have caused more damage and deterioration to mobile homes than anything else. Each manufacturer has an installation manual that prescribes a simple design procedure for the home's foundation, and this procedure should be followed precisely. The Manufactured Housing Institute has a model installation manual (see Bibliography) that can be used to design the foundation if the original installation manual is not available. HUD has published a design manual (see Bibliography) for permanent foundations. This manual, available from HUD local offices, is used when lenders require that a foundation for a manufactured home be as permanent as a site-built home. Following the design procedure in any of these manuals will result in a good foundation and this section is not written to substitute for the voluminous information contained in the design manuals. Check with state building code officials before making any plans to find out if the state has adopted a code for foundations and installation of mobile homes.

Any person experienced at measuring, digging, and pouring flat concrete pads can construct the footings. However, the actual installation and leveling are fairly difficult and dangerous. A reputable mobile home service, often the same company that moves the home, is usually the best qualified contractor to install and level the home.

Foundations must resist the forces of gravity and water. If the ground beneath a footing settles or heaves up due to frost, the home may be damaged. Water is the worst enemy of foundations. Frost heave occurs when the water in the soil freezes and expands, raising the ground surface. Wet sites in very cold climates may rise as much as 4 to 5 inches. Settling occurs when the footings are too small to support the weight of the home. Settling or frost heaving can cause leveling problems which distort window and door openings, and buckle or even break structural materials. High and low areas in the floor, distorted window openings, and puddles of water on the roof are

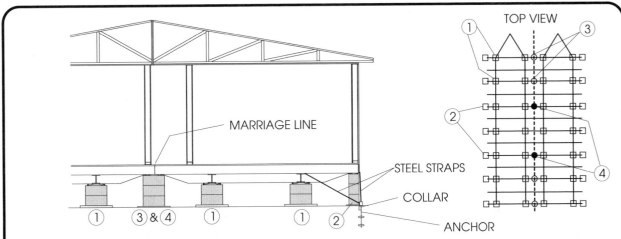

1-7 Pier Locations - 1) *Main Beam Pier: Required on all mobile homes usually, 8 feet apart.* 2) *Perimeter Support Pier: Required on both sides of doors or windows more than 6 feet wide and at regular intervals in northern and mountain regions with heavy snow loads. Also required on many double-section homes.* 3) *Marriage Line Pier: Required at regular intervals on most multi-section homes.* 4) *Ridge Beam Support Pier: Required in specific locations on the marriage line under walls serving as columns on either end of a span of unsupported roof.*

GETTING STARTED

signs that the home is not level.

Water in the ground also causes high relative humidity underneath a home after skirting is installed. Moisture in the air beneath the home can condense, wetting building materials in the floor. Moisture can also wick up into the walls. Wet insulation loses much of its thermal resistance and damp lumber may rot. Mold and mildew in the floor can lead to unpleasant smells and respiratory problems.

Mobile homes should be sited carefully, and the site should be prepared so that surface water runs away from the home and never collects underneath. Soil characterized by rocks, sand, and gravel drains better than soil with silt and clay.

The levelness and the condition of the foundation affect the decisions to repair or weatherize the mobile home. Repairs to the foundation should be done before any weatherization and repair projects to ensure successful and long-lasting results. Any continuing ground movement could negate the benefits of repairs, caulking, weatherstripping, and improvements to windows and doors.

1.5.2 Drainage and Site Preparation

Preparing the site is very important to the comfort, safety, and permanance of the home. Neglecting site preparation is courting a disaster. The first step is to stake out the exact location and orientation of the home (see Section 1.6.2, Orientation). Next remove all plants, roots, leaves, and other organic material in the area which will be underneath the home. Then answer these questions. Can the home be maneuvered into place? Are there obstacles to remove? What are the required distances from the street and from other homes?

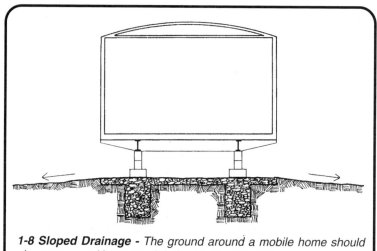

1-8 Sloped Drainage - The ground around a mobile home should slope away and have good drainage characteristics.

The home should be placed on the highest ground available at the site. If the home must be sited in a lower area, build the site up with gravel to provide an elevated base. You can also install a drain system with ditches or drain piping, if necessary, to direct water away from the ground underneath the foundation. It is essential that water cannot flow or collect under the home. If these conditions cannot be met, then the home should not be installed on the site.

A poorly prepared site is a difficult problem to correct and can seldom be as satisfactory as a site that is prepared properly in the beginning. If water is the main problem, a drainage system using gravel and drain piping may work if it is designed and installed by knowledgeable people. If settling is a problem because of inadequate sizing of footings, then adding more piers and footings may correct the problem if the repair workers re-level the home and make sure that all the piers are blocked tightly beneath the main beams. Severe drainage problems and frost heaving may require moving the home off the site temporarily and performing the correct siting and foundation procedures.

GETTING STARTED

The foundation can be simpler and less expensive if you can totally eliminate water from the soil underneath the home. Frost needs both water and cold. Without water in the soil, there is no frost and no frost heaving.

1.5.3 Foundations

Mobile homes have a maximum weight of 35 to 75 pounds per square foot of floor space. This range of weight includes the home's contents and an anticipated snow load of 20 to 40 pounds per square foot. Mobile homes are designed to support 20, 30, or 40 pounds of snow per square foot of roof, depending on their intended location and the typical snowfall there (see Appendix H). Homes with metal siding, metal roofing, and wood interior paneling are lighter than homes with shingle roofs, wood siding, and sheetrock interior paneling. Homes designed to support more snow are heavier than homes designed to support less.

1-9 Treated Wood Footing and Pier - On hard soils, the footing is often blocked directly on the ground or on a gravel base using a pressure-treated wood 2x12.

The manufacturer usually specifies the exact locations of the piers and footings depending on where the weight of the home is best supported. Piers and footings under the main beams are typically located 6 to 10 feet apart. Many homes require perimeter blocking, also, particularly on each side of large windows or sliding glass doors. Double-section homes need piers and footings under the marriage wall. The location of marriage-wall piers is critical because certain ones must support large sections of the roof through an interior wall. These special piers are called roof column support piers (see figure **1-7**). Information about footing location, spacing, and the weight footings must carry is found in the installation manual for the home. See Appendix H for more information.

The size (area) of a footing depends on the amount of weight that the footing must support and the type of soil upon which it rests. The installer may determine the supporting capacity of the soil with a device called a pocket penetrometer, which is sold through engineering suppliers. If this device is not available, then local experts such as a building inspector or an agricultural extension agent should be contacted to identify the soil type (see Appendix H). Deep, soggy topsoils and uncompacted fill may be unsuitable to support the weight of the home and require special analysis and design. If the home must be located on poor soil, or if ground water is near the surface, or if the site is near a lake or river, then you should contact an engineer to advise you about the foundation.

1-10 Large Concrete Footing with Pier - On soft and damp soils, footings must be large enough to spread the weight of the home over more area of ground. The concrete, or at least a base of graduated gravel, must extend below the frost line.

The frost line is the maximum depth (inches) of the soil where water will freeze during the coldest winter weather. Frost line is important to footings because when water

11

GETTING STARTED

in the soil freezes, it can move the ground. This ground movement is called frost heaving. If the ground moves, it can move the home. If the home moves, it can deform the structure, buckling floors and roofs and tilting window and door openings. The frost line at footings underneath main beams of skirted homes may be considerably less that the frost depth shown on the map in Appendix H. The sheltering effect of the home and skirting means that the frost line under the home may be only 40% to 60% of the regional depth.

The success of a foundation in supporting a home depends on the size, spacing, and depth of the footings. Poured concrete footings, which extend below the frost line, will be adequate for almost any type of soil including silt and clay. A 4- to 8- inch-thick, concrete pad laid on a gravel base which extends below the frost line will be adequate on most soils (see figure **1-10**). When pouring concrete footings, make sure that the wood forms, which will contain the concrete, are absolutely level from side to side and between footings.

1-11 Stabilized Pier System - These special steel piers may be cross-braced and anchored to concrete footings for resistance to earthquakes.

Gravel is the best material for fill beneath footings and to elevate the level of the ground, if necessary, because it compacts itself naturally and because it drains water away from the footings. Gravel can also absorb the movement of water freezing to ice within the spaces between the stones, and can absorb some movement from the surrounding ground without moving the footing.

Footings, set directly on the ground, may be adequate in the following soil types: 1) rock or hard pan; 2) dry sand and gravel soils; 3) any soil that remains absolutely dry from the surface of the soil to the frost line. The most common types of footings for installation on undisturbed ground are treated 1.5-inch, pressure-treated wood footings (see figure **1-9**), four-inch-thick, solid concrete blocks, and poured concrete pads.

Some dealers encourage customers to install manufactured homes on reinforced concrete slabs that cover the whole area underneath the home. These so called "floating slabs" have advantages over individual footings. Mistakes in locating the footings accurately are eliminated. Anchors are easy to install in the concrete and a permanent plastic vapor barrier can be placed below the slab. However, slabs are more expensive and more difficult to install properly. Many park owners use 2 strips of reinforced concrete to allow versatile placement of piers for different single-section homes. The reinforced concrete strips, poured on gravel bases 8.5 to 9.5 feet apart, are more economical than a floating slab. The strips are completely sheltered under the home, making them slightly less susceptable to frost than the edges of a concrete slab.

The most common type of pier is made of concrete blocks with the hollow cores aligned in a vertical direction. A single column of concrete blocks, used as a pier, can be up to 36 inches tall. A double column of blocks (one course rotated 90° to the next) can be up to 80 inches tall. Piers over 80 inches tall must be double-column, concrete blocks with the cores filled with concrete or mortar and with metal reinforcing steel rod through the blocks and into a concrete footing below.

The minimum height between the ground and the I-beam should be about 19 inches, which would be the height of the 1.5 inch treated wood pad, two 7.5-inch concrete blocks, a 1.5-inch thick

GETTING STARTED

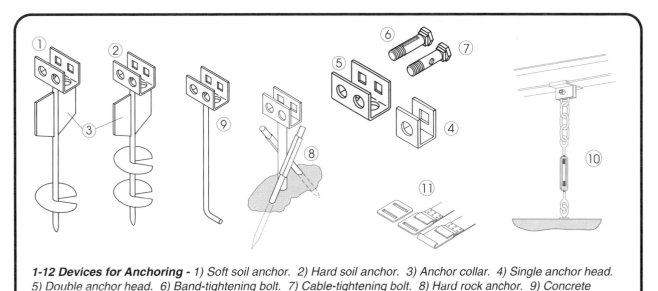

1-12 Devices for Anchoring - 1) Soft soil anchor. 2) Hard soil anchor. 3) Anchor collar. 4) Single anchor head. 5) Double anchor head. 6) Band-tightening bolt. 7) Cable-tightening bolt. 8) Hard rock anchor. 9) Concrete anchor. 10) Chain and turnbuckle anchor. 11) Hook and buckles for fastening banding to the frame.

plate on top of the pier and 1 inch for leveling wedges. Final leveling adjustments are made with two beveled, pressure-treated wood wedges at each pier (see figure **1-9**). Steel piers are also common and the best steel piers may offer some advantages in anchoring and stabilizing the home in areas with a high risk of earthquakes (see figure **1-11**).

1.5.4 Installing Anchors

Ground anchors are steel rods or screws that penetrate the ground and attach the home to the ground with steel strapping, cable, or chain (see figure **1-12**). Ground anchors prevent the home from moving during high winds or earthquakes. Even if your region is not affected by earthquakes or high winds, anchors will stabilize the floor and reduce slight movements and vibrations. An anchoring system diagram is usually included in the installation manual.

Screw-type anchors are screwed into the ground using a piece of metal rod for leverage. Some mobile home services have electric anchor drivers which make anchor installation easier. There are two types of screw-type anchors, the soft-soil anchor and the hard-soil anchor. The hard-soil anchor is installed about 30 inches into the ground. The soft-soil anchor and is installed 40 inches or more into the ground. **Each screw-type anchor should have a collar to resist the anchor rod slicing through the soil.** The collar can be the manufactured plate shown in the illustration, or it can be a concrete block buried next to the anchor, or a collar of poured concrete. This collar is absolutely essential for all screw-type anchors which connect to the home at an angle.

Rock anchors are pinned to the ground with steel stakes. There are a variety of anchors sold for use with concrete footings or slabs. Figure **1-12** shows a variety of anchoring devices.

You can place the anchors 8 to 24 feet apart at pier locations, depending on the recommendations in the installation manual and the danger of high winds in your area. Fasten the anchors to the frame with steel strapping or cable at any angle between 45 degrees and vertical. Attach the strapping to the steel framework of the chassis or over the roof, not to wood framing. The chassis may have slots or steel fittings in the main beams to attach the strapping or cable. Anchor kits contain buckles or cable connectors that aid in attaching the strapping around the main beam or over the roof. Anchors have special brackets with slotted or drilled tension bolts that the straps or cables are inserted into. These bolts are rotated to wind the end of the strap around the bolt. Don't

GETTING STARTED

overtighten the bolts because that could deform the chassis by pulling too hard on the main beam. Tighten tie-down straps alternately on opposite sides of the home during installation.

Many installation manuals recommend that strapping be installed over the roof in high-wind areas but this practice is not common. Many single-section homes built in recent years have built-in anchor straps that go over the roof and hang out underneath the siding in several places. The installation manuals usually suggest that the anchor be attached both to the built-in strap and to the main beam by another strap using a double-headed anchor (see figure **1-12** and **1-13**). Over-the-roof strapping was developed to prevent the home from blowing off the chassis during a hurricane.

1-13 Double Tie-Down - *A double-headed anchor connects both a built-in over-the-roof strap and a strap tied to the main beam to the ground for stability in high winds.*

1.5.5 Installation Procedures

Drainage and site preparation work are completed and the foundation is ready before the home is delivered to the site. Water, sewer, electrical, and gas utilities must be ready for connection too. Professional home installers follow a procedure, with steps like those outlined below, to set the home on the site.

- Step 1: Mark the corners of the home and lay out materials for the piers and temporary blocking. Prepare the jacks, the steel plates for support between the beam and jack, and the blocking for under the jacks.

- Step 2: Position the home over the footings making sure that the main beams are directly over the center of the footings. Raise the home to a level slightly higher than its final intended position, first at the hitch then near the axels, installing stable temporary blocking in 6 to 10 locations under the main beams, as you jack.

- Step 3: Erect the piers and level them with a water level (see Section 1.5.5, below). Lower the home carefully using wedges to adjust the final level and remove the temporary blocking.

- Step 4: (For double-section homes only.) Prepare the utility connections between the sections. Install the mating gasket. Push the home into position and follow Step 2, moving the second section into contact with the first. Follow manufacturer's instructions formoving and fastening the sections together and installing closure materials at the interior and exterior of the joint. Connect the utility crossovers.

- Step 5: Check pier level and stability. Inspect utility crossovers on double-section units. Connect utility systems according to local codes and factory instructions.

Caution: These procedures require skill and previous experience.

1.5.6 Leveling a Mobile Home

Mobile homes are leveled during installation and should not need to be leveled again unless the footings move. Mobile homes are leveled by jacking underneath the two main steel beams. The best places to jack are at the hitch and at the axle cross members where the chassis is strongest. It is important to lift the home slowly using two jacks underneath a single main beam to prevent the

GETTING STARTED

beam from buckling. **Caution:** *Do not attempt to level a mobile home unless you are experienced, because you might damage the frame or even topple the home onto yourself.*

The tools used for leveling are two 12-ton hydraulic jacks, a 4-foot bubble level, a water level, pressure treated wedges, and large wood blocks to temporarily support the main beams The water level is ideal for leveling the main beams because it is easy to use over long and short distances from point to point (see figure **1-14**). Professional installers set the level of the first pier and then set the level of the liquid in the jug of colored anti-freeze at the exact level of the top of the first pier. The installer then determines the level of the other piers using the level of the liquid in the clear hose, which remains naturally level with the top of the liquid in the jug.

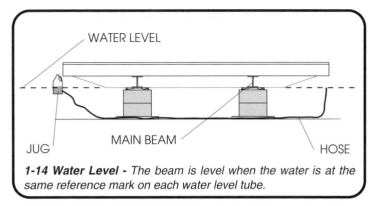

1-14 Water Level - The beam is level when the water is at the same reference mark on each water level tube.

A correctly designed and installed foundation will not move. Re-leveling is unfortunately a common repair practice for homes with poor foundations. The home may require some time for window and door openings to return to a rectangular shape after it is re-leveled. Additional footings and piers should be added and necessary drainage work performed during re-leveling to prevent the home from moving again.

Caution: *Beams being jacked should always be blocked temporarily to catch the home if a jack slips. The blocks must be strong and placed at right angles to the ground directly under the main beams.*

1.5.7 Installing a Ground Cover

The ground cover should be at least 6-mil black polyethylene or a similar material. Black poly is preferable to clear poly because it prevents plants from growing under the home. Fiber reinforced polyethylene is preferable for ground covers because it is resistant to tearing. All joints should overlap 12 inches. If the ground cover is installed during placement of the foundation during set-up, place it under the piers. If the ground cover is laid down around the piers, cut and piece it closely around the piers. If the home is skirted, the ground cover should extend at least 6 inches up the inside of the skirting (see figure **1-15**). Fasten the polyethylene ground cover securely against the skirting with a reliable construction adhesive.

Remove any sharp objects beneath the mobile home so the ground cover will not be punctured. During installation, you may want to put a light covering of pea gravel or sand on the ground cover to help hold it down and keep it from being punctured.

1.5.8 Skirting

Skirting is the sheeting attached to a lightweight frame around the bottom perimeter of the mobile home. Skirting improves the appearance of the home and is required in many mobile home parks. It keeps animals out of the crawlspace, which is very important because animals like to tear the underbelly. Skirting provides a windbreak that lessens the likelihood of frozen pipes in cold climates and it prevents snow, rain, and debris from blowing underneath the home.

Skirting can be constructed out of a variety of materials. Figure **1-16** shows site-built skirting

GETTING STARTED

with plywood or composite sheeting which needs to be treated with several coats of an effective waterproofing sealant. Good drainage around the base of the skirting is very important to protect wood skirting. Wet sites are better served by vinyl or metal prefabricated skirting shown in figure **1-15**. Drainage is not as important with the vinyl or metal system. Building a rigid framework between the ground and the edge of the mobile home floor in cold climates is not recommended because water running off the roof and sides of the home concentrate around the base of the skirting and could cause frost heaving that can move a mobile home with a rigid framework. Vinyl, metal or wood skirting can be insulated.

Figure **1-16** shows an inexpensive and easy-to-assemble skirting frame that uses less lumber than the 2x4 stud wall that many people use. The 2x4 post should be an inch or two short so that frost heaving doesn't push the edge of the home up. The plywood foot on the bottom of the foot provide the flexibility to attach the somewhat loose post. Prefabricated skirting comes with its own frame that is pinned to the ground and fastened to the rim joist of the mobile home as shown in figure **1-15**.

The skirting should be vented approximately every 20 feet to remove accumulated moisture. The vent openings should be screened to keep pests out. Keep the openings away from plumbing to prevent freezing in cold climates. Thermally activated vents that open automatically at about 50° F are available for cold climates.

Skirting should never be installed around a crawlspace that has water puddling or ground moisture problems. A ground cover should be installed whenever skirting is erected. These precautions ensure that the crawlspace will not become a source of high humidity that will produce moisture problems inside the home.

Insulated skirting can save some energy, but it is not a good substitute for floor insulation. If you decide to install insulated skirting, use thermally activated vents to limit ventilation during cold weather. Insulated skirting is not a very cost-effective energy conservation measure, which may come as a surprise to many people. Even with insulated skirting, the crawlspace under the home is likely to be about the same temperature as the outside, so there is not much heat flow between the

1-15 Vinyl or Metal Skirting - This prefabricated skirting system is sold by mobile home suppliers and is easy to assemble.

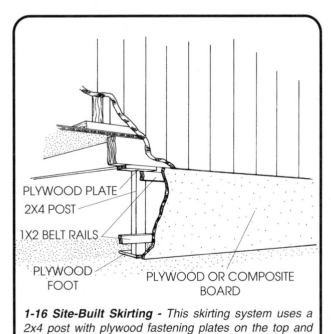

1-16 Site-Built Skirting - This skirting system uses a 2x4 post with plywood fastening plates on the top and bottom. The posts are preassembled on site and tied together by 1x2 belt rails.

GETTING STARTED

crawlspace and outdoors for the insulation to resist.

In warm wet climates, the outdoor air that comes into the crawl space through vents may carry unwanted moisture with it that can condense in the relatively cool crawl space. Closable vents are an option for warm wet climates to allow residents to ventilate during drier periods of the year and close the vents during wetter months.

If you install tight skirting with thermally activated or closable vents you must duct air through the skirting, to the combustion air intakes for the furnace, water heater, and woodstove if they draw combustion air from the crawl space. The combustion appliances must have combustion air. The dryer vent must be connected to intake fittings mounted in the siding. **Dryer vents terminating in the crawl space, even if the skirting is vented, may cause serious moisture problems.**

1.6 Landscaping

Landscaping can save energy through proper siting and orientation of your mobile home, as well as through the use of trees, shrubs, vines, groundcovers, fences, and other structures. Siting and landscaping your homesite correctly can conserve heat in winter and reduce cooling needs in summer. Landscaping is not a substitute for the other energy conservation methods described in this manual, but it is another cost-effective way to lower your energy costs.

You can use the landscaping methods discussed in this section for a single mobile home or a group of mobile homes located together. If you are setting up a new mobile home park, follow the guidelines for siting and landscaping for all the sites. If you are working with an existing mobile home park, evaluate each site and consider the guidelines. In addition to applying landscaping or orientation concepts to individual sites, you may be able to use landscaping or windbreaks that will benefit more than one site.

Your landscape can be developed gradually, so there does not need to be a large initial investment. You can start by planting some strategically placed vines and shrubs near the mobile home and progress

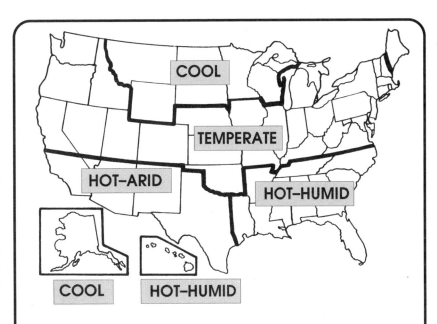

1-17 Four climatic regions of the United States
Temperate: This region has equal overheated and underheated periods, seasonal winds from the northwest and south, and periods of high humidity and high precipitation rates.
Hot-Arid: This region has clear skies, dry air, and extended periods of overheating with large daily temperature fluctuations. Wind generally is along the east-west axis, varying from day to evening.
Hot-Humid: This region has high temperatures and consistent vapor pressure. Wind speed and direction vary throughout the year and daily. Wind speeds of up to 120 mph may accompany hurricanes, which generally come from the east-southeast direction.
Cool: This region has hot summers, cold winters, and persistent winds year-round, generally out of the northwest and southeast. Northern locations receive less solar radiation than southern areas of the country.

GETTING STARTED

to planting shade trees or an evergreen windbreak as your budget allows.

Simple landscaping can shield the mobile home from temperature extremes by creating a buffer zone around the perimeter. Well-planned landscaping requires little maintenance and most landscape improvements can be performed by the homeowners. Landscapes are inexpensive and improve with age. Low cost is one of the most attractive aspects of landscaping as a means to save energy. An eight-foot shade tree will cost about the same as an awning for one large window.

1.6.1 General

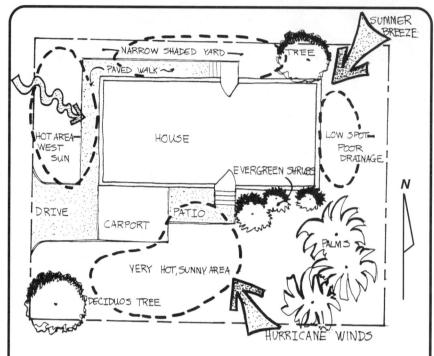

1-18 Sample Site Analysis for Hot and Humid Regions - This example shows a double-wide mobile home facing south. Dotted lines indicate potential problem areas. This home is exposed to hurricane winds.

1-19 Sample Site Analysis for Temperate Region - This example shows a single-section mobile home with problem areas on the west and the south where the home is exposed to the sun.

Climatic Considerations

Climatic factors determine how you should proceed with your siting and landscaping. The United States can be divided into four climatic regions: temperate, hot-arid, hot-humid, and cool (see figure **1-17**). Energy conserving landscape objectives and strategies are different for each of these regions.

Temperate: Maximize warming effects of sun in winter. Maximize shade in summer. Reduce winter winds near buildings, but allow air circulation in summer.

Hot-Arid: Maximize shade in late morning and all afternoon. Maximize humidity. Maximize air flow in summer.

Hot-Humid: Maximize shade.

GETTING STARTED

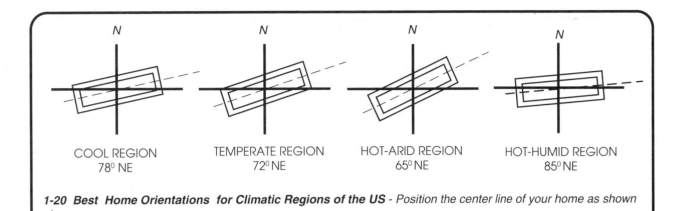

1-20 **Best Home Orientations for Climatic Regions of the US** - *Position the center line of your home as shown above.*

Minimize air flow for cooling, drying effects.

Cool: Maximize warming effects of sun. Reduce winter winds. Cool air is heavier than warm air and acts much like water, flowing downhill to low points on the site. At night, this causes "cold air puddles" which, in cool regions, can be very unpleasant. Avoid sites in valley bottoms and depressions if you can.

The climate in the area right around your home is called the microclimate. You may live in a cool region but have a warm microclimate near your home if you are located on a warm, sunny south slope. Or you may live in a hot-humid region but have a comfortable microclimate due to drying summer breezes that are channeled your way by a forested area. Before you begin to plan your landscape, find out about your microclimate. Ask yourself the following questions about your home, the site, and local weather patterns:

—Where are the sunny spots on your site? The shaded areas?

—Which direction does the wind usually come from in the summer? In the winter?

—Is your site exposed to cold winter winds? Cool summer breezes?

—Are there other structures nearby which would block the wind or sun?

—Do you have water bodies such as a stream or lake nearby which would either increase humidity or cool the summer breezes as the air flows over the water?

—Is there a drainage problem around your home? Does the ground slope away from your home or toward it?

—Paving near your home will reflect or radiate solar heat onto the walls and windows. Note the location of any paved surfaces (drives, patios, sidewalks) near your home.

—What kind of plants (species, evergreen, deciduous, height, location) are already growing on your site?

Draw a simple aerial map of the site and put the microclimate information on this map. You can also include views you want to preserve or block,

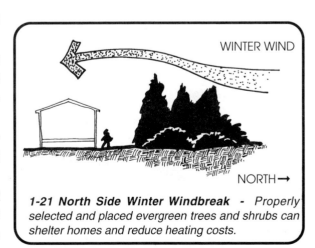

1-21 **North Side Winter Windbreak** - *Properly selected and placed evergreen trees and shrubs can shelter homes and reduce heating costs.*

GETTING STARTED

noise you want to block, and access to roads and walkways. See sample site analysis drawings in figures **1-18** and **1-19**. Now, you can decide the best orientation for your home as well as the most efficient energy conserving landscaping strategy.

1.6.2 Orientation

The orientation of your home is one of the most important factors determining energy costs. If you are looking at sites on which to locate your mobile home, make sure the site allows you to orient your home for maximum access to the sun, protection from wind, or access to cooling breezes. If you own a mobile home on an existing site and it

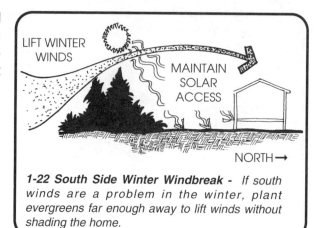

1-22 South Side Winter Windbreak - If south winds are a problem in the winter, plant evergreens far enough away to lift winds without shading the home.

is oriented poorly, for example with a long window wall facing west, you might consider reorienting it to take full advantage of the sun or shade available to you. The cost of rotating a mobile home may be relatively low, especially if your heating and cooling costs are extremely high. You may have to change or add to exterior structures such as drives, walks, carports, or entryways, but you can still realize a payback very shortly because of the energy saved.

Figure **1-20** shows the best orientation for your home with respect to the sun for each of the major climatic regions. If your climate is dominated by cold winds and long winters, you may want to point the shortest wall directly at the prevailing winter wind to minimize exposure.

1.6.3 How Plants Affect Microclimate and Energy

One of the most obvious advantages to having trees and shrubs planted around your home is that they immediately make the outside living areas more comfortable and pleasing. Plants also act as buffers to temperature extremes inside the home.

Evergreen trees planted to the north of the home help block winter storm winds and, in the summer, cool the air as it passes through the branches. Windbreaks, if properly selected and placed, can reduce heating expenses considerably when the trees and shrubs are mature (see figure **1-21** and **1-22**). In the summer, trees also shade the ground around buildings, cooling the air before it reaches the walls and windows of your mobile home. Consider planting evergreen shrubs as a buffer around the entry to your mobile home if it

1-23 Reflected Heat and Light - Paved areas reflect the sun's heat and light toward the home.

1-24 Natural Ventilation - Deciduous trees can channel and cool summer breezes.

GETTING STARTED

faces cold winter winds. Be careful not to plant evergreens to the south of your home or you'll have shade there in the winter when you want the sun. If winter winds are a problem and come from the south in your area, plant evergreens far enough away from your dwelling so that they will lift the cold winds up and over the house without shading it (see figure **1-22**).

1-25 Natural Cooling With Vegetation - To cool south and west sides of home, reduce paved areas, plant shade trees, or add a trellis.

Deciduous trees, when planted to the south, east, and west of your home, will shade the walls, roof, and windows during the cooling season, which corresponds to their leafing season. A tree located to shade the walls and roof in the afternoon may reduce the wall and roof temperature by as much as 20° to 40° F. Trees can also channel cool summer breezes toward the house (see figure **1-24**). In the late fall and winter, the bare deciduous trees allow the sun's heat to warm the surfaces of your home and surrounding earth (see figure **1-23**). If you have drainage and humidity problems around your home, be careful not to aggravate those problems by planting too many trees which would prevent evaporation of water from soggy soils.

Paving reflects or absorbs solar energy and radiates the heat to the walls of your home, increasing the heat load on the home (see figure **1-23**). Low shrubs and groundcovers around buildings reduce the reflection of solar energy from roads, walks, patios, or water bodies. Trees can also be placed so that they shade paved areas, reducing the heat that radiates from the paved surface (see figure **1-25**).

Plant vines and shrubs next to your home to create a dead air space which helps insulate the home in winter and stop solar heat from hitting the wall in summer (see figure **1-26**). A lattice, a trellis with climbing vines, or a planter box with trailing plants will form a screen, blocking the sun yet allowing cooling breezes to flow through (see figure **1-27**).

Consider planting fast-growing trees or larger specimens of medium-fast growing trees. A six to eight foot deciduous tree planted near the home will begin shading windows the first year and,

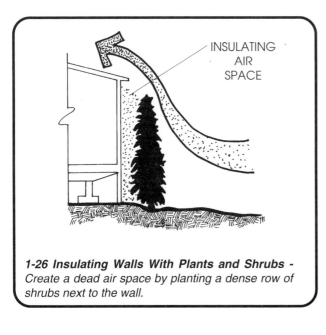

1-26 Insulating Walls With Plants and Shrubs - Create a dead air space by planting a dense row of shrubs next to the wall.

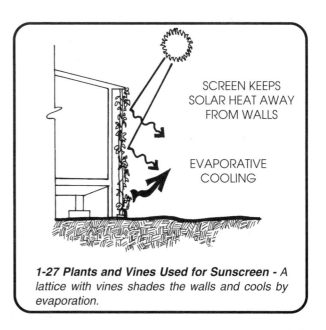

1-27 Plants and Vines Used for Sunscreen - A lattice with vines shades the walls and cools by evaporation.

GETTING STARTED

depending on the species, will shade the roof in five to ten years. Foundation plantings of shrubs will fill in rapidly and shade walls or windows within a couple of years. Vines will provide shade beginning with the first growing season. You may choose to plant annual vines or climbing plants (such as runner beans, sweet peas, morning glories), or perennials and permanent plantings (such as wisteria and clematis).

It is beyond the scope of this manual to provide you with plant lists for each climatic region. For information about hardy plants for your area, contact your County Extension agent, local nurseries, or university and public libraries. Most areas have landscape architects who can help you plan your landscape. Nurseries and landscape contractors are other sources for design and planning assistance. The bibliography lists several of the best gardening references. Check your library or bookstore for other references that may be specific to your region.

1.7 Moisture and Ventilation

Mobile homes are more prone to moisture problems than other housing types for the following reasons:

1. The metal exterior siding and roofing present in many homes cause condensation because the metal stays at a low temperature during the heating season.

2. Moisture originating indoors travels through a wall or ceiling driven by humidity differences and air leakage, then condenses on the inside of the metal skin.

3. Mobile homes are also more likely to be sited directly above bare wet ground than site-built homes.

Water vapor travels through building materials through a process called vapor diffusion, which is driven by the difference in humidity levels between the indoors and outdoors. Vapor diffusion increases the humidity of the air in building cavities and increases the moisture content of building materials. Water vapor diffuses through different building materials at different rates. Materials known as vapor barriers allow almost no water vapor to diffuse through them. Plastic films, metal foils, and metal sheeting are common vapor barriers.

Water vapor is also carried by air leaking out of and into cavities of the building envelope. Air infiltration usually carries several times as much moisture into building envelopes as vapor diffusion. Vapor barriers do not stop air leakage unless they are completely airtight. When warm moist air encounters colder areas of building envelopes, water can condense wetting building materials, particularly insulation. Water reduces the effectiveness of insulating materials and provides an environment for the growth of microbes and insects that decay building materials and can be a health hazard to occupants.

Plumbing leaks and leaking rain water are important sources of moisture problems in mobile homes. Plumbing leaks are relatively easy to find and are com-

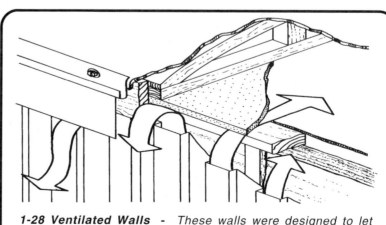

1-28 Ventilated Walls - These walls were designed to let ventilation air remove moisture from insulation, but they also contribute to air leakage in the home.

GETTING STARTED

monly found in the hot and cold water supply lines (see Section 5.2.3 Plumbing Leaks). However, water leaks in the envelope can be difficult to find because it's often unclear whether the moisture you observe is caused by leakage or condensation. Also, the wet area of the home may be some distance from the leak. Many mobile homes have no eaves and so the walls are exposed to more rainwater than site-built houses. The small holes and cracks around windows and holes around fasteners can leak water through capillary action. Capillary action is the tendency of water to adhere and pull itself through small spaces.

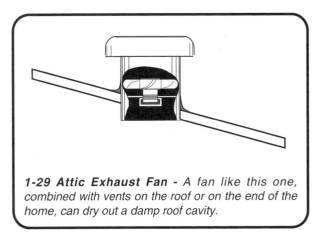

1-29 Attic Exhaust Fan - A fan like this one, combined with vents on the roof or on the end of the home, can dry out a damp roof cavity.

Venting attics of site-built homes to remove moisture has been standard practice in building technology for many years. However, many mobile home roofs, especially the metal roofs, are unvented. Most mobile homes have a vapor barrier located at the ceiling to limit the moisture diffusion into the attic. Water stains on the ceiling are a sign of a roof leak or a condensation problem. An isolated water stain is often the sign of a nearby air leak into the ceiling or a nearby flaw in the roof. Sealing air leaks in the ceiling is the first step in eliminating condensation problems in the roof. Persistent roof cavity condensation problems may require a fan-powered (see figures **1-29** and **1-31**) or passive ventilation system for the roof. (see also Section 2.3.2, Natural Air Changes, Moisture, and Ventilation and Section 2.5.3, Wall Insulation and Moisture.)

In the past, the metal-sided walls of many mobile homes were designed to let ventilation air into them. The idea of ventilating walls was a controversial one. The infiltrating air could bypass and short circuit the insulation and even contribute to moisture problems in walls. You can recognize a ventilated wall by the vertically applied metal siding that is not sealed at the top or bottom horizontal joint (see figure **1-28**). One benefit of this design is that the unsealed bottom wall joint on vented walls does allow water to escape. Lately, building scientists have emphasized the need to prevent moisture from entering building cavities rather than depending on vented outdoor air to dry out moist building materials. This prevention approach employs vapor barriers to stop vapor diffusion and, more importantly, air sealing to stop air leakage into building cavities. If you can prevent moisture from entering the building cavities then the typical non-airtight building cavity should receive enough incidental ventilation to keep the cavities dry.

Condensation indoors can originate from a number of different sources. Dryers that do not vent outdoors or that have leaky vents are a very common problem. You should always vent the dryer outdoors through the skirting because of the moisture and pollutants from soap and lint that the dryer exhaust puts into the air. Some other common sources of moisture are wet shoes, boiling water without lids, operating the washing machine with the top open, storing wood indoors, many house plants, and hot showers. There are two strategies for reducing moisture: 1) reducing moisture at its source and 2) ventilating and using dehumidifiers to remove moisture.

The most common ways of removing moisture are exhaust fans and dehumidifiers. The 1985 revisions to the HUD Code require exhaust fans in all mobile homes. Many mobile homes have fresh air intakes near the furnace that provide fresh air while the furnace blower is on. Newer venti-

GETTING STARTED

lation systems, designed to comply with the 1985 changes in the HUD Code, provide intermittent ventilation.

1.8 Exhaust Fans and Dehumidifiers

Every mobile home should have a properly operating bathroom exhaust fan and ducted kitchen range hood or wall exhaust. If you coordinate the installation of new exhaust fans with roof, wall, or ceiling repairs, you may eliminate extra labor. You may need to hire a licensed electrician to wire and install electrical exhaust fans.

A bathroom exhaust fan should be wired to its own switch except when moisture is a chronic problem. Then the fan should be wired to the same switch as the bathroom light to ensure its frequent use. Special controls, called humidistats, cycle the fan on and off as needed to remove moisture and are becoming more common.

Backdraft dampers are located either in the fan housing or in the exhaust fitting on the exterior wall or roof (see figure **1-30**). The roof and wall mounted fittings with backdraft dampers are available separately. These fittings can be connected to a fan that either doesn't have a backdraft damper or one with a disabled damper. Propeller-type bathroom fans in some homes cannot be fitted with backdraft dampers because they are not powerful enough to open the damper. In these cases the air leakage can be tolerated or the fan can be replaced with a squirrel-cage exhaust fan rated a minimum of 100 cubic feet per minute. Make sure, before you order a new fan that there is enough space in the roof cavity to install it. Wall-mounted exhaust fans are another option.

1-30 Backdraft Damper Locations - All exhaust fans should have a backdraft damper to keep heated or cooled air in the home when the fan is not in use.

Another way to reduce moisture to acceptable levels is by using a dehumidifier. This should be considered only after moisture sources are reduced and exhaust fans are installed. Dehumidifiers are an energy-efficient way to remove moisture in winter when heating is needed, because they release heat as they remove moisture. A dehumidifier extracts moisture from the air in the same way as a mechanical air conditioning system (see Section 4.4, Air Conditioning).

In addition to exhaust fans and dehumidifiers, a third option is a central mechanical ventilation system. The two leading manufacturers of mobile home heating and cooling equipment make central, active (fan-powered) and passive (no fan) ventilation systems for mobile homes. Passive ventilating systems bring in outside air through a duct with an adjustable damper. Active ventilation systems (see figure **1-31**) pressurize the attic and force ventilating air into the home through the attic by way of a ventilating duct with a backdraft damper. The systems have the tradenames Blend-Air™ and VentilAire™. These systems can provide a remedy for serious and persistent moisture problems in mobile homes. They provide fresh air to the furnace whenever the furnace blower is operating. These systems also ventilate the home independent of the furnace at intervals

GETTING STARTED

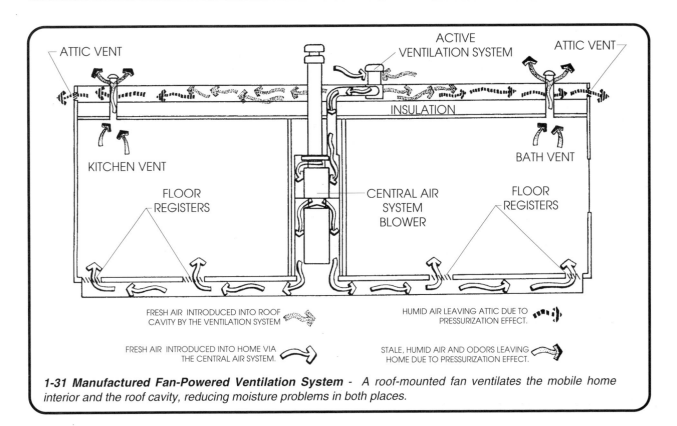

1-31 Manufactured Fan-Powered Ventilation System - *A roof-mounted fan ventilates the mobile home interior and the roof cavity, reducing moisture problems in both places.*

determined by the system's controls. For example, the Blend-Air™ system turns on to provide air to the house every four hours and stays on for a four-hour interval. The VentilAire I™, which is a passive system, eliminates the fan and uses only a tube with an adjustable damper that feed outdoor air into the furnace compartment. Vents on the roof let fresh air into the roof cavity to replace the air that flows into the home.

1.9 Indoor Air Quality

Many weatherization measures, like caulking and insulation, reduce the amount of fresh air that ventilates the home. Pollutants and moisture tend to be more concentrated indoors, than outdoors and the more pollutants that are released into the indoor air, the more ventilation is needed to keep the air healthy. Mobile homes may have a smaller volume of air than site-built homes and, if properly weatherized and insulated, have lower natural air infiltration rates than conventional homes. Breathing polluted indoor air can cause respiratory problems or aggravate existing ones. It is important to ventilate the home regularly by opening windows as weather permits to keep the air fresh.

Combustion appliances may cause the most serious indoor air quality problems. Under certain conditions, gas, propane, kerosene, and oil-fired appliances can produce the poisonous gas, carbon monoxide. Combustion appliances can also deplete the oxygen that we breathe if they are open to the living space. Combustion appliances all produce water vapor along with nitrogen oxides and sulfur oxides which are respiratory irritants, especially to children. For these reasons, HUD has required heat producing appliances to be sealed-combustion units. HUD also requires heating appliances to meet specific testing and certification for use in mobile homes. Combustion space heaters, gas and propane ranges, and wood stoves that are not sealed combustion appli-

GETTING STARTED

ances may cause indoor air pollution and associated health problems.

High moisture levels can encourage the growth of dust mites, mold, and fungus that cause allergic reactions in many people. Many building materials contain formaldehyde which, in the vapor form, is a respiratory irritant. HUD limited the amount of formaldehyde that building materials were allowed to contain in the 1985 HUD Code revisions.

Many people suffer poor respiratory health that's caused primarily by inhaling pollutants. Every individual has a different tolerance for pollutants and, after that point is passed, health may be noticeably degraded and the individual may become "environmentally sensitive." If odors linger in your home or if you have had persistent respiratory problems, your indoor air quality can probably be improved. Listed below are some recommendations for reducing indoor air pollution and keeping the air in your home healthy.

1. Never use unvented combustion space heaters.
2. Use an exhaust fan in the kitchen when cooking.
3. Use an exhaust fan in the bathroom when showering.
4. Keep relative humidity as low as possible.
5. Ventilate continuously when the smell of smoke, cleaners, paint, or other pollutants is noticeable.

Environmentally sensitive persons may need to take stronger measures (to avoid severe reactions to pollutants) like the following.

1. Prohibit smoking indoors.
2. Eliminate the use of gas or propane ranges.
3. Eliminate the use and storage of paints, solvents, strong cleaners, and other chemicals indoors.
4. Eliminate wood heating.
5. Keep pets outside.
6. Reduce the use of cosmetics.

ENVELOPES

2.1 Introduction to Mobile Home Envelopes

The envelope of a mobile home consists of the exterior walls, floor, and roof surrounding the living space. Heat flows from indoors to outdoors through the envelope during the winter, and from outdoors to indoors through the envelope during the summer. Heating systems produce heat to counteract heat loss in the winter, and cooling systems remove heat to counteract heat gain in the summer. This section of the manual is devoted to explaining how to reduce heat flows through the envelope by insulating, weatherizing, and making associated repairs. Improvements to the envelope, which slow the flow of heat into and out of the home, will save energy and money by reducing the amount of heat lost or gained.

2.2 Air Leakage Control

In discussions about air leakage, most people blame windows and doors for most of the problem. However, recent research at SERI and the field experience of many weatherization technicians have revealed that the major air leaks in older mobile homes are not usually concentrated around windows and doors. The following is a list of places where the air leaks in older homes are found:

1. Return air plenums in the floor and ceiling associated with heating and cooling systems (see Section 3.4.1, Improving Supply and Return Air Systems).

2. Joints and holes in forced air supply ducts (see Section 2.4.3, Design and Construction Characteristics and Section 3.4.1, Improving Supply and Return Air Systems).

3. Torn or missing underbelly material (see Section 2.4.4, Repairs to the Floor Area).

4. Plumbing access areas under bathtubs, behind washing machines, under sinks, in walls adjoining water heater closets, etc.

5. Joints between the halves of double-section homes and joints between the main structure and building additions.

6. Gaps around water pipes and flue pipes, especially where they penetrate the floor, walls, and ceiling (see figure **2-1**).

7. Hidden openings in closets and cabinets.

8. Older jalousie and awning windows, especially those with malfunctioning closer mechanisms.

9. Loose siding, paneling, and trim (see Section 2.5.4, Wall Repair and Renovation).

10. Electrical service panel boxes.

11. Light fixtures, electrical receptacles, and exhaust fans.

2-1 Gap Around Chimney - Large gaps around chimneys, pipes, and vents are common in older mobile homes.

The two main reasons for sealing air leaks are to prevent warm moist air from entering building cavities and to prevent energy waste caused by excessive air leakage. Preventing moist air flow into building cavities is essential to protecting insulation and other building materials from water damage. Reducing excess air infiltration in all climates, especially hot humid ones, should be a top priority.

ENVELOPES

Caulking or weatherstripping small cracks around doors and windows, while at the same time ignoring large air leaks in hidden locations will have practically no effect on energy consumption. The most important idea for air sealing in homes is to seal the biggest leaks first. The largest and most predictable air leakage reductions come from sealing up ducts and return air plenums in the floor and ceiling, patching underbellies, and plugging major leaks around plumbing, wiring, flues and joints in the building sections. Adding insulation to wall, floor, and ceiling cavities reduces air leakage to a surprising extent, also.

There is a large selection of materials available for patching large leaks in walls, floors, and ceilings that are similar in structure and appearance to the existing materials. Adhesives packaged in caulking tubes and spray cans are very useful for attaching patches. Cracks and small holes more than 1/8 inch wide should be stuffed with foam rubber or another compressible material before caulking is applied (see figure **2-2**). Use caulking and foam rubber wherever you find noticeable drafts coming from small and medium-sized cracks on the interior side of walls, floors, and ceilings. Apply caulking to the outside of the home only to seal window and door frames from water. Some people are sensitive to the odor from caulking and adhesives. It's best to ventilate the home regularly for a day or so after application to remove any odors.

2-2 Air Sealing Pipes - Stuff foam rubber or another suitable material in gaps around openings before caulking them. Follow the same procedure with cracks and small holes in the walls, floor, and ceiling.

The main challenge in controlling air leakage in homes is in determining how large of a problem air leakage presents in a particular home. Most of what is known about the effectiveness of air sealing methods comes from the use of blower door testing. Blower door tests produce approximate air leakage estimates by measuring how much air flow is required to keep the home depressurized to a specific pressure — usually 50 pascals (or 0.2 inches of water). A wind of approximately 30 miles per hour blowing against the side of a home would produce about 50 pascals of pressure difference between indoors and outdoors and would be similar to a house pressure of 50 pascals produced by a blower door.

2.2.1 Blower Door Testing

Blower door testing is a practical and effective technique for estimating air leakage in homes. Some homes are very leaky while others are very tight, and it's difficult to distinguish the difference without measuring. A blower door is an air-leakage testing device used by weatherization crews and energy researchers. The blower door consists of a large fan that is positioned in a sealed doorway (see figure **2-3**). The pressure created by the fan draws air from outdoors through holes and cracks in the house and forces that air through the fan housing where the air flow rate is measured by guages.

Blower door testing is used to determine how much air leakage a home has and to help decide if air-sealing work is necessary. A high air flow reading on the blower door at 50 pascals house pressure would point out the need to seal air leaks. A low reading would mean that the home is allowing only enough air leakage to keep the air fresh and relatively dry. In this case, air-sealing

ENVELOPES

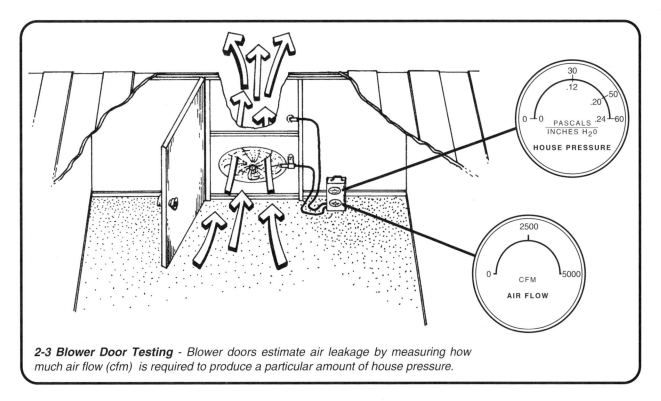

2-3 Blower Door Testing - *Blower doors estimate air leakage by measuring how much air flow (cfm) is required to produce a particular amount of house pressure.*

procedures will not be cost-effective and may create a health hazard. If the decision is made to seal air leaks, the blower door helps to locate specific areas in the home that allow air leakage and require air sealing. You can feel air coming in from the various leaks around the home. You can seal a leak temporarily or permanently and then measure the reduction in air flow. **The use of blower door testing is the only practical and accurate way to determine whether or not you need to seal air leaks.**

The blower door measures two factors: 1) the pressure difference between indoors and outdoors, referred to as the "house pressure" and measured in pascals; and 2) the air flow rate in cubic feet per minute (cfm) required to maintain a specific house pressure (see figure **2-3**). Calculations are applied to the exaggerated air flow, produced and measured by the blower door, to estimate the natural air flow under typical wind and barometric conditions.

There is one common factor that is measured by a blower door and two others that are calculated from these measurements. These factors are discussed as follows:

1. The 50-Pascal Air Flow Rate is expressed in cubic feet per minute (CFM50) and is the actual flow rate measured at 50 pascals of house pressure. CFM50 is the simplest and most direct measurement of the airtightness of a building.

2. The 50-Pascal Air Change Rate is expressed in air changes per hour at 50 pascals (ACH50) and is calculated by dividing the CFM50 by the house volume in cubic feet, and then multiplying by 60 minutes per hour.

3. Natural Air Change Rate is expressed in air changes per hour (ACHn) and is roughly estimated by dividing the 50-Pascal Air Change Rate by a number between 10 and 20 depending on geographic location, wind, and shielding by nearby objects. The Environmental Protection Agency (EPA) suggests a natural air change rate of at least 0.35 ACHn.

ENVELOPES

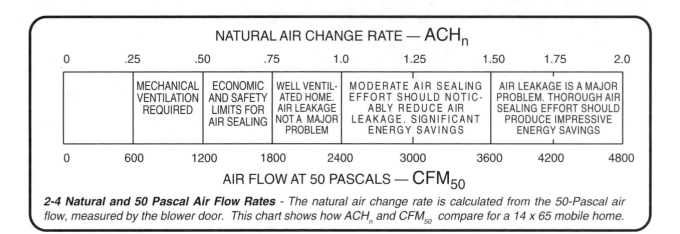

2-4 Natural and 50 Pascal Air Flow Rates - The natural air change rate is calculated from the 50-Pascal air flow, measured by the blower door. This chart shows how ACH_n and CFM_{50} compare for a 14 x 65 mobile home.

To protect indoor air quality, the American Society of Heating, Refrigeration, and Air Conditioning Engineers (ASHRAE) and the EPA set guidelines, for minimum natural air flow rates in buildings. The recommendations in figure **2-4** are based on the ASHRAE and EPA guidelines and they add a small safety allowance to compensate for inaccuracy of estimating natural air flows from blower door measurements. The home must have enough air leakage to remove moisture and pollutants and to ensure healthy indoor air or it must have a mechanical ventilation system.

2.3 Insulation Methods and Materials

This section will provide general information to home owners and technicians on characteristics of various types of insulation and on techniques which are unique to installing insulation in mobile homes. While there are many types of insulation on the market, the insulation types discussed here are only those used most often for insulating mobile homes.

Insulation slows the movement of heat through the envelope of the home. Insulation is added to cavities in the building envelope to slow heat loss in the winter and heat gain in the summer. Insulation materials work because they have millions of tiny air cavities that reduce the flow of heat.

Many mobile homes, especially those built before 1976, are not well insulated. Walls, floors, and roofs typically have from 1 to 4 inches of insulation. The wall, floor, and ceiling cavities are often partially void of insulation. When building cavities are partially empty, air can circulate around the insulation reducing its resistance to heat flow. These facts point to the opportunity to add insulation, which can bring the home up to modern standards of energy efficiency. However, adding insulation to building cavities can be difficult and requires some skill and specialized equipment.

In cold climates, it makes good economic sense to add insulation to building cavities where there is room for more insulation. Roof cavities, with their high solar heat absorbance, are good candidates for more insulation in hot climates, too. However, it is much less cost-effective to add insulation to the walls and floors of homes in hot climates when those cavities already have a couple of inches of insulation.

2.3.1 R-Values

The R-value of a material is its resistance to heat flow. The higher the R-value of a material the longer it takes heat to travel through the material. Single-pane glass has an R-value of R-1; wood doors, R-2; and uninsulated walls, R-4. Insulating materials have R-values that range from R-2 to R-6 per inch of thickness (see figure **2-5**). Adding insulation to a wall, floor, or ceiling increases its

ENVELOPES

R-value. More compacted insulation produces a slightly higher R-value per inch of thickness and stops air more effectively from moving through and around it. Compacting insulation is important in blowing wall cavities to achieve maximum R-value and to stop air movement in walls. (see Section 2.5.5, Wall Insulation.) It is less important in ceilings and floors because these areas are horizontal and do not experience a chimney effect like walls do.

The ideal installation of insulation, especially blown insulation, has uniform coverage and density (see figure **2-6**). Uniform coverage means that there are no voids and that all areas of the building cavity are evenly blanketed with insulation. Uniform density means that the insulation is uniformly compacted or fluffed in all areas of the cavity. You may not be able to achieve uniform density and coverage in all areas of the floor and ceiling, which vary in depth and access, but it's worth striving for because the uniformity of coverage and density have a significant influence on the effectiveness of the insulation. Various types of fill tubes, inserted into the cavities, help to achieve uniform coverage and density for blown insulation.

2.3.2 Natural Air Changes, Moisture, and Ventilation

Installing insulation in the cavities of the building envelope reduces air flow through the cavities and air flow into and out of the home. Since air leakage is a natural form of ventilation, a lower air leakage rate can produce higher humidity levels, moisture problems, and possibly indoor air pollution. These issues are discussed more thoroughly in Sections 1.7, Moisture and Ventilation and Section 1.9, Indoor Air Quality.

Adding insulation to the envelope reduces air flow through the cavities. With less air flowing through the cavities, there is less air to bring moisture into the insulation and also less air to carry moisture away. However, there is little or no evidence to indicate that installing insulation either aggravates or relieves moisture problems inside the cavities. Experience from professionals who are performing the insulation work, described in this section, indicates that moisture problems have not been aggravated by insulation.

R-VALUES OF COMMON ATTIC INSULATION MATERIALS PER INCH OF THICKNESS	
Fiberglass Batts	2.0-3.0
Fiberglass Blowing Wool	2.5-3.5
Mineral (Rock) Blowing Wool	2.5-3.0
Cellulose Blowing Insulation	3.0-4.0
Polystyrene Beads	2.0-2.5
Urethane Foamboard	5.5-6.5
Polystyrene Beadboard	3.5-4.0

Figure 2.5

2.3.3 Fiberglass Insulation

Fiberglass is a versatile insulating material for adding insulation to mobile homes because it is non-combustible and it absorbs only a little water. Fiberglass is not organic so it does not provide food for pests. The R-value of fiberglass is around 2.9 per inch at a density of 0.65 lbs./cu.ft. (pounds per cubic foot), and R-4.0 per inch at 4 lbs./cu.ft.

The main advantages of using fiberglass batts are that they are inexpensive and readily available. The best kind of fiberglass batt to use in a mobile home is the unfaced batt. Most facings are partial vapor barriers and they make the batts harder to install and less resistant to moisture. The purpose of facings is to resist moisture and to make fastening easier in new homes but the facings

ENVELOPES

are a hindrance in reinsulating mobile homes. Facings are flammable too, unlike fiberglass itself which is non-combustible. One disadvantage of using fiberglass batts is that their low density (light weight) may not reduce air flow in the building cavities as well as denser blown insulation. Compressing the batts, or installing them in narrower cavities than the batt is designed for, will resist air flow better than installing them at the lower density.

Fiberglass batt or blanket insulation was installed in most manufactured homes in service today. The batt insulation was either installed between studs, trusses, and floor joists or blanket insulation was installed over the outside of the framing in large pieces. Fiberglass batts can be compressed in walls by removing the exterior wall and adding the batts to uninsulated or partially insulated cavities. Or you can stuff batt insulation into the cavities from the bottom of the wall. For ex-

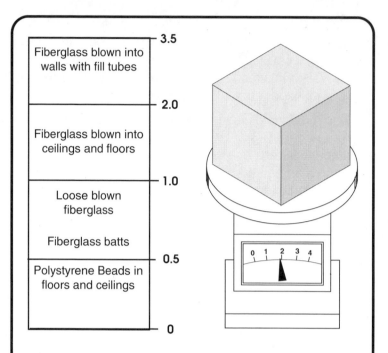

2-6 Density of Insulation - Density of insulation affects its R-value and resistance to air flow. Wall insulation should be denser than floor and ceiling insulation because walls are vertical like chimneys and air flow inside wall cavities is a bigger problem than in floors and ceilings. Numbers on the above graph are density in pounds per cubic foot of insulation.

ample, you can compress a batt designed for a 3.5 inch wall into a 1.75 inch wall approximately doubling the insulation density, slightly increasing the batt's R-value per inch, and significantly increasing its resistance to air flow (see Section 2.5.5.2, Stuffing Fiberglass Insulation). However, the batt, optimistically rated by the manufacturer at R-11, becomes about R-7.

The advantages of fiberglass blowing wool are that it can be installed in roof and floor cavities at a lower density than cellulose, and it puts less pressure on the ceiling or underbelly during installation, reducing the danger of damaging paneling or belly board. Fiberglass absorbs much less water in the event of a roof leak or condensation. The disadvantages of using fiberglass blowing wool are that it requires more skill to install, and it readily catches on obstacles inside the cavities. (see Section 2.4.5, Insulating Floors).

Fiberglass for blowing is packed in a very compressed 30 to 40 pound bale and requires a blowing machine with an agitator that will tear up the fiberglass bale into small pieces. Smaller pieces of fiberglass will fly fluidly through the blower hose without plugging up. Some less expensive blowing machines are not suitable for blowing fiberglass.

Caution: *Fiberglass insulation irritates the skin and lungs. Always wear a respirator when working with fiberglass.* Powdering exposed parts of the body before handling fiberglass will reduce itching and skin irritation.

2.3.4 Polystyrene Beads

Polystyrene beads are lightweight, moisture-resistant plastic foam beads. Beads used for blow-

ENVELOPES

ing are made by shredding polystyrene foam board waste. The largest particles of shredded foam board should be no more than 1/2 inch in diameter.

One advantage of using polystyrene beads is that they pose the least risk of contributing to moisture damage of any common insulation. Beads are easy to install in floors and ceilings because they can flow past barriers that would stop fiberglass or cellulose. Beads don't produce much dust and will work well with almost any blowing machine. They are less likely than cellulose or fiberglass to plug the hose on the blowing machine. Beads have a relatively low R-value of about 2.3 per inch but their other good qualities make them a practical choice for mobile home roof and belly insulation.

Beads have several disadvantages. They are not packaged in compressed form so they are very bulky to store and transport compared to other blowing insulations. Beads may not be appropriate for roof cavities of homes in very hot and sunny climates because polystyrene starts to soften and shrink at temperatures above 130° F. Beads should not be used in wall cavities with interior wood paneling because the HUD code states that all plastic foam insulation must be separated from indoors by at least 5/16 inch gypsum board or 2 inches of mineral fiber insulation or equivalent materials. This standard is important because polystyrene beads are combustible and produce toxic smoke when they burn. Beads would be difficult to install in walls anyway because they will flow out of the bottom of a wall cavity through any small holes.

2.3.5 Cellulose Blowing Material

Cellulose blowing insulation is inexpensive, has a high thermal resistance (R-3.5 to 4.0 per inch) and is easy to install. Cellulose is easier for a do-it-yourselfer with a rented blowing machine to use than fiberglass. The major disadvantage of cellulose is that it absorbs a great deal more water than fiberglass or polystyrene beads. Another disadvantage is that the fire retardants in the cellulose can corrode metal siding and roofing. Cellulose also puts more pressure on the siding, roofing, and underbelly during installation than fiberglass or beads, increasing the likelihood of damage. Because of these disadvantages, cellulose is only practical for mobile homes in very dry climates. It is necessary to use cellulose with fire retardants that are compatible with metal, if the insulation will be in contact with metal siding or roofing.

2.3.6 Rigid Foam Board

Foam board (1/4 inch thick), faced with cardboard or foil, is a common exterior insulated sheathing for many mobile homes. You can buy this type of foam board at mobile home suppliers in long folding sheets up to 9 feet wide. This material is excellent for belly repair and sealing air leaks in areas that do not face a living space. Thicker 4 x 8 foot sheets of polystyrene foam and polyurethane foam are useful for patching bellies below pipes and ducts to enclose them within the heated envelope. White polystyrene bead board is the least expensive of the foam boards and is installed over metal roofs and capped with rubber or metal roofing (see Section 2.6.4.1, Insulated Rubber Roof Cap).

Caution: Building codes do not allow the interior application of plastic foam board because it produces toxic smoke during a fire. The HUD Code requires that foam board be separated from the interior by 5/16 inch gypsum board or 2 inch mineral fiber insulation or equivalent materials.

2.3.7 Blowing Insulation

Blowing insulation into wall, floor, and roof cavities can be the easiest and most practical insulation method available. Types of blown-in insulation used in mobile homes include fiberglass, cellu-

ENVELOPES

lose, and polystyrene beads. There are two major challenges to blowing insulation with an insulation-blowing machine.

The first major challenge is gaining access to cavities. **Plan ahead.** Before you remove a section of the wall, floor, or roof cavities or cut any holes into the cavity, you should know how you are going to replace it or patch the holes. A key element in this strategy is to have the right tools and materials to do the job. Power tools are essential to the modern professional tradesman. You can accomplish most jobs with hand tools though, if you have the skill and the patience.

The second major challenge is obtaining a suitable blowing machine and learning to use it with the accessory equipment like: hoses, fittings, and fill tubes (see figure **2-7**). To install blowing wool insulation with a uniform density and coverage, the technician must learn to use blowing equipment and select the right insulation for a particular job. After a few mobile home insulation blowing jobs, a technician should be confident enough to handle any blowing job that is judged to be cost-effective.

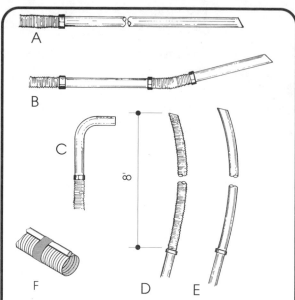

2-7 Fill Tubes for Blowing Insulation:- A. Long 1 1/2-2 inch rigid pipe used for floor and roof insulation; B. Semi-rigid, semi-flexible fill tube used for roof insulation; C. 1 1/2-2 inch muffler pipe fitting for blowing through ceilings, roofs, and bellies; D. Wall insulation fill tube made of flexible recreational vehicle sewer pipe; E. Wall insulation fill tube using flexible heavy-duty agricultural tubing; F. PVC water pipe is taped to the blower hose to stiffen the last 4 to 8 feet of hose.

Using fill tubes correctly is important to maintaining uniform density and coverage of the blown insulation. The density of blown fiberglass and cellulose insulation will be lower the farther away from the end of the fill tube that the insulation is blown. The denser you want the insulation, the closer you want the end of the fill tube to the part of the cavity you are blowing. The density of blown insulation should be 1 to 2 pounds per cubic foot in floors and ceilings and the fill tube should be held so that the insulation will travel no more than 24 inches from the end of the fill tube. Wall insulation should be at least 3 pounds per cubic foot and the fill tube should be held so that the insulation will travel no more than 12 inches from the end of the fill tube (see Section 2.5.5.1, Blowing Insulation Into Wall Cavities). However, depending on the power of the blower, the insulation can travel 24 inches or more without losing too much density or creating voids in floor and ceiling cavities.

Static electricity can build up in insulation hoses and fill tubes and cause painful static shocks to technicians. Fill tubes made of PVC plastic pipe are the worst. Fill tubes made of lightweight electrical conduit or copper drain pipe are more static free than PVC. You can also attach a piece of #8 bare copper wire to the metal connector between the hose and the fill tube and drag the wire, clamped to a piece of copper tubing for weight, on the ground to discharge the static electricity into the ground. The wire must be attached tightly to the connector and tubing. Spraying small amounts of water, mixed with just enough antifreeze to keep it from freezing, into the hopper of the blowing machine will also reduce static electricity. Make sure that the home itself is grounded properly before blowing insulation.

Graphite dust is an excellent lubricant for blowing equipment. The best way to use graphite is to mix a of a half pint or so of graphite dust with a half hopper of insulation, and then blow the

ENVELOPES

mixture through the blower and hose and back into the hopper of the blowing machine a few times. Then blow the mixture back into a sturdy plastic bag to be used to lubricate the equipment again.

Caution: Blowing insulation creates dust that may irritate the skin and lungs. Technicians blowing insulation should always wear respirators.

2.3.8 Radiant Barriers/Reflective Coatings

Radiant barriers are reflective coatings and foils that are effective at reducing solar heat gain in hot climates. There isn't much, if any, evidence that radiant barriers are cost-effective in cold climates. Radiant barriers are designed to reflect heat rays and are not insulating materials. Most foil radiant barriers are not practical for manufactured homes because you would have to remove the wall, ceiling, or roof coverings to install them.

The exterior walls and roof of a mobile home should be reflective in warm climates to prevent the skin of the home from absorbing too much solar energy in summer months. Dark colors are inappropriate for walls and roofs in hot climates because they absorb too much solar heat. Mobile home siding can be repainted a lighter color (see Appendix D, Maintenance Tips).

Roofs can be coated with a variety of reflective coatings. The most common is an asphalt-based coating with aluminum particles and mineral fibers mixed in, that reflects about 60% of the solar heat hitting the roof. The asphalt coatings are reasonably priced and vary in quality, mainly by the amount of aluminum material in each 5-gallon container. The better coatings, which are more expensive, contain more aluminum and may offer a little improvement in reflectivity. This asphalt/aluminum coating must be stirred vigorously and often during application. The bright white latex rubber coatings, which reflect as much as 80% of the solar heat that strikes the roof, are better for warm, sunny climates. Most large hardware stores and lumber yards carry both types of roof coating. Be sure to follow the manufacturer's instructions for surface preparation and application carefully. (see Section 2.6.7, Roof Repair).

2.4 Floors

2.4.1 Introduction To Floors

Mobile home floors that have insulation levels of 3 inches of fibrous insulation or less can be an important source of heat loss in cooler climates. Floors are often the major source of air leakage, leaking more air into and out of the home than the windows, doors, and walls combined. The floor is the most vulnerable area to damage from plumbing repairs, moisture, animals, and other causes. The heating duct system, housed in the floor assembly, is often the source of the most serious air leakage anywhere in the home.

Floor insulation may not be cost-effective in warm climates with long cooling seasons where the crawl space remains cooler than the outdoor air in the summer. However, even in warm climates you still have to be sure that the floor is in good repair and that ducts are sealed to limit air leakage. Sealing ducts is doubly important in hot humid climates because cooled air leaving the ducts can cause moisture problems in the underbelly (see Section 4.4.5, Distribution Systems).

There are five main energy problems related to mobile home floor assemblies.

1. Inadequate floor insulation. Three inches or less is common.

2. Air leakage into the home caused by holes in the underbelly and insulation.

3. Movement of outdoor air around and through the insulation caused by damage to the

ENVELOPES

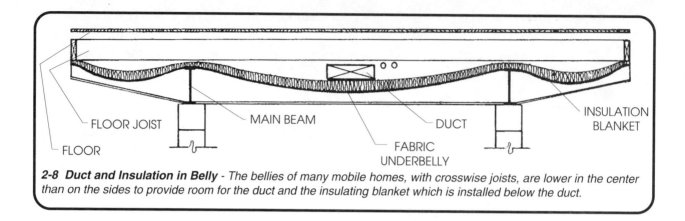

2-8 Duct and Insulation in Belly - *The bellies of many mobile homes, with crosswise joists, are lower in the center than on the sides to provide room for the duct and the insulating blanket which is installed below the duct.*

underbelly. This airflow can decrease the insulation's ability to resist heat flow.

4. Leaks in the heating/cooling ducts. These leaks can cause heated or cooled air to escape through holes in the underbelly and insulation (see Section 2.4.4, Repairs to the Floor Area).

5. Return air plenums in the floor (in some homes). These plenums allow the introduction of large amounts of outside air directly into the heating or cooling system (see Section 3.4.1, Improving Supply and Return Air Systems).

For the reasons listed above, floors are the key element for mobile home weatherization, especially in cold climates. Floor insulation and the associated repairs to the underbelly can effectively solve the first three problems. You have to repair the underbelly anyway to contain the new insulation and to protect it. Those repairs reduce air leakage and reduce convection of outdoor air through and around the insulation. The new insulation fills the floor cavity, greatly increasing the R-value of the floor and further reducing air circulation in the cavity.

2.4.2 What To Look For

The floor should feel solid when you walk around on it and should not have soft spots. Water damaged and weak areas should be repaired (see figure **2-12**). The underbelly should be nearly airtight with no open holes or cracks. The heating supply duct should be enclosed within the heated envelope or should be insulated to R-4. Plumbing, wiring, and other penetrations should be sealed from the top and bottom of the floor assembly. Drain pipes and supply pipes should be protected from freezing by being enclosed within the insulated floor cavity, or be insulated to R-4. Heat tape, approved for use in manufactured housing (see Section 5.3.5, Special Safety Precautions), is also an option in cold climates.

In Zone 1 (see the map in figure **1-2**), the underbelly should be airtight and the floor insulated to at least R-6.5. In the colder regions of Zone 1, the floor should be insulated to at least R-11. R-11 is a minimum for the warmer regions of Zone 2 and R-19 is recommended for the cooler areas of Zone 2 and Zone 3. R-values higher than R-19 are difficult to achieve in mobile home floors unless the floor cavity is filled with fibrous insulation and rigid foam board is attached to the outside of the underbelly. This is an option to be considered only in the severest northern climates, like Alaska. These recommendations are based on minimum standards by HUD, DOE, and others for conserving energy in homes, and also on the cost and difficulty of insulating mobile home floors.

Skirting is important to protect the underbelly from damage from rodents and cats. Skirting also breaks the wind in cooler climates and prevents pipes from freezing.

ENVELOPES

![Figure 2-9 diagram]

2-9 Duct Location For Lengthwise Joists - The main duct is up against the flooring in mobile homes with lengthwise joists.

2.4.3 Design and Construction Characteristics

The floor assembly of a mobile home is more complex than that of a conventional home. The floor has 2x6 floor joists (2x4s on some older models) that are spaced at 16, 18, or 24 inches on center and supported by the metal chassis (see figure **1-3**). The floor joists run lengthwise along the long axis of the home or crosswise across the width of the home. Floors with crosswise joists have underbellies bellies that are dropped 4 to 10 inches below the bottom of the floor joists because the main duct is located below the joists (see figure **2-8**). On floors with lengthwise joists, the duct is between the floor joists up against the flooring (see figure **2-9**) and the belly board or rodent barrier is attached to the bottom of the floor joists.

Fibrous insulation is installed either between the floor joists or attached in a large blanket to the bottom of the floor joists. Since the 1976 HUD Code, the heating/cooling duct must either be insulated or be included in the heated envelope by having the insulating blanket of the floor installed underneath it as shown in figure **2-8**.

The bottom of the floor is covered with a material that protects the floor during moving and keeps animals out of the floor once the mobile home is installed. Older mobile homes use an underbelly of asphalt impregnated fiberboard or heavy tar paper. Newer mobile homes use an asphalt-impregnated fiberglass cloth or fiber-reinforced polyethylene. The fiberboard, paper, plastic, or fabric underbelly material is attached to the bottom of the floor during construction. Particle board flooring (5/8 or 3/4 inch) is fastened to the top of the floor joists. The wood floor, with the insulation, duct and belly board is then placed on the steel frame so the underbelly material is pinned between the chassis and the wood floor. The floor joists are fastened with lag screws to the steel chassis which is as long and wide as the home.

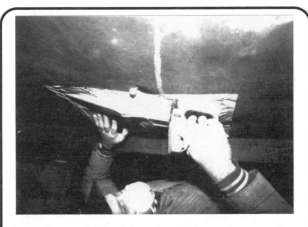

2-10 Outward Clinch Stapler - This stapler, sometimes called a stitch stapler, fastens paper and fabric underbelly to patches made of the same material.

2-11 Underbelly Patch - A technician puts caulking around the perimeter of a patch made of an air infiltration barrier material.

ENVELOPES

2.4.4 Repairs to the Floor Area

There are a variety of effective methods used to patch the underbelly. A key fact to remember is that the underbelly material is sandwiched between the metal chassis and the wood floor. You cannot always fasten a patch to a floor joist because the metal frame under the floor may be in the way.

Paper and fabric bellies are the easiest to patch. A combination of mechanical fasteners and adhesives provides the most secure patch. Many professional technicians and mobile home repair services use outward clinch staplers (also called stitch staplers) (see figure **2-10**) and common construction adhesive to fasten a fabric or paper patch to the existing belly board when there is no wood backing to fasten the patch to (see figure **2-11**). Standard construction adhesive works very well and some spray adhesives and tape, sold by mobile home parts suppliers, are also acceptable. Large fabric patches may be reinforced with wood lath screwed into available floor joists so that the force of blown insulation doesn't loosen the patches.

2-12 Floor Patch - Cut damaged sections of flooring out between joists where you can reattach a plywood patch.

Solid fiberboard bellies can be patched using a variety of materials including plywood, paneling, reinforced polyethylene, and rigid insulation. Power staplers and screw guns are handy for fastening patches to solid underbellies.

Damaged areas in the particle board flooring can be repaired using plywood or particle board (preferably plywood because it's stronger and more waterproof) of the same thickness as the floor, usually 5/8 or 3/4 of an inch. To repair the hole, locate the centers of two floor joists at or beyond the damaged area (see figure **2-12**). Remove the nails or staples along the line where you'll be cutting. Use a circular saw with the blade set to a depth of 5/8 or 3/4 inch to avoid damaging the floor joist. You should make your cut over the center of the joist. Some professional repair specialists cut on the edge of the joist and attach a 2x4 nailer to the side of each of the floor joists bordering the patch.

Cut out a rectangular section of floor and patch with a piece of the same size minus about 1/8 to 1/4 inch in length and width for fit and expansion. Fasten the new patch with screws, countersunk to make the heads even with the floor.

Sqeaky floors can usually be fixed by driving a flathead all-purpose screw into the squeaky area but sometimes you need to drive a small wedge between the floor joist and the particle board floor from under the floor to stop the squeak. Humps and sagging areas caused

2-13 Leveling the Floor - Illustrates how to level floors if the floor joists are bowed causing the floor to hump or sag.

ENVELOPES

by humping or sagging floor joists can be repaired using a 2x4 or 4x4 wood beam or an angle iron beam (see figure **2-13**). Lag screws provide the force to pull the floor joists into a level plane. A small hydraulic jack can provide some extra lift for stubborn joists.

2.4.5 Insulating Floors

The crawl space area under a mobile home may be cramped, dark, and dirty, but it is the best access point for floor repair and insulation. You can make the crawl space a more tolerable place to work by installing a polyethylene moisture barrier on the ground. This moisture barrier reduce moisture transmission from the ground and will make the area more comfortable to work in (See Section 1.5.7, Installing a Ground Cover). You may need protective gear such as a respirator, safety glasses, and coveralls. Always inspect the entire area underneath the home before deciding which repair and weatherization projects you will do.

The most effective insulating materials for floors include unfaced fiberglass batts, rigid foam insulation, blown fiberglass, and polystyrene beads. Mobile home floors vary in construction, accessibility, and state of repair so you may have to use more than one insulation technique.

When large sections of the underbelly are damaged or missing and where access to the crawl space is easy, you can stuff fiberglass batts into the floor cavity. It is important to get full coverage with no gaps in the fiberglass. Do not hesitate to buy fiberglass batts designed for a thicker cavity and compress them because this practice will give a slightly higher R-value and inhibit air circulation in the cavity. Damaged areas of the underbelly can also be access points for blowing insulation. You can blow insulation into the areas you can reach through existing holes and tears in the underbelly before patching it.

Sheeting over the underbelly with rigid foam insulation is also a good option, either by itself or combined with the fiberglass batts. You can use 1/4 inch foam board common to mobile homes as a convenient replacement belly board when you install new fiberglass batts. Thicker rigid foam board insulation can be fastened with screws or nails with large washers that prevent the fastener from pulling through the soft insulation material.

Blowing fiberglass, cellulose, or polystyrene beads is the easiest and fastest way to insulate the floor cavity. Before beginning to blow insulation into the floor cavity, follow the 4 preparatory steps listed below.

Step 1: Tightly seal all openings in the floor from above to prevent loose insulation from entering the living space. Inspect and seal the ductwork thoroughly, as described in Section 3.4.1, to prevent blown insulation from entering the ductwork.

Step 2: Repair the belly board as necessary using the techniques described in Section 2.4.4. Consider blowing insulation through damaged sections of the rodent barrier before you patch any holes. You may be able to fill several cavities through one large tear in the belly using a flexible fill tube.

Step 3: Locate the plumbing supply pipes

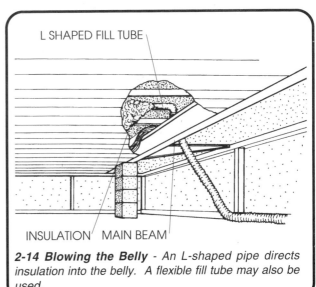

2-14 Blowing the Belly - An L-shaped pipe directs insulation into the belly. A flexible fill tube may also be used.

ENVELOPES

and note where they run. If they are installed up close to the floor or next to the heating duct, you don't have to worry about them freezing after you add insulation. Check the pipes for leaks and repair any leaks before adding insulation.

Step 3A: If the supply pipes are separated from the warmth of the home, they may freeze. If the pipes are below the floor and away from the heating duct, you'll have to find a way to strap them up closer to the floor to avoid insulating above them.

2-15 Cutting a Hole at a Floor Joist - A hole directly beneath a floor joist gives the technician access to two joist spaces.

Step 3B: If you cannot move the pipes close to the floor or a heating duct, you'll have to take an additional step after you blow in insulation. Slit the belly to access the pipes. Reach up and push the insulation away from the pipe so that it is not between the floor and the pipe. This will allow heat to escape through the floor and prevent the pipes from freezing. Place the remaining insulation below the pipes and patch the belly. Another option is to sheet over the rodent barrier underneath the water pipes with foam insulation board.

Step 4: In floors with crosswise joists and a dropped belly, you may want to push the dropped belly up and brace it to reduce the volume of insulation that the belly will consume. With fabric bellies, you can pin the fabric up to the floor joists with wood strips. With rigid bellies that rest on the lip of the I-beams, you can use wood spacers. Leave a 2-4 inch space under pipes and ducts which can be filled with insulation.

The following are three good options for blowing insulation into the floor cavity. Carefully inspect the floor to familiarize yourself with the construction characteristics and the condition of the underbelly, before deciding how to proceed. You can add insulation to almost any floor using the methods described below or else a combination of these methods.

Option 1: Blowing insulation into the closed floor cavity through the underbelly underneath the home is a simple and practical method for persons experienced in blowing insulation. If there is at least 18 inches of vertical space under the home, cut small holes in the belly board, blow in insulation, and then patch the holes. Another alternative is to cut a V-shaped slit in the belly board. The V-shaped slit in fabric and paper underbelly works well if you are blowing with an L-shaped metal fill tube (see figure **2-14**).

2-16 Blowing Through the Rim Joist - This technician has drilled a hole through the rim joist in order to blow insulation through a 12 foot metal pipe into the floor.

Option 2: With crosswise floor joists and a paper or fabric underbelly, cut an

ENVELOPES

H-shaped 6 by 12 inch slit in the fabric or paper belly material right across a joist just outside the main beam. This produces two holes about 6 inches square, one on each side of the joist, giving access to two adjacent joist spaces (see figure **2-15**). Or with lengthwise joists, simply make the same H-shaped slits through the belly paper or fabric across the width of the belly every 6 to 12 feet depending on the length of the fill tube. With rigid belly board, you would need to cut a rectangular hole directly under a floor joist. Either of these methods leave fewer openings because of accessing two or more cavities from one hole. The larger opening allows the use of a semi-flexible 4-8 foot-long fill tube. The fill tube ensures uniform coverage and density.

Option 3: Loosen or remove the metal trim piece at the bottom of the wall. Drill a hole at least 2 inches in diameter through the rim joist into each joist cavity. A long plastic or metal tube is then attached to the end of the blowing hose and inserted into the cavity until it is 18 inches or less from the rim joist on the opposite side (see figure **2-16**). One disadvantage of this method is that these holes may weaken the rim joist to an unacceptable degree, especially when the mobile home is moved again or when it has 2x4 floor joists, or in areas with high snow loads. At worst, you might have to add several piers and footings under the rim joist for added support (see Section 1.5.3, Foundations).

2.5 Walls

2.5.1 Design and Construction Characteristics

Many existing mobile homes have only 1 or 2 inches of fiberglass insulation installed in the wall cavity or over the outside of the studs. In other homes, the insulation has settled down the wall a couple feet or more from vibration in transit. These homes are good candidates for wall insulation if they are located in areas with cold winters. The three most common wall types that would benefit from increased wall insulation are shown in figures **2-17, 2-18,** and **2-19**. A majority of mobile home walls have 2x4 studs (vertical framing boards) that measure 1-1/2 x 3-1/2 inches in width and depth. The next most common type of wall stud is the 2x3 which measures 1-1/2 x 2-1/2 inches. Construction of 2x3 and 2x4 stud walls is similar, as shown in figure **2-17**. Some newer mobile homes built for cold climates have 2x6 studs which measure 1-1/2 x 5-1/2 inches (see figure **2-18**).

Many older mobile homes built before 1976 have 2x2 studs which measure 1-3/4 x 1-3/4 inches (see figure **2-19**).

Many mobile home walls have belt rails of 3/4 inch thick lumber that is applied horizontally

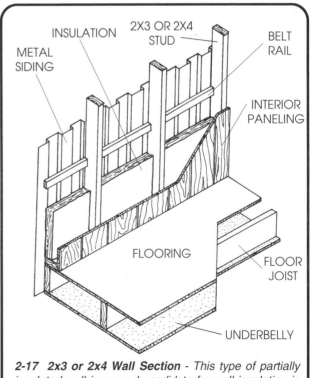

2-17 2x3 or 2x4 Wall Section - This type of partially insulated wall is a good candidate for wall insulation in cold and temperate climates.

ENVELOPES

across the studs to provide a nailing strip for the siding. The belt rails are either fastened on top of the stud or fastened into rectangular slots cut in the studs (see figures **2-17** and **2-19**). The studs and sills are usually not doubled up around windows and doors as they are in site-built houses.

2.5.2 What To Look For

It is usually easy to inspect a wall cavity and usually takes only a few minutes. Look for a joint in the metal siding where it is easy to remove a few screws and partially unfasten a panel. Or find an electric outlet or switch inside where the hole under the outlet cover is large enough to see around the box into the wall. If neither of these options will work, you can cut a hole in the outside wall from inside a closet, that can be patched when you are finished. If you suspect that insulation may vary in different parts of the mobile home, inspect several walls. Use a flashlight to inspect the wall cavity to determine if there is any wall in-

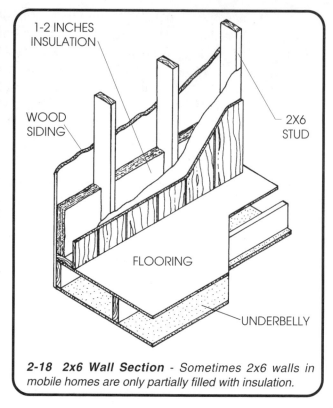

2-18 2x6 Wall Section - Sometimes 2x6 walls in mobile homes are only partially filled with insulation.

sulation and, if so, how much. You may actually need to partially remove a few exterior wall panels to clearly see the insulation and other features of the wall. A good indication of settled or missing insulation is a wall section that is colder than other wall sections in the winter. An uninsulated wall section would feel colder to the touch and would be more likely to have water condensation or frost deposits during very cold weather.

2.5.3 Wall Insulation and Moisture

Condensation in walls has been a common problem in mobile homes. Water leakage can also be a serious problem. Water damage is often observed at the bottom part of the wall cavity and at window sills. While there is the slight possibility that wall insulation will aggravate existing moisture problems by reducing the flow of dry air through the cavity, it is more likely that wall insulation should reduce wall moisture problems. By completely filling the cavity, insulation reduces the mixing of warm moist air and cooler drier air because the insulation stops most of the air movement. Moisture will still move into and out of the wall but at a slower rate.

If you want to insulate your walls and not have wall moisture problems:

1. First identify existing moisture problems and their causes and provide effective solutions for those problems.

2. Do not seal the exterior siding, especially horizontal joints at the top and bottom of the wall. Many mobile home walls were designed with a ventilated wall system to remove moisture. One benefit of this system is that the unsealed bottom joint does allow water to escape. (see Section 1.7, Moisture and Ventilation and figure **1-27**.)

ENVELOPES

2.5.4 Wall Repair and Renovation

If wall framing has been damaged by moisture or by impact in transit, you should remove and replace the damaged framing pieces. If you have to re-size a window or door opening, the job is similar to repairing a wall. The mobile home is designed to be lightweight, so every piece is important to the structure. New pieces of the framework should be the exact same size as the damaged pieces that you remove. Make sure that wall studs are fairly straight so they don't create bulges in the wall. Fastening the framing pieces is the key to wall frame repair. Construction adhesive and all-purpose screws are better than nails because nails can split the wood and reduce the strength of the wall frame. Be sure to drill holes in lumber before driving the screws to prevent splitting.

Paneling and trim indoors should be re-fastened if loose. A standard construction adhesive will help to fasten paneling and trim permanently. When you re-nail paneling and trim, don't use the existing nail holes because the nails will come loose again. Nail holes can be covered by colored putty available at most lumber and hardware stores.

2-19 2x2 Wall Section - This older type of wall is a good candidate for wall insulation in cold and temperate climates, however installation can be a tight squeeze.

Pressed fiberboard siding deteriorates quickly when exposed to water from condensation or water leakage from the outside. The damage to fiberboard is often concentrated near the bottom of the wall. One idea for repairing the damage is to cut a straight horizontal line with a power saw around the home just above the damaged areas and then remove the damaged siding. While this continuous gap in the bottom of the wall cavity is open, you can stuff or blow more insulation into the cavity. Then replace the siding with a more moisture-resistant material like: vinyl lap siding; steel lap siding; plywood treated on all sides and edges with a sealer and paint; or fiberboard siding treated on all sides and edges with wood sealer and paint. Use metal or plastic flashing between the existing siding and the new siding to shed water. The flashing should go under the existing siding and over the new siding.

2.5.5 Wall Insulation

Wall insulation is a practical energy retrofit and can be cost-effective depending on fuel cost, climate, and the thickness and condition of existing insulation. Wall insulation has often settled so that the top part of the wall is empty. Voids in insulation due to poor supervision on the assembly line are not uncommon. Based on the experience of SERI and others, increasing wall insulation will save around 10% of existing heating costs in homes that have 2 inches or less of wall insulation and are located in cold climates. It may not be cost-effective to re-insulate walls in warmer climates if the cavities have some insulation already.

Three different methods of wall insulation are discussed and each has advantages and disadvantages when compared to each other. On some mobile homes, the three methods might even

ENVELOPES

be used in combination with each other due to the variations in walls caused by doors, windows, vents, and other obstructions in the walls.

Insulating the walls with fiberglass batts by removing the siding is an option, especially during major renovations. Stuffing fiberglass insulation into poorly insulated wall cavities with a flexible stuffing tool is usually the fastest way to insulate walls, although this method is not as versatile as blowing. One disadvantage of stuffing is that it does not usually provide uniform coverage and density because it is difficult to fill corners, narrow cavities, and areas around doors and windows. The stuffing method works well when combined with blowing or removing siding. Blowing insulation into a wall cavity with existing fiberglass batt insulation will work well most of the time. Removing the exterior wall panels is the most time consuming method but it facilitates wall repair, if needed, and does not require a blowing machine.

Any type of wall insulation project should include repair and re-fastening of interior and exterior wall panels when necessary.

2.5.5.1 Blowing Insulation Into Wall Cavities

Fiberglass insulation can be blown into walls using a blowing machine with a special fill tube attached to the end of the hose (see figure **2-7** and Section 2.3.7, Blowing Insulation). The best fill tubes for mobile home walls are stiff but flexible plastic pipes about 8 feet long and 1 to 2 inches in diameter. Tubing used for agricultural pumping or recreational vehicle sewer pipe works well. You can take the 2-inch size and drive over it with a car to flatten the round shape of the tube into an oval. This oval shaped tube has more cross-sectional area and a higher rate of delivery of insulation than smaller tubes but still fits in most mobile home wall cavities.

For homes with wood siding, the procedure for insulating walls is the same as for site-built houses. You can drill holes into each cavity a foot or two from the bottom of the wall and insert the fill tube up into the wall. Or, you can cut 6-inch square holes centered over the studs to gain access to two wall cavities through one hole. With this method you cut only half the number of holes compared to drilling. Patch the holes with individual patches, plastic plugs, or a continuous piece of trim beveled at the top to shed water and sealed carefully with caulking.

With metal siding the procedure is different and somewhat easier and is described in the steps below.

Step 1: Check the inside paneling and trim to make sure it is securely fastened to the wall. Caulk all cracks and repair holes to prevent indoor air from entering the wall. Note the location of electrical boxes and wire so you can try to avoid damaging them as you push the tube up the wall.

Step 2: Remove the bottom horizontal row of screws from the exterior siding. If the joints in the siding interlock, fasten the bottom of the joints together with sheet metal screws to prevent the joints from coming apart. Pull the siding and existing insulation away from the studs and insert the tip of the fill tube into the cavity. It is important to insert the tube so that the bow of the tube presses the tip against the interior paneling. When the tip of the tube, which is cut at an angle like

2-20 Inserting the Fill Tube - The technician has removed the bottom row of screws and is inserting the fill tube into a metal-sided wall cavity.

ENVELOPES

that shown in figure **2-7**, is pressed against the paneling (see figure **2-20**), it is least likely to snag on any existing insulation on its way up the wall. If the tube hits a belt rail or other obstruction, twisting the tube will help the point of the tube get past the obstruction.

Step 3: Push the tube up into the wall cavity until it hits the top plate of the wall. The tube should go in the wall cavity 7 to 8 feet. Mark the tube in 1 foot intervals to let you know how much of the tube remains in the wall when you are pulling the tube out. It's a good idea to stuff a piece of fiberglass batt into the bottom of the wall cavity around the tube to prevent insulation from blowing out of the bottom of the wall cavity. Leave the batt in place at the bottom of the wall when you pull the tube out of the cavity.

Step 4: Draw the tube out of the cavity about 6 inches at a time listening for the blower fan to indicate strain and watching for the insulation to slow its speed of travel through the blower hose. These two signs will tell the installer when to pull the tube down.

Because the fiberglass tends to cling to wall surfaces and to the existing insulation, the wall cavity will fill and pack from top to bottom. The installed density and the speed at which the cavity fills depends on the feed gate setting on the blowing machine and the blower speed. If the feed gate is open too far, the hose may clog. If the feed gate is closed too far, the cavity will take too long to fill and the high density insulation may bulge the interior or exterior paneling. Select a blower speed and feed gate that fills the wall quickly and steadily without bulging the wall or clogging the hose.

Unless care and judgment are exercised, the bottoms of the insulated wall cavities will over-fill because the siding is loose on the bottom. Marking the fill tube every foot and listening to the insulation filling the wall cavity will help you in withdrawing from the last two feet without over-filling. Holding the siding closely around the fill tube and inserting a piece of fiberglass batt around the tube will help you keep the insulation in the wall and avoid over-filling the bottom of the cavity. If you do over-fill the bottom of the cavity you can reach up inside the wall and remove some insulation.

Above windows you can fill the cavities from the inside by drilling holes in the paneling and blowing insulation into them through a swivel nozzle. Some mobile homes have a wide trim piece on the upper part of the wall that allows easy access to the area above windows. However, the areas above windows are small and may not be worth the effort it takes to fill them with insulation.

2.5.5.2 Stuffing Fiberglass Insulation

Unfaced fiberglass batts can be stuffed into empty or partially insulated wall cavities with a strong but flexible metal or plastic panel sized to provide a strong flexible stuffer about 8 feet long and 12 inches wide. Galvanized sheet metal of the same gauge used for ducts can be folded for stiffness and to produce smooth edges (see figure **2-21**). 3/8 inch thick clear polycarbonate plastic sheet makes a very strong and flexible stuffer.

Step 1: Check the inside paneling and trim to make sure it is securely fastened to the wall. Caulk all major cracks

2-21 Stuffing Batts - Fiberglass batts can be stuffed into a partially filled wall cavity using a flexible metal or plastic plate.

ENVELOPES

and repair holes to prevent indoor air from entering the wall. Remove anchoring screws from the switch and outlet boxes and pull the boxes temporarily out of the wall to clear the cavity for batt stuffing. Don't remove the boxes from the wall unless you're sure that you can fasten them back in place again.

Step 2: Remove the bottom two horizontal rows of screws from the siding. If the joints in the siding interlock, fasten the bottom of the joints between pieces of siding together with sheet metal screws to prevent the interlock from separating. If necessary, use wood blocks to temporarily hold the panels of siding away from the studs.

Step 3: Cut an unfaced fiberglass batt at least 8 inches longer than the height of the cavity and a piece of flexible plastic sheeting the same size as the batt. Lay the plastic on the ground and place the batt on top of the plastic. Then put the batt stuffer on top of the batt with the top of the batt stuffer 4-8 inches down from the top of the batt.

Step 4: Fold the batt and film over the top of the batt stuffer, pull back the siding, and put the side with the plastic sheeting against the interior paneling (see figure **2-21**). Then push the batt up into place. Cut off any excess or fold it up into the wall.

The disadvantage of the stuffing method is that it does not work well near corners or doors because the siding is difficult to loosen in those areas. If there is existing insulation, it must often be removed from the wall or compressed by the new insulation as it is stuffed into the wall. The coverage and density of the insulation inside the walls is not as uniform for stuffing as it is for blowing but the stuffing method is much faster than either blowing insulation or removing siding.

2.5.5.3 Removing Exterior Siding

Removing the exterior siding is more time-consuming than the other methods but it requires less skill and equipment. In most mobile homes, the door and windows have to be removed to get the siding off because they are installed over the siding, pinning the siding to the wood frame of the window or door. This method is practical if you have to remove doors and/or windows for repair and replacement or if you have to make structural repairs to the wall. It's also practical for a home owner or technician to examine and re-insulate a wall section that has missing or damaged insulation. Mobile home siding has a few different ways of being attached at the top and bottom which will determine how difficult removal will be. Study the siding details or remove an easy panel which has no window or door to find out how much work siding removal will be.

Step 1: Decide how far you can progress during a day of work. Two experienced people, using power screwdrivers to remove siding, doors, and windows, may be able to re-insulate half of an averaged size single-wide mobile home in an 8-hour day. Mark the joints between siding panels and between siding and trim with tape. Place the tape across the joint, write a number on the tape on each side of the joint, and then cut the tape. These tape marks will make re-assembly easier.

2-22 Sealing Walls - A technician caulks around electrical outlets and seams from the outside when wall panels are removed to insulate.

ENVELOPES

Step 2: Remove the windows and doors. They are usually attached with screws and have a putty tape seal that will have to be replaced when they are reinstalled. Label the windows and doors noting locations and the direction they were mounted to ensure correct reinstallation.

Step 3: Remove the siding and trim as necessary after you mark it. On most older mobile homes with bowstring truss roofs, the metal roof overlaps the siding or trim and is fastened by staples and a j-rail that clamps and seals the joint. Don't loosen the joint between the roof and siding or between the roof and trim unless you have to, because this joint must be sealed very

2-23 Installing Fiberglass Batts in an Open Wall Cavity - Batts designed for a 3 1/2 inch cavity are installed in a 1 3/4 inch cavity with the siding removed.

carefully upon reinstallation. The smallest leak in this area can let a lot of water into the building. You may choose to let the siding remain attached at the top and to prop the loose siding out in order to install insulation underneath it. This method can be dangerous on a windy day and should only be done in calm wind conditions.

Step 4: If a vapor barrier is present on the cold side of the wall, remove it. With the wall cavities exposed, examine the studs, window sills, and plates and repair any damage. Caulk and seal all visible holes and cracks around outlets and other openings and seams in the interior paneling (see figure **2-22**).

Step 5: (Optional). Install a vapor barrier by gluing polyethylene to the interior paneling between the studs. This will protect the insulation from condensation and takes little extra time. Insulate the cavity with unfaced fiberglass batts (see figure **2-23**).

Step 6: Install the air infiltration barrier. Wrap the newly insulated walls with an air infiltration barrier with a perm rating of at least 5. Staple it in place (see figure **2-24**), joining the edges of the air infiltration barrier at studs for support. Repair any tears in the barrier. Use construction adhesive to seal the edges, seams, and patches.

Step 7: Replace the siding and trim using larger screws if necessary. The old siding may not align perfectly with the existing holes in the wood. This will not be a problem because the new screws will bore their own new, tight holes. The siding should be flat and tight and be installed exactly as it was removed.

Step 8: Reinstall windows and doors with new putty tape, then caulk carefully around the frames to prevent water leaks. Also caulk over the screw holes to prevent them from leaking water.

2-24 Air Infiltration Barrier - When installing batts in an open wall cavity from outside, an air infiltration barrier is stapled and sealed tightly over the insulation.

ENVELOPES

2.6 Roofs

2.6.1 Design and Construction Characteristics

Many mobile home roofs are constructed with a shallow roof cavity that has 1 to 4 inches of insulation installed between the trusses on top of the ceiling. Other roofs have insulation installed over the top of the trusses. Some homes have insulation at the ceiling and at the roof. Since roof trusses are usually not built much stronger than required by code, there are limitations to the weight that they can carry. The arrangement of the framework of the roof will dictate what methods are used to add insulation to the roof cavity or how to fasten insulation to the roof surface. Mobile home roofs are built with either bowstring, standard pitched, or half trusses (see figure **2-25**). Figure **2-26** shows construction details for metal and wood roofs. The materials used for the waterproof surface of the roof and the sheathing (if the roof has sheathing) will determine the tools needed to cut through the surface of the roof if it is necessary.

On metal roofs without sheathing, you can determine the location of trusses, strongbacks, and belt rails by walking on the roof and feeling where the roof is most solid. Look for vents or other openings in the roof where you can actually look into the roof cavity. There may also be some convenient access inside the home where you can see the construction and amount of insulation in the roof. If there isn't any convenient place, you can drill a 4 to 5 inch hole with a hole saw in the ceiling of a closet. Don't cut through the vapor barrier or insulation with the hole saw; you can slit the insulation and vapor barrier with a knife to see up into the cavity at the insulation. Then replace the plug of ceiling tile with some caulking or construction adhesive around the edge to stick it in place.

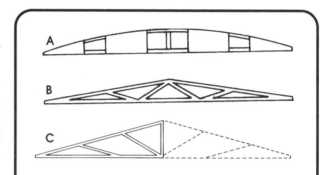

2-25 Three Common Types of Mobile Home Roofs - A. Bowstring trusses are common with metal roofs; B. Low-sloping standard pitched trusses are common with shingle roofs; C. On double-wides each unit has a half truss roof which combines with the other half to form a gable roof.

2.6.2 Moisture and Roof Insulation

Moisture problems in mobile home roof cavities happen for two main reasons: condensation of water from moist air in the roof cavity; and roof leaks. The main causes of roof leaks are water puddles on the roof and the failure of seams on the roof. Condensation in roof cavities is often mistaken for roof leakage. The main cause of condensation in the roof cavity is warm moist air escaping from the home into the roof cavity. This air from the home encounters the cold interior surface of the metal or plywood roof and cools, causing condensation like that which forms on the outside of a cold beverage glass. In this condensation process, the droplets of water that form on the underside of the roof, will often roll down to the edge of roof and cause staining at the edge of the ceiling.

Roof insulation may have either a positive or negative effect on existing moisture problems in roofs. Loose fill insulation may restrict the flow of warm moist air from the home into the roof cavity producing a positive effect. Insulation can also have a positive effect by keeping the roof cavity warmer so that condensation does not occur as much. Many mobile home roofs are not vented so that the new insulation restricting air flow through the roof cavity is not a problem.

ENVELOPES

Loose-fill insulation, installed inside a vented roof cavity, might reduce the ability of outside air to ventilate and dry the insulation in the roof cavity. Or, increased insulation could provide more material to soak up water. Moisture has not been a significant problem in reinsulating mobile home roof cavities in dry and moderate climates. However, it is important to select the less absorbent insulation materials for roof cavity insulation in case condensation or roof leakage do occur. Cellulose is probably too absorbent to be used in all but the very driest temperate climates. Fiberglass absorbs considerably less water than cellulose. Polystyrene beads absorb hardly any water.

2.6.3 Safety and Roof Insulation

The two main fire dangers associated with roofs are recessed light fixtures and flue pipes from furnaces and water heaters. Recessed light fixtures are designed to be surrounded by air which ventilates the housing of the fixture cooling it. Installing insulation around a recessed light fixture could raise the temperature of the fixture high enough to start a fire. So, when considering blown insulation in mobile home roof cavities, you must construct a barrier of noncombustible material around each recessed light fixture to ensure that the blown insulation does not pack around the fixture.

2-26 Corner Details of Mobile Home Roofs - A. Construction detail of a metal roof; B. Construction detail of a standard pitch roof with asphalt shingle.

Mobile home flue pipes are usually double or triple wall pipe assemblies. The surface of the outer pipe is not likely to ever exceed 350° F. However, a combustible insulation like polystyrene beads should never be blown up against a flue pipe assembly. The flue pipe assembly should be protected by an additional sleeve of metal pipe or by wrapping the flue pipe assembly with unfaced fiberglass batt insulation which is noncombustible. The fiberglass batt can be stuffed in from the roof after removal of the chimney flashing (see figure **2-27**).

Many mobile home fires burn through the ceiling and then spread through the roof cavity. A roof cavity filled with insulation is safer from a fire safety perspective because it would inhibit a fore from spreading.

2-27 Protecting the Chimney - This technician is stuffing unfaced fiberglass batts around the chimney forming a dam to prevent combustible insulation from touching the chimney.

ENVELOPES

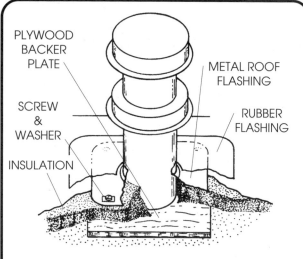

2-28 Flashing Detail for an Insulated Rubber Roof - Note the plywood plate that was fastened to the old roof under the insulation and new roofing to give solid backing for the screws that hold the metal flashing down.

2.6.4 Rooftop Insulation

There are three common ways to add insulation to the top of a mobile home roof.

1. Installing at least 2 inches of rigid insulation with a synthetic rubber cap over the insulation.

2. Installing at least 2 inches of spray-applied polyurethane over the existing metal roof.

3. Installing at least 2 inches of rigid insulation with a metal roof over the insulation.

2.6.4.1 Insulated Rubber Roof Cap

An insulated synthetic rubber roof cap significantly reduces heat loss and heat gain through a roof. In this system insulation board and then a rubber roofing material are installed directly over the existing roof. The rubber roof cap is an expensive option and has not performed quite as well as blown insulation in tests performed by SERI. However, the roof cap covers the home with a roof that will last 30 years or more, if it is installed correctly. The insulated rubber roof is more economical when major roof repairs are needed in addition to insulation or when the climate is hot in summer and cold in winter. The following are some general instructions for installing an insulated rubber roof system.

Step 1: Remove existing pipe and vent flashing around plumbing and heating vents and set it aside. Remove roof mounted coolers and raise their mounting blocks. Extend plumbing, heating and exhaust vents at least 10 inches above the new roof level. Do not assemble the vent extensions permanently until after the membrane is installed because they will be in the way.

Make sure that you have wood backing underneath the pipe and vent flashing so that you can fasten the flashing back to the roof solidly after the insulation and roofing membrane are in place. You can fasten a piece of plywood on the existing roof surface as shown in figure **2-28** to provide a wood backer for fastening if you think you may have trouble finding a solid surface which to fasten the vent pipe flashing.

Step 2: Install the insulation board leaving at least 3 inches clearance around hot vents like wood stove flues. Fasten the insulation to the roof trusses using screws that are long enough to penetrate the truss 1/2 to 1 inch.

2-29 Fastening Insulation - A crew installs beadboard insulation over a metal roof, fastening the insulation down with screws and large washers.

ENVELOPES

2-30 Rubber Roofing - Technician drags the continuous sheet of rubber roofing across the roof.

2-31 Flashing Around a Chimney - The lifespan of the roof depends on the careful installation of flashing around chimneys, pipes, and vents.

Use large washers, called fender washers or roof deck plates, to prevent the screws from pulling through the insulation (see figure **2-29**). Cut the insulation to fit around all the vent holes. You can stuff fiberglass tightly around pipes and vents to insulate spaces left for fire safety or by mistake.

Step 3: Pull the rubber cap up on the roof by using two people to lift the leading edge over the edge of the roof and to drag the membrane up onto the roof (see figure **2-30**). Two strong people can accomplish this but it is easier with three people. Lay the membrane out so that at least 6 inches overhangs on all sides. Then locate all the vent holes and cut an opening in the membrane for each vent.

Step 4: Assemble the vent extensions permanently and put the new flashing around the vent pipes. New flashings can be purchased from a mobile home dealer or made on site. Examples of vent pipe flashings are shown in figures **2-31** and **2-32**.

Step 5: Install the new termination rail just above the existing j-rail. Begin at the center on both sides of the roof and work towards the ends of the roof. Straighten the membrane and work out any wrinkles as you proceed. Do not fasten the termination rail the last 10 inches at the corners. Follow the same procedure for the ends of the roof. Begin in the center and work towards the corners. Again, do not fasten the termination rail the last 10 inches at the corners.

2-32 Manufactured Vent Flashing - This type of vent flashing is manufactured for easy installation at the site.

ENVELOPES

Step 6: Fold the membrane at each corner and fasten the last 10 inches of the termination rail. Then trim off the excess membrane hanging below the new termination rail.

Note: Because most roof leaks occur at seams and flashings, the careful installation of seams and new flashing around vents will determine how long the roof will function without leaking. It is important that you apply the adhesive evenly and continuously and keep the roof cap clean during the installation procedures. All seams and edges of the membrane on the roof should be sealed with a special seam sealant. The membrane might last 50 years with good workmanship but it could leak in 10 years or less with poor workmanship. Follow the manufacturer's instructions carefully.

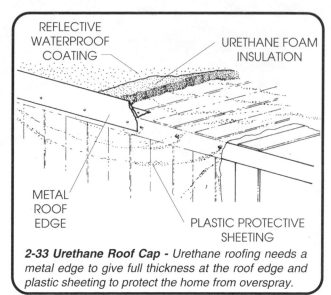

2-33 Urethane Roof Cap - Urethane roofing needs a metal edge to give full thickness at the roof edge and plastic sheeting to protect the home from overspray.

2.6.4.2 Sprayed Urethane Roof Cap

A urethane foam roof cap can be professionally installed for about the same cost as an insulated rubber roof. The urethane foam roof cap is not as durable as the rubber roof cap. The urethane should have a grainy surface like an orange peel and not look like the surface of a popcorn ball. The contractor should install a metal edge around the perimeter of the roof to maintain the thickness of the insulation all the way out to the edge of the roof (see figure **2-33**). Insulation should not be installed on windy days or when the temperature is below 50°. Vents should be extended and the urethane must be protected from contact with hot vents. The contractor should use plastic or paper masking to prevent over-spray from damaging the walls and other objects around the home. The urethane should be coated with at least 20 mils (thousandths of an inch) of a reflective coating specially designed to protect urethane from sunlight and water. The quality of urethane foam installation varies widely so it is important to check the insulation contractor's past work history before signing a contract.

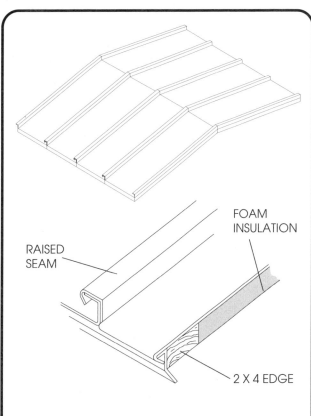

2-34 Metal Reroofing System - These replacement roofs are durable and they offer the option of a small overhang, but they are expensive.

ENVELOPES

2.6.4.3 Metal Roof Caps

Insulated metal roofs for mobile homes are generally the most expensive type of rooftop insulation. They combine rigid foam board insulation with a metal roofing system and are attractive and very durable. Metal roof caps are available through roofing contractors and mobile home contractors.

One advantage to some metal roof systems is that the technicians can allow the new roof to overhang using the strength of the metal roofing. The overhang provides a little shading and partially shelters the wall from weather.

2.6.5 Roof Cavity Insulation

Before you blow any insulation, follow the preparatory steps listed below. Both preparatory steps are very important in preventing moisture problems from occurring.

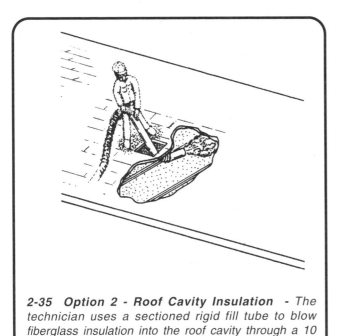

2-35 Option 2 - Roof Cavity Insulation - The technician uses a sectioned rigid fill tube to blow fiberglass insulation into the roof cavity through a 10 inch square hole.

Step 1: Inspect the ceiling of the mobile home. Do not neglect closets and cabinets. Seal around all openings in the ceiling and repair all damage. Look for signs of moisture damage and find out why the damage occurred.

Step 2: Inspect the roof for leaks and water puddling. Then repair the roof, if necessary. It is very important to the effectiveness of the insulation to keep it dry. See Section 2.6.7, Roof Repair, for instructions on roof repair.

Four options for getting access to the roof cavity and blowing insulation into it are (see section 2.3.7, Blowing Insulation):

Option 1: Drill two long rows of 2-1/2 inch holes in the ceiling from indoors along the length of the home. Drill the holes 3 feet in from the end of the truss in each of the spaces between the trusses and blow in fiberglass or polystyrene bead insulation through an L-shaped fill tube (see figure **2-7**). Then cement 2-1/2 inch white plastic plugs into the holes with construction adhesive.

Option 2: Cut 10-inch square holes in the roof surface on top of alternate trusses to allow access to the roof cavities on both sides of the trusses and then blow in fiberglass insulation through a 2 or 2-1/2 inch diameter fill tube (see figures **2-7** and **2-35**). Centering the 10 inch square

2-36 Option 3 - Standard Pitched Roof Insulation - There is usually more room to maneuver the hose when blowing insulation into a standard pitched roof.

53

ENVELOPES

hole on top of the truss produces two 4 inch x 10 inch holes providing access into adjacent truss spaces. These holes are large enough to allow you to inspect the roof as you blow the insulation and to move the fill tube around to provide good coverage. See Section 2.6.7, Roof Repair, for patching instructions.

Option 3: For pitched truss shingle roofs on double- and single-section homes, you can blow insulation through existing roof vents and cover large areas of the roof from a few vents (see figure **2-36**). The roof vent holes are usually about 10 inches square and provide enough room to move the hose around, blowing in all directions through each hole. Wherever you can't reach with the blower hose, you can cut another square hole in the roof and install a new roof vent to close the hole.

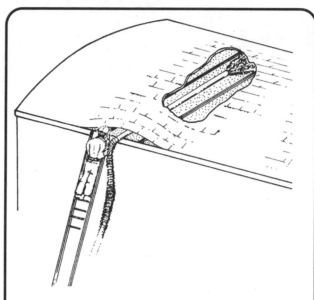

2-37 Option 4 - Blowing From the Edge of the Roof - *This technician is using a fill tube that is 10 to 12 feet long to blow insulation underneath a metal roof.*

Option 4: Remove the metal rail along the edge of the length of the roof and pull the metal roof up far enough to insert a fill tube. Then blow fiberglass insulation through a rigid pipe 10 or more feet long into each truss space (see figure **2-37**). foam rubber and sealed with an acrylic latex caulk. You can buy foam rubber at an upholstery shop.

Option 5: Drill 2-1/2 inch holes in either the roof or ceiling as needed and blow polystyrene beads into the roof cavity (see figure **2-38**). You can patch the roof holes with 2-1/2 plastic plugs, cemented in place with exterior caulk. Then cover the plug with a 6 inch square butyl and foil tape patch, designed for patching metal and asphalt roofs (see Section 2.6.7, Roof Repair).

2.6.6 Sealing the Ceiling

The ceiling of any a mobile home should be inspected and sealed, if necessary. It is not unusual to find areas around flues and plumbing vents where gaps will allow considerable air exchange between the home and the roof cavity.

The problem with patching ceilings is that the fiberboard or sheetrock ceiling material does not hold nails or screws well. Luckily, there are a variety of adhesives, some packaged in caulking tubes and others in spray

2-38 Option 5 - Blowing Beads - *This technician is using an L-shaped fill tube to blow polystyrene beads into the roof cavity through a 2-1/2 inch hole.*

ENVELOPES

cans, that are designed to work without fasteners. You simply make a patch of any suitable material (preferably a non-flammable one). Next, test the patch without adhesive to see if it fits and then apply the adhesive and put the patch in place.

Smaller gaps can be sealed with acrylic latex caulk. Medium-sized gaps can be stuffed with foam rubber and sealed with an acrylic latex caulk. You can buy foam rubber at an upholstery shop.

2.6.7 Roof Repair

Roofs on mobile homes develop leaks because of the severe weather conditions that roofs have to endure. There are two main causes of mobile home roof leaks: the failure of seams around penetrations in the roof; and water puddles on roofs. The failure of seams occurs on all types of roofs, especially at vents and other openings in the roof.

Water puddles are a particular problem on the metal roofs of single-section homes because they don't have much of a slope and water will collect in the smallest indentations. If water stands in puddles on a roof, eventually the roof will leak there. Large indentations or creases in metal roofs may indicate a leveling problem (see Section 1.5.6, Leveling a Mobile Home). Sometimes you have to cut out a section of the metal roof where the water puddles and reinforce the area with plywood attached to the trusses. The plywood builds up the low area so the water drains off. After screwing the plywood to the trusses cover the whole area you cut out with a metal patch that overlaps 4 inches in all directions. The edge of the patch should be bedded in roof cement. Screw the metal patch to the existing metal roof and to the plywood reinforcing panel. Then follow the instructions below for installing asphalt or latex roof patches along the seam of the metal patch.

The most universal patching system for mobile home roofs is asphalt-based black mastic, reinforced with fabric webbing. The black mastic is spread in a thin, even base coat with a brush or trowel. Then the webbing is laid in the base coat and covered with one or two top coats. Patches should be covered with an asphalt-based reflective coating that has reinforcing fibers and aluminum particles mixed in. The reflective coating is brushed on to protect the patch from the damaging effects of sunlight and it prevents patched areas from absorbing excessive solar heat in the summer. This system can be used easily on metal and asphalt shingle roofs and is inexpensive.

2-39 Applying a Patch - The technician is installing a foil-faced butyl rubber patch to a hole where the polystyrene beads were blown into the roof. A standard 2 1/2 inch plug was placed in the hole first.

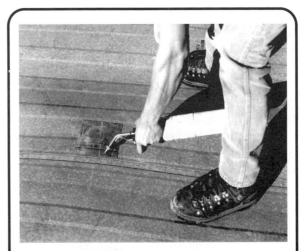

2-40 Adhering the Patch - The butyl rubber patch is heated with a propane torch to permanently adhere to the metal roof surface.

ENVELOPES

There are a variety of butyl rubber tapes with aluminum foil skins that are used for quick patches on metal roofs (see figure **2-39**). These tapes stick tenaciously to warm roofs but may need to be heated with a propane torch during cooler weather to make them stick (see figure **2-40**). This tape isn't as messy as asphalt mastic and reflective coatings, and it works well for small holes or cracks.

The most flexible and longest lasting patches are the fabric reinforced latex rubber. However, surface preparation is critical and the manufacturer's instructions must be followed exactly to ensure success. These latex rubber systems usually employ a primer coat and one or more top coats painted onto the roof. Latex roof patch and coating is used primarily on metal roofs but can be used to coat asphalt roofing too.

The latex rubber coatings reflect about 80% of the solar heat falling on the roof and the aluminum / asphalt coatings reflect about 60%. **It's important to have a reflective roof, particularly in warmer climates, so that the mobile home roof will be a solar reflector not a solar collector.** Other coatings that are much more expensive and claim to be much better, should be looked upon skeptically. Its a good idea to hose dirt off of the roof each spring to prevent the reflective surface from darkening and collecting more solar heat.

The asphalt shingles on low-sloping roofs on single- and double-section homes may leak prematurely especially in windy, rainy, and/or cold climates. Asphalt shingles are more appropriate for slopes of more than 4 inches per foot. If you have to replace an asphalt shingle roof, consider stripping the existing shingles and applying 90-pound, granular-surface roll roofing. Roll roofing will probably out-last shingles, is less expensive, and leaks are easy to find and fix. Or, 40-mil synthetic rubber makes a very permanent, if somewhat expensive, replacement roof (see Section 2.6.4.1, Insulated Rubber Roof Cap). If you need to patch an old shingle roof, caulk underneath all loose shingles and caulk all seams with roof cement. You can even coat the shingle roof with asphalt/aluminum coating or latex rubber coating if appearance is not an issue.

Roof rumble is a common complaint about metal roofs. Metal mobile home roofs are typically attached only at the perimeter of the roof along the top of the wall. The metal roof skin lays loosely on top of the trusses. Some metal roofs move and rumble in the wind. If you look up on the roof on a windy day you can see what areas are making noise. Then later, you can get up on the roof carefully, using plywood walkboards, and attach the rumbling areas to the roof trusses with screws and rumble washers every 2 to 4 feet. A rumble washer is large washer with a rubber gasket and a small hole for a sheet metal screw in the center. Use a roofing sealant over the rumble washer to prevent it from leaking.

If you live in a windy area, it's wise to inspect the perimeter of the roof carefully to make sure that the j-rail (see figure **2-26**) fits tightly. There should be no places around the roof/wall junction

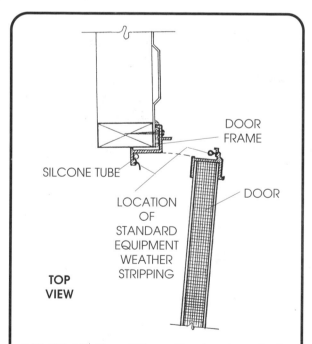

2-41 "Mobile Home" Door - Drawing shows the two locations of weatherstrip that is standard equipment on these outwardly opening doors and one location for retrofit silicone tube weatherstrip.

ENVELOPES

that are protruding, open or loose. The wind can pry under protruding areas and eventually cause significant damage.

2.7 Doors

2.7.1 Design and Construction Characteristics

Most doors in mobile homes are uninsulated, but heat loss or gain through the door is a minor problem because of the door's relatively small area. Doors can be repaired, weatherstripped to reduce air leakage, or replaced with insulated doors.

Before 1980, most mobile home doors were made of wood or aluminum sheeting on a wood frame. Most were uninsulated, and they typically had an approximate R-value of R-2. New replacement doors typically have insulation values of R-6 to R-7, although foam-filled steel doors, boasting up to R-15, are available.

2-42 "House-Type" Door - Drawing shows three locations for weatherstrip on this inwardly opening door. Weatherstrip is needed at only one of the perimeter locations (door jamb or door stop).

There are two types of doors common to mobile homes, outwardly opening doors and inwardly opening doors. The outwardly opening door has been traditional for mobile homes since the 1940s and will be referred to here as a "mobile home door." When mobile homes were only 8 feet wide, it was an inconvenience and a waste of space to have an inwardly opening door. These doors are shorter than house-type doors and are usually located in hallways as a second door and fire exit. Outwardly opening "mobile home doors" are weatherstripped with a vinyl flap mounted in the metal frame that seals against the inside surface of the door (see figure **2-42**). Mobile home doors are usually made so that the corners of the door contact the frame first when closing. The rest of the door seals against the frame with a push and is held in place by the latch.

Inwardly opening doors, called "house-type doors", are mounted to wood jambs with standard butt hinges and usually have sloping aluminum thresholds. The door bottoms have a single or double vinyl flap that seals to the threshold (see figure **2-42**). The assembled pre-hung door unit consists of side jambs, a head jamb, threshold, door, hinges, and weatherstrip. Homes with house-type doors often have standard outwardly opening storm doors. The storm door is hinged in an aluminum frame which is fastened onto the wooden door jambs and through the exterior siding (see figure **2-44**).

2.7.2 Doors - What to Look For

The door should open and close smoothly without binding and it should fit closely against the doorstop with no significant gaps. Check the door opening for squareness. Either place a framing square in the corners or measure the opening from corner to corner (the measurement should be identical if the opening is square). A door opening that is significantly out of square usually indicates that you should inspect the foundation and re-level the home if necessary (see Section 1.4,

ENVELOPES

Foundations and Installation, and Section 1.4.6, Leveling a Mobile Home). An extra footing and pier may be necessary near the door to prevent it from moving again.

Repairs to the door should precede weatherstripping. The paneling on the faces of the door should not be loose or damaged. Tighten the hinges, lockset, and strike plate if necessary. When the door opening is square and the hardware is tight, then you can weatherstrip the door if necessary. Seeing daylight around the door or noticing uncomfortable drafts is an indication that the weatherstripping needs to be improved.

Replace a door only if it is worn out or if the repair cost, which is mostly labor, exceeds the replacement cost. The decision to repair or replace depends on the condition of the door, the possibility of repair, and the home owner's budget.

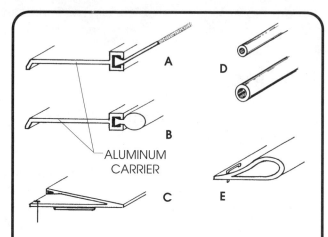

2-43 Examples of Weatherstrip - A. Flap-type weatherstrip in aluminum carrier; B. Tube-type weatherstrip in aluminum carrier; C. Rigid bronze V-strip; D. 2 sizes of of silicone tubing that is attached to the door jamb with silicone caulk; E. Silicone tube with a lip for stapling.

2.7.3 Weatherstripping Doors

You can choose from a variety of weatherstripping materials available for doors depending on the style of door and its condition. Flexibility is important for door weatherstrip because doors move slightly with changes in temperature and humidity. New materials like silicone rubber, neoprene rubber, and foam rubber with a plastic jacket are very flexible. These weatherstrips will allow door movement of 1/8 inch or more in either direction and still provide a good air seal.

Many common types of weatherstrip, sold in lumber yards and hardware stores, are not very flexible or permanent. Vinyl tubing, roll spring bronze, felt, and foam tapes are not recommended for doors on mobile homes.

Silicone tube weatherstrip is particularly effective on mobile home doors. It's available in several sizes, so you can close a variety of gap sizes around doors. The silicone tubing sits in a corner out of the way, so it is not likely to be damaged (see figure **2-42**).   Silicone caulking adheres the silicone tubing to the door frame. You simply squirt a bead of silicone caulking into the corner and press the silicone tubing into the corner with a small roller. The roller works better than your finger because your finger will drag and stretch the tubing. You can install the silicone tubing in any corner of the door or frame where it will be compressed when the door closes.

If you are using an adhesive to fasten weatherstrip, clean the surface with alcohol or some other effective cleaner that won't leave a film. Self-adhesive weatherstrip should be stapled because its adhesive doesn't stick well to rough surfaces and is not permanent. Automotive weatherstrip adhesive and construction adhesive will stick permanently and tenaciously whenever you need to fasten weatherstrip without nails, staples, or screws.

With outwardly opening mobile home doors, the weatherstrip carrier is an integral part of the door frame and/or door. The vinyl flap is the most common type of seal for these doors. You can replace the vinyl by either sliding it in from one end or by prying it into the track with a tool. The

ENVELOPES

silicone rubber tubing and some types of rigid plastic or bronze V-seal are useful, as well, for mobile home doors.

House-type doors are weatherstripped the same way as doors on site-built homes. Mount V-seal type weatherstrip on the jamb where the edge of the door will compress the V. Rigid metal carriers with flexible tubing or rubber flaps are effective for sealing house-type doors. The more flexible the carrier-mounted weatherstrip is, the better it will seal the door and allow for some movement in the door. Mount the metal carrier on the door stop as shown in figure **2-41**.

2.7.4 Replacing Doors

Replacement doors are available in inwardly opening and outwardly opening pre-hung units. Pre-hung means that the door is hung on hinges in a frame. The house-type replacement door unit often includes a storm door. The better outwardly opening mobile home doors are double weatherstripped and have an extruded aluminum channel around the door. The better pre-hung house-type doors are have steel face panels and are filled with urethane foam insulation. These house-type doors have flexible jacketed-foam weatherstrip and are designed to seal the perimeter of the door very tightly.

Clear communication between the installer and the supplier is very important in measuring doors. The installer and supplier must understand how the door was measured to avoid mistakes in sizing. Although there is no rigid industry standard, mobile home doors are usually sized by the rough opening into which they are installed. Replacement door sizes begin at 28 x 72 inches and increase in 2 inch increments for width and height to 36 x 80 inches. House-type doors are generally larger than mobile home doors. A door is either left-hand or right-hand, and you must specify a left or right-hand door when ordering. A left-hand door has the hinges on your left side as you pull the door open toward you.

Before you install a new door, check beneath the threshold for damage. If any part of the flooring has to be replaced, use exterior plywood for repairs. Mobile home doors are replaced like windows. Remove the existing door and its metal frame, then remove the caulk or putty tape from the home's siding to provide a clean, smooth mounting surface. Put new exterior caulk or putty tape on the backside of the door flange. Screw the new door in place making sure the door is plumb and level.

House-type doors are a little more difficult to replace. First remove the existing door and frame. Make sure the threshold is level, then

2-44 Door Installation - Pre-hung mobile home doors and house-type doors often have a frame that is thicker than the mobile home wall. The frame juts out past the inside wall paneling and a spacer is needed to bring the wall out for installing trim.

check the door jambs for plumb. If necessary level the home. Since the opening is larger than the door frame you should use shims to align the door frame. Place the shims behind each hinge, at the latch, and at the top and bottom of the frame. Fasten the frame to the opening with screws through the shims. Then nail the trim securely to the door frame and to the wall.

Many mobile home specialists prefer to use doors designed for site-built homes because these

ENVELOPES

doors are sturdier. Insulated steel doors and solid-core wood doors are readily available in lumber yards as pre-hung units. The frame of the house-type door may be thicker than the wall. In this case, the door jamb will be flush with the exterior wall and will extend beyond the surface of the inside wall. So, you will need to fasten a wood spacer to the wall around the frame so that the spacer is flush with the edge of the door jamb (see figure **2-44**). Then, nail the door trim securely to the door frame and to the spacer. The trim and spacer strengthen the wall and help support the extra weight of this heavier house-type door.

Repairing doors and replacing doors are necessary maintenance projects but do not save much energy.

2.8 Windows

Heat loss and gain through windows in mobile homes is a major energy conservation problem. In some cases, windows are also ma-

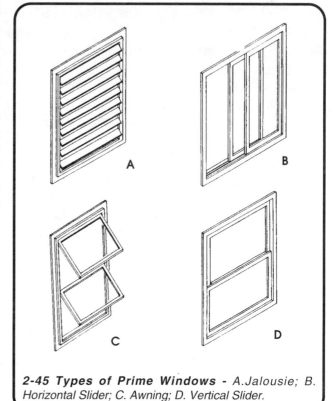

2-45 Types of Prime Windows - A.Jalousie; B. Horizontal Slider; C. Awning; D. Vertical Slider.

jor sources of air leaks. Windows cause energy and comfort problems in four important ways.

1. Hot or cold window surfaces radiate heat in the summer and absorb heat in the winter.

2. Windows cool the air around them in winter and heat the air around them in summer causing drafts that reduce comfort.

3. Poorly sealed windows allow air to leak through them, especially during windy conditions.

4. Sunlight penetrates windows during the cooling season adding direct solar heating to the home.

2.8.1 Design and Construction Characteristics

Windows on mobile homes usually have metal frames and sashes. Prime windows are

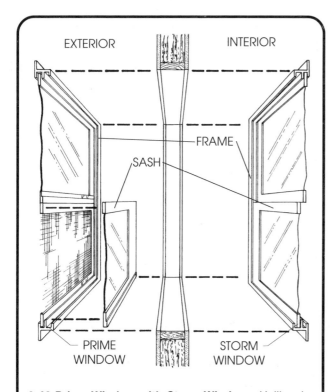

2-46 Prime Window with Storm Window - Unlike site-built homes, mobile home storm windows are installed on the inside.

ENVELOPES

fastened to the outside wall of the home. Storm windows are fastened to the inside wall or window trim. The prime windows on most mobile homes are metal-frame, single-pane windows fastened to the outside of the wall. Storm windows are either removable panels or self-storing sliding windows that slide up and down or sideways (see figure **2-46**).

2.8.2 Prime Windows

Most window types have a metal frame with an external flange for mounting. The prime window frame is fastened onto the exterior siding and into the rough framing. There are four types of windows that are common to mobile homes, jalousie windows, awning windows, vertical sliders, and horizontal sliders (see figure **2-45**).

Jalousie windows and awning windows the most common type of window on homes built before 1976. The jalousie is the best ventilator for hot weather and the poorest cold air infiltration barrier of any window type. Jalousie and awning windows have special storm window assemblies. If the window does have a storm, it is a clip-on type. The storm window frame allows the window crank to protrude through the frame of the storm window. Awning windows work like jalousie windows but have just one or two panes of glass rather than multiple panes.

2-47 Fixed Sash Storm Window - Many mobile homes have storm windows that clip to the interior window trim or a metal frame fastened to the interior paneling. Glass, rigid plastic, or flexible plastic may be used as glazing.

The horizontal or vertical sliding windows are the most common on newer homes. Horizontal or vertical sliding window sashes slide open and closed in similar double-track metal frames. Each window has a movable sash and a fixed sash. Vertical sliding windows have a spring counterbalance to keep the movable sash up, when it is open. The movable sash of a sliding window slides on the bottom of the metal frame.

2.8.3 Storm Windows

Storm windows come in a variety of materials and mountings. Fixed storm windows which are mounted and removed seasonally are common in older homes. However, self-storing horizontal and vertical sliders are more popular and practical. Storm windows are usually installed on the interior window trim or the paneling around the window open-

2-48 Fixed Storm Window with Flexible Film - This detail shows a low-cost interior storm window panel with an aluminum frame and flexible plastic film. This storm window is held in place by clips which rotate to install or remove the window

ENVELOPES

ing. The storm windows that are standard equipment in mobile homes are horizontal or vertical sliders or fixed panels with metal sashes and frames. Newer types of storm windows use plastic frames and sashes with plastic sheet or plastic film window panes.

Storm windows save substantial energy and make a noticeable difference in comfort in the cooler temperate regions and in cold regions. The payback for storm windows typically ranges from 5 to 15 years in these climatic regions. In warmer climates that are dominated by cooling, storm windows are not as effective as the shading strategies discussed in Section 4.2, Shading.

The fixed-sash storm window clips to the window trim or to a metal frame with rotating clips. Fixed storm windows that are weatherstripped with 1/8 to 1/4 inch closed-cell foam tape seal very tightly if the clips hold them tightly against the wood or metal frame (see figure **2-43**). However, the fixed storm window has to be removed seasonally for ventilation and, in the process, the sash is sometimes damaged or lost.

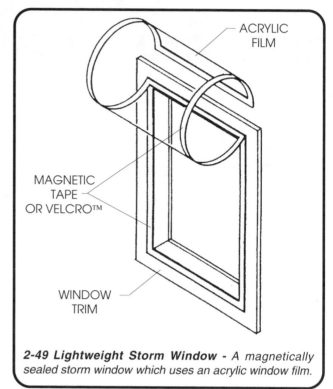

2-49 Lightweight Storm Window - *A magnetically sealed storm window which uses an acrylic window film.*

Storm windows with movable sashes, either horizontal or vertical sliders, are lightweight relatives to prime windows. They resemble exterior aluminum storms on site-built homes. Usually, no improvement is needed to this type of storm window. The movable sash of horizontal or vertical sliding storm windows usually has a spring-loaded sliding latch to lock it in place.

Newer light-weight interior storms use acrylic plastic instead of glass. They are available in fixed panels, horizontal sliders, and vertical sliders. The fixed plastic storm windows are the most common because they are very inexpensive. Although rigid acrylic plastic storm windows are lighter and stronger than glass storms, they are difficult to clean and the plastic scratches easily. Use water and a soft cloth to clean acrylic plastic or use a special acrylic cleaner and polisher. These interior storm windows have tight seals and resist heat flows slightly better than metal and glass storms.

Flexible, clear vinyl and acrylic film is the least expensive of all window materials. It is fairly durable and very lightweight, too (see figure **2-49**). It can be cut with scissors or a utility knife to the exact size needed. The lifespan of storm windows made with flexible film will depend on the care used in mounting, removing, and storing them.

Rigid and flexible plastic storms have magnetic, Velcro™, or snap-together mechanical mounting and sealing systems. The Velcro™ system uses an adhesive hook tape adhered to the interior wall surface and an adhesive loop tape adhered to the rigid acrylic sheet. The magnetic system uses magnetic tape on the plastic sash rail and magnetic tape or a metal strip on the interior window frame. This magnetic attraction forms an excellent seal, but the magnetism is not strong enough to support the weight of the window frame and the rigid plastic window pane. The bottom

ENVELOPES

of the plastic sash should rest on the sill, on a strip, or on rotating sash clips. The problem with magnetic tape, Velcro™, or plastic frames which are stuck to paneling or trim by a thin adhesive, is that most thin adhesives eventually fail. You should clean the surfaces carefully if you want a thin adhesive to last more than a couple of years. If the adhesive does fail, you can re-attach the material with construction adhesive or automotive weathershrip adhesive, which is more reliable than thin adhesives.

2.8.4 Windows - What to Look For

Single-pane glass is a serious energy liability in cold climates. Storm windows are a good investment in the northern tier of the United States and cooler regions of the central United States as long as the installed price is reasonable (see Appendix G and use lower square-foot costs for storm windows). Shading the windows is a more important consideration in warmer climates, and if you live in the south you should find a way to block 50% to 80% of the solar heat falling on the window (see Section 4.2, Shading).

The wooden window openings should be free from rot and other moisture damage. The prime window should fastened firmly to the wall with no significant gaps which are not sealed with putty tape or caulking. The interior storm window if present should be sealed tightly to the wall. The sashes should close completely without gaps of more than 1/16 inch. Some air leakage around the sash is tolerable.

Inspect the window opening and repair any moisture damage to the framing and trim before doing any work on the windows. It is common on many older homes to find window jambs and trim with serious moisture damage. Replace all structurally weak and rotting material (see Section 2.5.4, Wall Repair and Renovation). Also, inspect the condition of exterior caulking around the window frame and re-caulk if necessary. Any broken or missing glass should be repaired. The decision to repair or replace a window depends on the type and condition of the window, the labor required to repair it, and the cost of materials.

2.8.5 Windows and Condensation

Condensation occurs on window panes when warm humid air indoors is cooled by the cold sur-

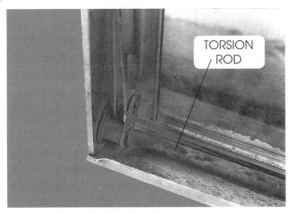

2-50 Awning Window - Note the torsion rod at the bottom of the photo and the torsion rod holder at the bottom left. The torsion rod holder can break causing the window to remain slightly open.

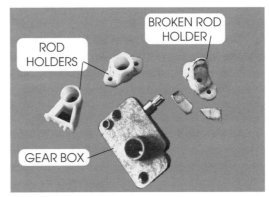

2-51 Torsion Rod Holders and Crank Gear Box - Several types of torsion rod holders are shown, including a broken one. The gear box shown is available in replacement units for existing gear boxes that are stripped out.

ENVELOPES

face of the window. As the humid air cools, it loses its capacity to hold water and the water collects on the window. Condensation is more of a problem when the outdoor temperature drops below freezing because the glass gets colder and more condensation collects. The only two ways to beat condensation are to lower the humidity in the home or to raise the temperature of the inner pane of glass. In very cold weather, the air must be very dry to avoid condensation. New windows may not cure window condensation problems.

Interior storms will reduce condensation because the inside surface of the glass in the storm window is warmer than the glass in the primary window. However, if an interior storm window is installed loosely, condensation may then occur between the storm and primary window. This condensation is caused by moist air inside the home leaking around the edges of the interior storm into the air space between the two windows and condensing on the inside of the prime window. The presence and extent of a condensation problem depends on relative humidity inside the home, outdoor temperature, and the tightness of the interior storm. If you notice water stains or water standing on the window sill, you may want to drill some weep holes in the window frame, level with the sill, to drain the water away (see figure **2-52**).

Water can also get in between the storm and prime windows from the outside where the prime window and the exterior siding meet. Examine the top and sides of the window between the frame and the siding for cracks and re-caulk if necessary.

2.8.6 Repairing Windows

Since replacing an old single-pane window with a new single-pane window is not going to save much energy or money, repairing the old unit may be a practical alternative. Aluminum and glass do not suffer much wear and anyone with home repair skills should be able to make some basic repairs on mobile home windows. Regular maintenance should include lubricating the moving parts of the window to reduce the strain of opening and closing.

If a sliding window doesn't slide easily, first clean out the channel, then spray the channel with silicone lubricant to make the sash slide easier. Lubricate awning and jalousie gear boxes and all the moving joints in the opening mechanism regularly. If a sliding window has pile weatherstrip that is worn out, you can replace the weatherstrip. Take a sample of the weatherstrip to your local glass dealer to see if they can match it. The pile weatherstrip slides or folds into a slot in the sash rail during assembly. To replace the pile, either take the sash rail off the glass and slide the pile in from one end, or place one side of the pile's plastic backer in the slot and fold the other side in with a spline roller or screwdriver.

If an awning or jalousie window will not close tightly, check to see if the torsion rod bearing is broken. Often this plastic or metal bracket, which holds the torsion rod as it turns, will break preventing the window from closing tightly. The torsion rod transfers the force of the closing mechanism to a push bar on the opposite side of the window from the crank. When the torsion rod bearing breaks and the

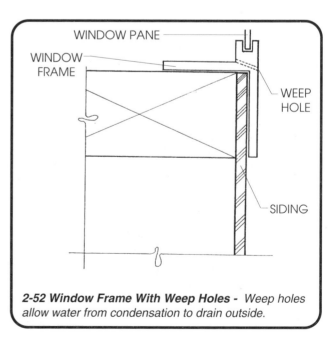

2-52 Window Frame With Weep Holes - *Weep holes allow water from condensation to drain outside.*

window doesn't close tightly, people may get frustrated and turn the crank until the threads in the crank or the gears in the gear box strip out. Replace stripped cranks with plastic replacement cranks to avoid stripping out the notched shaft which extends out of the gear box. A metal crank might strip the shaft if the window malfunctioned, causing a more expensive repair. Figure **2-50** shows the torsion rod and bearing in the bottom corner of an awning window and figure **2-51** shows a broken torsion rod bearing, two types of replacement bearings, and a replacement gear box.

The hinges on the awning window have 3 holes in the end of the hinge that pushes the window open and pulls it closed. Moving the small screw from one hole to another is a method of adjusting the window operator so that the window closes tightly.

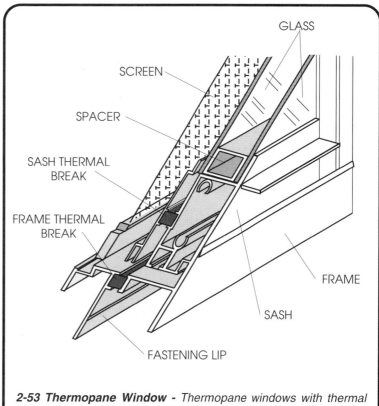

2-53 Thermopane Window - *Thermopane windows with thermal breaks are the replacement window of choice for cold climates. For hot climates, window shading is more important than layers of glass.*

As a last resort, you can install a clip on the exterior jalousie or awning window frame or siding to keep the window closed if you can't repair the mechanism. Most hardware stores carry rotating clips or spring-loaded clips that are used to hold storm windows and screens. These clips may work well to hold a jalousie or awning window closed until the window can be repaired or replaced.

To replace broken glass in horizontal or vertical sliding windows, remove the sash from the frame. Most prime sliding windows have to be completely removed to replace glass, but most sliding storm windows do not. If you have to remove the sash, the easiest way to replace the glass is to take the sash to a glass shop and let a glazier do it. The glass slides out of awning and jalousie windows for easy removal and replacement without removing the window. If you replace it yourself, be careful to compensate for the correct inset of the glass into the sash rail when you measure. If the rubber gasket that cradles the glass is missing or deteriorated, you can fill in and stabilize the glass with silicone caulk. The prime window must be carefully sealed with new putty tape or caulking underneath the perimeter of the flange, when the window is re-installed. Caulk between the edge of the flange and the siding with an exterior caulk after installation, too.

2.8.7 Replacing Windows

Some older windows, especially jalousie and awning windows, leak a lot of air and are worn beyond maintenance and repair. In this case, window replacement makes good sense. However, even replacing leaky jalousie windows may not have a noticeable effect on heating costs unless the new window assembly has more layers of glass than the old one.

Replacing an old single-pane window with a new single-pane window neither improves the R-

ENVELOPES

value of the window area, nor does it save much energy. The new window will probably not leak as much air as the old one, but that won't make much difference in the heating bill. If you plan to replace your existing windows and you want to reduce heating costs, you'll need to increase the R-value of the window in one of the following ways:

1. Replace existing single-pane window with a new double-pane window.

2. Replace existing single-pane window and storm window with a new double-pane window. The existing storm window must be retained or a new storm window installed to achieve any savings in heating cost.

3. Select a double-pane window with a heat reflecting coating (called Low-E coating) that reflects heat back into the home during the winter.

Replacing a single-pane window with a double-pane window will cut heat loss in half and result reduce air leakage too. Replacing a double-pane window assembly with a new triple-pane window assembly will save about 1/3 of the heat loss through the double-pane assembly. This option, described in #2 above, is cost-effective only in cold climates with high energy costs. Consider ordering Low-E glass in the new double-pane window, because the Low-E double-pane window will insulate like a triple-pane window. If you install a double-pane window with a metal frame, the frame should have a thermal break. A thermal break is a joint around the perimeter of the window frame that acts as a barrier to heat conduction through the metal frame and also reduces condensation on the frame (see figure **2-53**).

If you want to save cooling costs too, you have to order reflective glass or heat-absorbing glass in new windows. Adding another layer of glass will not save much cooling energy during the summer. Windows are a major source of unwanted heat during the summer by admitting solar heat into the home. Section 4.2, Shading describes how to reduce this solar heat gain.

When replacing a window, visualize the exact location and position of the new window. The new window will probably be installed in the same location and position as the old window even if the replacement window is a different type from the window it replaces. The metal or vinyl frame of the new window fits inside the window opening and the flange fits over the exterior siding.

Measuring for a replacement window is similar to measuring for a new door. You simply measure the opening that the window will fit into. Be sure to communicate to the supplier that you have measured the opening and give the supplier the dimensions of the opening by stating the width first, then the height. Check the opening for squareness by measuring the diagonals or by placing a framing square in the corners. If the opening is not square, you may need to level the home before replacing the window.

Know the thickness of both the existing window and replacement window and note how any difference may affect the installation. Also, measure the thickness of the wall to make sure it is thick enough to accommodate both the replacement window and the storm window that you intend to install in the window opening.

When installing a new window, apply enough putty tape or caulking to the perimeter flange so it squeezes out from between the flange and siding to provide a tight seal. Apply caulking over the screw holes too. Follow all manufacturer's instructions when installing the storm window. Be certain the storm window seals tightly. If you plan to install fixed-pane, removable storms in the existing storm mounting trim (commonly found on mobile homes), then use a compression type weatherstrip where the storm and trim join. Most of these trims are merely stapled to the wall paneling and leak between the trim and paneling. Remove the trim, caulk the surface underneath, and re-attach the trim to the wall. Or carefully caulk the cracks on both sides of the trim.

HEATING SYSTEMS

3.1 Heating Systems

This section discusses the operation, maintenance, and efficiency of mobile home heating systems. Proper maintenance and repair of home heating equipment is important because inefficiency can cause high energy costs. Systems that are not properly serviced and maintained can present fire or safety hazards, too. Even though much of the work on these systems should be done by a qualified technician, there are steps a home owner with basic home repair skills can take to increase the efficiency of a home heating system.

This is an introduction to mobile home heating equipment and is not intended to be a complete repair and energy conservation reference. The manufacturers of heating devices have complete service manuals for each piece of heating equipment. These parts and service manuals have operating instructions, troubleshooting procedures, detailed drawings, and wiring diagrams. Manufacturers of mobile home heating equipment are listed in Appendix A, Businesses and Organizations.

Combustion furnaces, combustion space heaters, and electric furnaces must be specifically designed and rated for use in mobile homes. The HUD Code lists the specific codes to which heating equipment must conform in order to operate safely in mobile homes (see Section 1.2, Codes and Standards).

3.2 Fuel-Burning Furnaces

Older furnaces in site-built homes are open-combustion furnaces. Open combustion means that the combustion air is pulled into an open firebox and flue from inside the home. Since many mobile homes are small and tightly constructed, open-combustion furnaces would be a poor design and possibly dangerous. For this reason, sealed-combustion furnaces have been standard equipment since the early 1970s.

Sealed combustion means that all the combustion air comes from the outdoors, and that the firebox and flue have no openings to the interior of the home. Almost all mobile home furnaces are downflow furnaces. Downflow furnaces take the return air in at the top of the furnace, heat the air, and force it into ductwork below the furnace in the floor. Return air from the rooms is pulled back to the furnace through the hallway by the blower, which creates a large suction at its inlet.

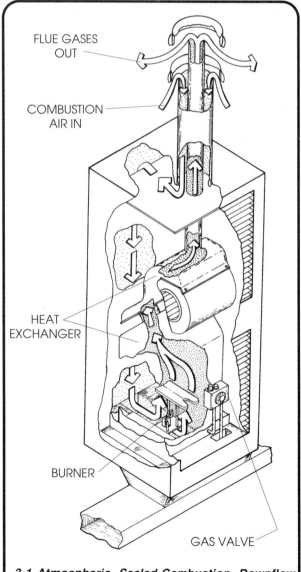

3-1 Atmospheric, Sealed-Combustion, Downflow Furnace - Combustion air from the roof comes down the outside of the flue pipe, around the furnace cabinet, and into the heat exchanger where it mixes with gas during combustion.

HEATING SYSTEMS

The blower inlet is close to the flue so it could suck flue gases into the home if the flue or the firebox were open.

3.2.1 Natural Gas and Propane Furnaces

Natural gas and propane furnaces are actually the same except for the burner orifices, the pilot orifice, and the pressure setting on the automatic gas valve. A conversion kit comes with every furnace. The furnace should be marked with a tag to indicate which type of fuel it is equipped for.

Gas furnaces are classified as either atmospheric (see figure **3-1**) or forced-draft (see figure **3-2**). Atmospheric gas furnaces employ the differences in weight between the cool combustion air and the hot flue gases to move combustion air and the exhaust gases through the firebox. Most atmospheric gas burners on mobile home furnaces are not adjustable, so there is really no way to improve the efficiency of the furnace by adjusting the burner. The burner assembly may need to be cleaned periodically. The presence of black soot should always be a cause for concern because soot indicates incomplete combustion and the formation of the poisonous gas, carbon monoxide. One-eighth inch of soot on the heat exchanger will reduce combustion efficiency about 10%.

Figure **3-1** shows the flow of combustion air and gases from the inlet outdoors to the outlet which is also outdoors in an atmospheric furnace. The illustration shows how the chimney cap of one type of atmospheric furnace contains both the combustion air inlet and the flue gas outlet. The combustion air travels down through a doughnut-shaped cavity created by a double-pipe assembly as shown. The flue gases travel up through the inner pipe. The combustion air flows out of the double pipe assembly into a narrow duct space around the furnace and into the bottom or backside of the heat exchanger. The air mixes with the gas in the flame, and the products of combustion (flue gases) rise up into the inner flue pipe because they are lighter than air. On leaving the firebox, the gases create a vacuum which pulls more combustion air in through the inlet, down the pipe, around the furnace cabinet, and into the firebox.

Forced-draft furnaces use a fan called a draft booster to help pull combustion air into the firebox and to push exhaust gases out. Gas furnaces with draft boosters are adjustable, but only by a trained technician using combustion-testing equipment. The draft boosters are set at the factory to provide adequate draft for combustion, but only combustion testing of the burner can determine whether the draft is correct. Too much draft will waste energy by moving too much heat-absorbing air through the firebox. Not enough draft will starve the flame for air and produce soot and carbon monoxide.

Most oil and gas forced-draft burners bring combustion air in from the crawl space under the floor through ducts connected directly to the draft booster or the firebox (see figure **3-2**) However, some oil furnaces have the combustion air delivered into a closed burner compartment. The interior of combustion air passageways should not be visible from inside the home. Don't confuse these combustion air ducts with other small metal ducts in the floor

3-2 Forced-Draft Mobile Home Furnace - *A small fan called a draft booster pulls air from the crawl space, through a metal duct, and forces the combustion air into the heat exchanger.*

HEATING SYSTEMS

that bring fresh ventilation air into the furnace blower (see figure **3-9**).

3.2.2 Oil Burning Furnaces

An oil burner fires into a refractory combustion chamber that sits inside the steel heat exchanger and protects it from the intense heat of the oil flame (see figure **3-3**). The pump in the gun-type burner pumps the oil through a nozzle that sprays the oil into the combustion chamber. A sparking electrode lights the spray of oil and a fan in the burner housing pulls combustion air from the crawlspace and mixes it with the oil to produce combustion. The refractory combustion chamber radiates heat back towards the flame to aid in vaporizing and burning the oil. The combustion chamber is shaped to match the particular pattern of flame that the burner produces.

The oil burner is more complicated because oil does not burn as easily as natural gas or propane. For these reasons oil furnaces require more maintenance than gas furnaces. Unlike propane and gas combustion efficiency, which remains stable over periods of years, oil combustion efficiency deteriorates as more soot and sludge are deposited around the nozzle, combustion chamber, and heat exchanger. It is important, therefore, to have an oil furnace serviced annually by a qualified technician.

3-3 Typical Oil Burner - Oil sprays from a nozzle and mixes with combustion air that is pulled from the crawl space by a fan in the gun-type oil burner. The combustion chamber radiates heat back to the flame keeping it hot enough to burn all the oil.

A flame-retention burner is a newer type of burner that gives a higher combustion efficiency by swirling the mist of oil and air in a way that produces better mixing (see figure **3-4**). Flame-retention burners waste less heat and have combustion efficiencies of 80% or slightly more. Replacing an existing burner with a flame retention model is usually cost-effective if the existing combustion efficiency is less than 75% or if the burner needs major repairs. Another change that may make sense, especially in cold climates, is an oil preheater. The oil, which is sprayed at the nozzle, must vaporize before it will burn cleanly. The oil preheater aids this vaporization and produces a cleaner flame in cases where colder, thicker oil is retarding vaporization.

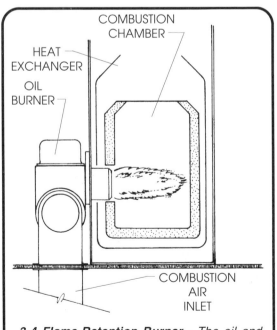

3-4 Flame-Retention Burner - The oil and combustion air swirl and mix better in a tight flame pattern which leads to more complete combustion and a better combustion efficiency.

The difference in fuel usage between an efficient oil burner and a very inefficient one may be as great as 30%. This is one reason why annual maintenance and combustion testing are so important. Oil burners should be cleaned, tested, and adjusted every year.

HEATING SYSTEMS

Adjusting an oil burner is a job for a specialist because of the need for specialized training and test equipment. The oil service technician should have combustion test equipment and know how to use it. Two combustion test measurements are particularly important:

1) A measurement of both carbon monoxide and smoke will give the technician information on whether the combustion process is burning all the fuel. If there are excessive amounts of unburned or partially burned oil in the flue gases, then steps should be taken to clean up the combustion process.

2) A measurement of carbon dioxide or oxygen will tell the service person how much heat is escaping up the flue so adjustments can be made to adjust the fuel/air mixture and improve efficiency.

Yearly Oil Service Checklist

1. Replace nozzle
2. Replace fuel filter or install filter if none is present
3. Adjust electrodes
4. Clean blast tube, electrode, and burner fan
5. Check for soot accumulation in combustion chamber and heat exchanger and clean them if necessary
6. Test flame sensor
7. Perform combustion tests and make necessary adjustments (see figure **3-5**)

Caution: When you are trying to start an oil burner, do not push the reset button repeatedly. This practice will deposit a pool of oil in the bottom of the furnace that is difficult to remove and can be dangerous when the furnace finally restarts. If the furnace does not start properly, call a qualified service person to diagnose the problem.

Oil is stored in a tank outside the home. An approved and readily accessible shutoff valve should be installed at the outlet of the tank. The tank should be kept at least half full, especially in summer months. A nearly empty tank has too much cold interior surface area that will condense water out of the air inside the tank. Water can interfere with oil burner operation. Do not fill a nearly empty tank without first draining it. Moisture and sediment at the bottom of the tank may mix with the new oil and clog the system. When the tank is almost empty, drain it to remove the dirt and moisture before filling it again.

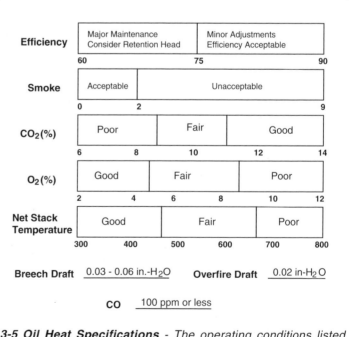

3-5 **Oil Heat Specifications** - The operating conditions listed above are rough guidelines used by oil heating technicians to measure and adjust oil heaters.

HEATING SYSTEMS

3.3 Heating Controls

Almost all mobile home heating systems use 24-volt control systems and bimetal thermostatic controls. The voltage that is commonly used in homes is 120 volts. This house power is reduced to 24 volts by a transformer to provide a safer and more convenient power source to control heating. The source of power for the 24-volt circuit is the transformer which transforms the 120-volt house power to the 24-volt control power. The other parts of the control circuit are the thermostat, safety switches (called limits), and a final operator that actually engages the heating. The final operator for gas and propane furnaces is a magnetically controlled valve. For oil furnaces, the final operator is a relay, which is a magnetically controlled switch that activates a 120-volt circuit. For electric furnaces, the final controller is a small heating element that activates a series of bimetal switches called sequencers.

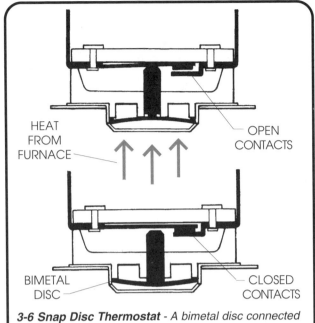

3-6 Snap Disc Thermostat - A bimetal disc connected to a switch snaps in and out with changes in temperature and opens or closes contact points with a rod attached to the disc. It is often used as a safety limit, fan control, or sequencer in heating equipment.

Bimetal controls work by employing a disc (see figure **3-6**), strip, or coil (see figure **3-7**) made of two different metals bonded together. The bimetal disc, strip, or coil moves as the temperature changes because the two different metals that compose the bimetal element expand and contract at different rates. The movement of the bimetal element opens and closes switches that control heating devices and fans. These bimetal thermostatic controls work like automatic light switches to turn heating components on and off.

Bimetal controls also control the staging of heating elements and fan speeds in electric furnaces and provide high-limit protection for all types of furnaces. Bimetal controls react to the temperature around them and they sometimes have small heating coils near them. These little heating coils make the bimetal control a time delay switch in staging the operation of fans and electric heating elements in electric furnaces. A miniature heating element inside many thermostats causes the bimetal element in the thermostat to turn the heating or cooling system off earlier in anticipation of the heated air that is left in the system after the heating element goes off. This small adjustable heater, called the heat anticipator (see figure **3-7**), is designed to prevent the temperature from exceeding the thermostat setpoint.

Most mobile home thermostats have metal contacts, one of which is attached to a bimetal strip or coil (see figure **3-7**). They are different from thermostats frequently found in site-built homes which have a bimetal coil attached to a vial where the contacts are connected and disconnected by a moving ball of liquid mercury. Mercury switch thermostats need to be level to control the temperature accurately. If the thermostat setting and the thermometer reading consistently do not match, the mercury switch thermostat probably needs to be leveled. Since mobile homes may move more than homes with permanent foundations, mercury switch thermostats are not common.

Thermostat location is very important to the functioning of a heating system. Localized sources of heat or cold can trick the thermostat. Troublesome locations for thermostats include outside walls and areas near windows, doors, light bulbs, registers, or near anything that can heat or cool

HEATING SYSTEMS

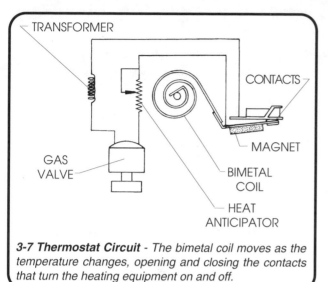

3-7 Thermostat Circuit - *The bimetal coil moves as the temperature changes, opening and closing the contacts that turn the heating equipment on and off.*

the thermostat. In cases where there are problems, the thermostat may need to be moved to an inside wall away from drafts and heat sources.

3.3.1 Burner Controls

The burners in oil and gas furnaces are controlled by a 24-volt circuit powered by a transformer. The transformer takes the 120-volt electricity and reduces it to a safer and more convenient voltage (24 volts). This lower voltage is used to open and close the automatic gas valve or to turn the oil burner on and off. The burner turns on when the contacts in the thermostat and the high-limit control are closed. Both sets of contacts must be closed at the same time. The contacts in the high-limit controls are always closed except when the furnace has reached a dangerously high temperature or when the high-limit control has failed. The contacts in the thermostat are closed when the temperature in the room is below the thermostat's set point. If the contacts in the thermostat or the contacts in the high-limit controls are open, then electricity can't flow through the circuit and won't turn the burner on. Gas and propane furnaces with draft boosters also have centrifugal safety switches that will not allow burner ignition unless the booster fan is operating.

The pilot safety thermocouple is a separate circuit. The pilot light heats a thermocouple which is a rod that generates a small electric current. The current energizes a magnetic valve stem called a solenoid in the automatic gas valve. The solenoid keeps the passageway open for the flow of gas to the pilot and to the burners in case the thermostat calls for heat. If the pilot goes out or if the thermocouple fails, the current stops flowing, a spring returns the valve stem to the valve seat like a cork in the neck of a bottle, and gas is prevented from flowing to the pilot and the gas burner.

Gun-type oil burners do not have pilot lights or thermocouples. Instead they have a flame sensor that will not allow the fan and oil pump to remain on unless it senses a flame. The flame sensor is connected to a switch in the 120-volt circuit that powers the oil burner.

3.3.2 Fan Controls and Furnace Operating Temperatures

All combustion furnaces have three operating temperatures that have a strong relationship to seasonal heating efficiency. These temperatures are: 1) the heat rise across the heat exchanger, 2) the fan-off temperature, and 3) the fan-on temperature. The heat rise across the heat exchanger is the number of degrees that the air is heated as it flows around the heat exchanger. If the return air temperature is 65°F and the supply air temperature is 125°F, the heat rise is 60°F. The temperature scales in figure **3-8** give rough temperature ranges for these three important operating temperatures.

It is important to test the fan control because it is often not working properly. Technicians measure the fan-on and fan-off temperatures with a thermometer to see if the fan (furnace blower) control is working properly. The fan-off temperature is the most important measurement and is directly related to the seasonal heating efficiency. The fan-off temperature is the measured temperature of the air in the closest register when the fan control turns the fan off after a burner cycle has ended.

HEATING SYSTEMS

The fan-on temperature is the measured temperature in the furnace (near the blower) when the fan control turns the blower on after the burner cycle has started.

Each time the burner cycles on and off, the fan should cycle on and off. The fan controls in most mobile home furnaces turn the fan on at a furnace air temperature of between 110°F and 150°F at the beginning of the cycle. The fan control turns the blower off at a furnace air temperature of between 100°F and 140°F at the end of the cycle.

The fan control is usually an inexpensive snap-disc type thermostatic control. These snap-disc fan controls in many furnaces do not hold the furnace blower on for long enough to get all the available heat out of each burner cycle. Unfortunately, these snap-disc controls are not adjustable, but fortunately the controls are inexpensive and easy to replace. The fan control is located in the furnace's electrical service box near a very similar control which is one of the two high-limit controls. Some of the replacement snap-disc fan controls are adjustable and these are better than the non-adjustable types. The fan control is usually held in place by two sheet metal screws and has two wires connected to it. These wires attach interchangeably to the terminals of the new control.

Many furnace blowers have several speeds. Increasing the speed can improve heating efficiency in cases where the heat rise is excessive. The larger volume of air, circulated by the higher fan speed, extracts more heat from the heat exchanger allowing less heat to escape up the chimney. However, if the fan speed is too high, the residents might complain of drafts, or the heat exchanger might cool too much, causing condensation and corrosion. Different speeds are represented by different-colored wires coming out of the fan motor. Increasing the fan speed usually involves removing a wire representing a lower speed from a terminal and replacing it with a wire representing a higher speed. The color coding should be noted in the wiring diagram attached to the furnace. On some furnaces, the speeds are more easily changed with a fan speed switch.

3.3.3 Automatic Thermostats

Automatic thermostats are a convenient and effective way to save heating and cooling energy. There are two types of automatic thermostats, electromechanical and electronic. The electromechanical thermostat employs an electric clock with a switching mechanism that is part of the movement of the clock. This type actually contains two thermostats with two different settings. The movement of the clock and the position of movable pins on a dial determines which thermostat is controlling heating or cooling at any time.

The electronic type, which is usually a little more expensive, is a digital clock with a small electronic brain that switches between high and low settings. Electronic thermostats have more features and are more con-

Inadequate heat rise - condensation and corrosion possible.	Heat rise good for both efficiency and avoidance of condensation in the flue. (Check mfgr's specs.)	Heat rise excessive. Check fan, heat exchanger, ducts, and fan speed.
20°	45°	70° 95°

HEAT RISE = SUPPLY TEMPERATURE MINUS RETURN TEMPERATURE

Excellent fan off temperature if comfort is acceptable	Borderline acceptable. Consider fan control change.	Unacceptable range. Large savings possible by replacing fan control.
85° 100°	115°	130°

FAN-OFF TEMPERATURE

Excellent - no action needed	Fair - consider fan control replacement only if fan off is unacceptable.	Poor - consider fan control replacement
90° 110°	130°	150°

FAN-ON TEMPERATURE

3-8 Furnace Operating Temperature - The operating conditions listed above are rough guidelines used by technicians to measure and adjust fan control and fan speed on mobile home furnaces.

HEATING SYSTEMS

venient but some are a little confusing to operate at first. Most electronic units will give two or more setback periods per day and will adjust for weekends. They usually give a wider range of temperature settings than the electromechanical models. And, the electronic models don't have mercury-buld thermostats inside them like many electromechanical models do. Mercury-bulb thermostats need to be level as mentioned in Section 3.3, Heating Controls.

Automatic thermostats are ideal for people who have regular schedules and who do not currently change thermostat settings for periods of occupancy or vacancy, and activity or sleep. You can save 5% to 15% of heating and cooling costs depending on the length of setback periods and the number of degrees of setback. Automatic thermostats will save the largest percentage in milder climates with both heating and cooling, but are effective energy savers in all climates. Be sure to ask for a heating and cooling thermostat if you have both central air conditioning and heating.

3.4 Air Circulation and Distribution

Forced-air heating systems take air from the home (called "return air"), and heat the air by forcing the air past a hot metal heat exchanger (see figure **3-9**). After it passes the heat exchanger, the heated air enters the supply duct and flows out of registers in the rooms. Most site-built homes have ducted return air but most mobile homes have unducted return air. Air from the rooms is pulled toward the furnace from the rooms and through the hallway by the suction created by the furnace blower. This return air flows through the door of the furnace, into the blower which pushes the air down past the heat exchanger, and into the main duct which runs lengthwise underneath the floor of the home (see figure **3-10**). The warm air flows through the ducts, out the registers, and into the rooms where it cools off by heating cooler air and by heating cooler objects in the rooms. The now cool air returns to the furnace where it is heated again.

One disadvantage of forced-air systems is that they contribute to air leakage. The suction near the furnace blower and the pressure in the supply ducts and registers pull outdoor air in through holes in the building and push indoor air out through holes in the ducts. The air exchange with the outdoors caused by the furnace blower can double the

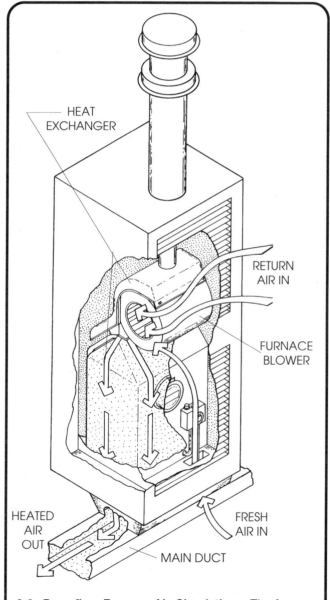

3-9 Downflow Furnace Air Circulation - *The furnace blower pulls air in from the hallway and blows the air down over the hot heat exchanger and into the main duct.*

HEATING SYSTEMS

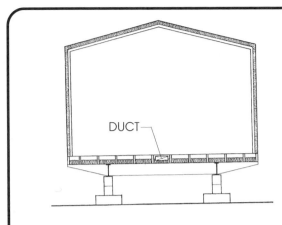
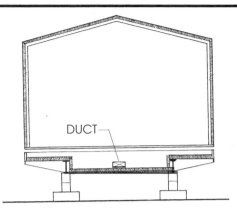

3-10 Duct Location - In homes with lengthwise joists, the main duct is installed between the floor joists, touching the flooring material. In homes with crosswise joists, the main duct is installed below the floor joists.

normal leakage rate. Some air exchange between indoor and outdoor air is necessary to remove moisture and pollutants from the home. For this reason, many furnaces have fresh air ducts that are designed to bring fresh air into the furnace through the floor of the furnace closet (see figure **3-9**).

A problem in air circulation systems is that supply ducts often have significant leaks at the joints between ducts and boots, branch ducts, the plenum (see figure **3-11**), and termination cap (see figure **3-12**). These leaks allow warm air to escape from the supply ducts lowering the overall efficiency of the heating system.

Another problem area is that some mobile homes bring the return air back to the furnace through the roof cavity (see figure **3-13**) or floor cavity (see figure **3-14**). These ceiling and

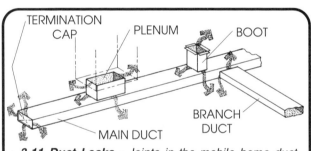

3-11 Duct Leaks - Joints in the mobile home duct system are a major source of air leakage.

floor return air systems are often very wasteful because they introduce excessive amounts of outside air into the home. The roof cavities of most mobile homes are not airtight and so routing the return air through the roof cavity mixes the return air from the home with outside air coming into the roof cavity. Floor return air systems often introduce excessive outdoor air through holes in the underbelly.

3-12 Leak in Duct Termination Cap - Leaks this large in main ducts are not rare in older mobile homes.

HEATING SYSTEMS

3.4.1 Improving Supply and Return Air Systems

Many of the major supply duct leaks can be patched from the registers and access doors in the furnace where these leaks are located. Other leaks, like those in crossover ducts and branch ducts, must be patched from underneath the home. Small mirrors, flashlights, and trouble lights are useful for inspecting ductwork. Laying the mirror on the floor of the duct and moving it around will show you the corners of the joint where the boot meets the main duct and if there are sizable leaks there. In homes with lengthwise floor joists, the main duct should be sealed to the floor at the register. You can attach a lightweight metal channel and seal it to the flooring and main duct as shown in figure **3-15**. With crosswise joists you must seal the boots that lead the air from the main duct to the floor (see figure **4-16,** page 97).

Putting a trouble light in one register and looking toward it at the next register using a mirror will enable you to see major leaks and obstructions. Using a blower-door test (see Section 2.2.1, Blower Door Testing) will locate air leaks in difficult locations inside ducts that cannot be seen by looking into the ducts. If you feel air entering through the ducts while the blower door is depressurizing the house, then the ducts are leaking. You can use pillows made of insulation inside plastic bags to systematically plug sections of the duct to locate the air leaks during the test.

Most common types of duct tape are not appropriate for sealing ducts because the adhesive does not stick permanently. There are, however, three very good materials for patching metal ducts. Silicone caulking works well

3-13 Roof Cavity Return Air - Air from the home enters the roof cavity through grilles and returns to the furnace through the roof cavity. If the roof is ventilated or if there are air leaks in the roof, excessive air leakage can result between the home and the outdoors.

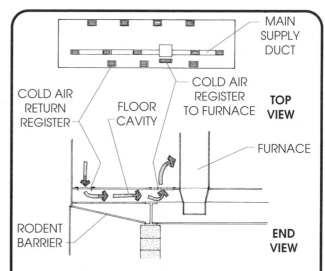

3-14 Floor Cavity Return Air - Registers near the wall let return air from the home into the belly where it travels under the floor and back to the furnace. Floor return air systems are often a source of excessive air leakage.

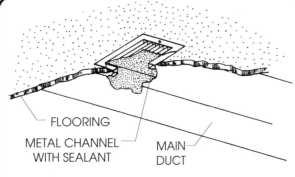

3-15 Duct Sealing at Register - In mobile homes with lengthwise floor joists, the main duct should be sealed to the floor at the register.

76

HEATING SYSTEMS

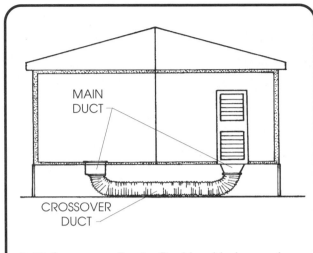

3-16 Crossover Duct - Double-wide homes have crossover ducts to take heated air from the side with the furnace to the side without the furnace. Crossover ducts can be a major source of air leakage.

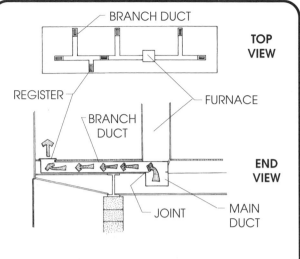

3-17 Branch Ducts - Some homes have branch ducts. Joints between branch ducts and the main duct should be inspected for air leaks.

for narrow cracks and small holes. A product which combines a 2-mil aluminum foil tape with a 20- to 40-mil butyl putty tape works well for larger holes and cracks, especially in corners. Possibly the best product is a latex mastic (a thin putty) combined with reinforcing tape that patches holes and cracks in ducts. This mastic has been used for years to seal ducts in commercial buildings. Fiber reinforcement added to some types of mastic may eliminate the need for the reinforcing tape when patching smaller holes and cracks. This mastic is easy to install with a brush or rubber glove, and it's available from heating wholesalers. For larger holes and cracks, use the reinforcing tape so the cracks do not reappear when the duct moves as it changes temperature. Always clean the area of duct to be patched with a solvent cleaner or steel wool.

When you're looking for duct leaks underneath the home, it may help to run the furnace fan so you can feel the air blowing out the leaks. Two locations that should always be inspected are crossover ducts (see figure **3-16**) and branch ducts (see figures **3-17** and **3-11**). The connection between the metal branch duct or the crossover duct with the main duct may not be airtight. For branch ducts, the connection between it and the main duct is often loosely attached with no sealant on the seam around the perimeter of the connection. To locate the joint, measure indoors using exterior walls and windows as landmarks, and then transfer the measurements to the underbelly so you know where to cut in order to access the duct for repairs.

For crossover ducts that use insulated flexduct, there are two different seams to seal. The first is the seam between the flexduct and the cone connector (see figure **3-18**). This seam can be sealed with caulking around the metal collar and a ratcheting plastic clamp. And the second seam is the seam between the

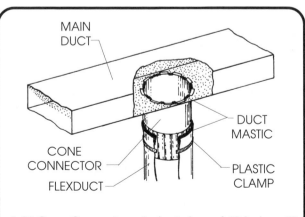

3-18 Cone Connector - A short piece of 10 inch or 12 inch metal pipe is often used to connect the flexible crossover duct with the main duct.

HEATING SYSTEMS

cone and the main duct (see figure **3-18**). This seam can be sealed with duct mastic and fabric, or silicon caulking. Duct tape is not appropriate for connections between flexduct and metal connections because it fails to permanently adhere.

When the registers are not screwed to the floor, children will often put toys and other objects into the ducts that partially block airflow. Blockages should be identified and removed from ducts during duct inspection. Supply registers can have severe blockages if the fins have been flattened by foot traffic (see figure **3-19**) or if they are dirty. Registers with flattened fins should be replaced or at least the fins should be straightened to allow maximum airflow. Dirty registers should be cleaned. All registers should be screwed to the floor after the inspection is complete.

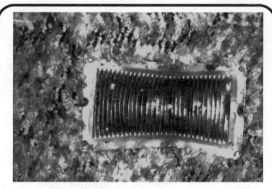

3-19 Obstructed Register - The louvers on supply registers become bent by foot traffic and restrict the delivery of warm air. Pry the louvers open or replace the register.

It is often best to eliminate return air systems in the floor and ceiling cavities because these systems can introduce excessive quantities of outdoor air. Seal the return air openings in the floor or roof cavity with wood or metal patches to prevent airflow between these cavities and the living space. Also seal the main return air opening in the floor or ceiling of the furnace closet.

When eliminating floor or ceiling return air systems, it is important to provide as large an opening into the furnace cabinet as possible. The amount of air flow through the furnace affects the efficiency of the heating system. The HUD Code specifies at least 2 square inches of return air area for each 1000 Btus of furnace capacity. This may involve installing one or two large grilles in the door to the furnace closet or even taking the door off permanently. Some metal furnace cabinet doors may not have adequate area for return air passage and installing grilles in solid sections of these doors may improve air circulation.

Cutting an inch or so off interior doors or installing louvers in the doors will allow return air to get back to the furnace from the rooms. Interior doors are hollow core doors that have a framing member at the bottom. It is best not to cut through the framing member when you cut off the door but to carefully remove and replace it at the bottom of the door after you cut the door off.

Supply air registers that are closest to the furnace often deliver more heat to rooms closer to the furnace than to rooms which are farther away. End rooms may not receive enough air to keep them comfortable because of the lower airflow they receive and because these rooms have more heat loss from their greater area of outside walls and windows. You may be able to change airflow by moving the adjustable vanes in registers or by sealing off portions of the registers which are closest to the furnace. It is not usually a good idea to block off registers altogether because this reduces airflow and furnace efficiency. Before you block off part of a supply register, be sure that the return air has an unobstructed path back to the furnace by cutting off doors or installing grilles in the doors, if necessary.

3.4.2 Cleaning the Blower and Heat Exchanger

Dirt on the fan blades of furnace blowers greatly reduces the blower's ability to move air over the heat exchanger. The amount of air flow, moving over the heat exchanger, strongly affects heating and cooling efficiency. Dirt on air filters reduces overall system efficiency. **Cleaning the blower and cleaning or replacing the air filter (if present) are two of the most effective en-**

HEATING SYSTEMS

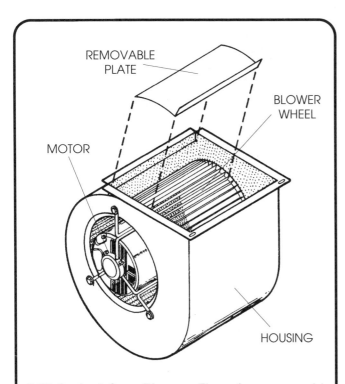

3-20 Squirrel Cage Blower - These fans are used in almost all furnaces, air conditioners, and evaporative coolers. Dirt on the blades of the blower reduces the efficiency of the cooling system.

ergy conservation measures for mobile homes.

Although the blower can sometimes be cleaned in place, you can do a much better job by removing it. *Caution: Before cleaning the blower, shut off power to the furnace at the breaker box or main switch.* With some blower motors, the wires from the motor are connected to wires in the main control box by a fool-proof plug that you pull apart. Other blowers have wires that are individually connected to terminals in the main control box. Label the wires and terminals as you disconnect them so that there is no possibility of reconnecting them improperly.

Most of the time it is not necessary to remove the blower wheel from the motor and housing, but you may need to remove a plate in the blower housing (see figure **3-20**) to get more space to work on the blades of the blower. The blower wheel can be cleaned with compressed air, pressurized water, or with a brush and vacuum cleaner. Inexpensive cylindrical hair styling brushes work well for cleaning blowers without having to remove the blower wheel from the housing.

While the blower is removed, a large portion of the heat exchanger is exposed. This is a good time to inspect the heat exchanger for cracks and dirt. Clean the heat exchanger with a brush or rag, using soap and water if necessary. You can use a long handled brush or tie a rag to a stick to reach further down into the heat exchanger if you see dirt down there. Also be sure to clean the blower motor thoroughly and add a few drops of 20-weight oil to lubrication ports.

3.5 Electric Furnaces

An electric furnace (see figure **3-21**) heats air by moving the air through a fan and over a series of electric resistance heating elements. Electric furnaces have 3 to 6 of these 5-kw elements that work like the elements in a toaster. The 24-volt thermostat circuit energizes devices called sequencers that bring the 240 volt heating elements on in stages when the thermostat calls for heat. Many mobile home furnace

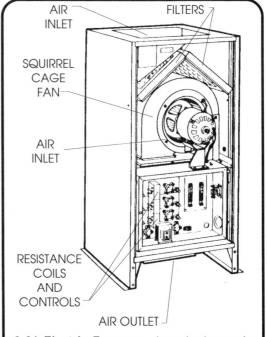

3-21 Electric Furnace - A squirrel-cage fan blows air over 3 to 6 electric resistance coils and down into the main duct of the mobile home.

HEATING SYSTEMS

blowers have multiple speeds to maintain a comfortable air temperature as the number of heating elements that are engaged changes. The variable speed fan switches to a higher speed as more elements engage to move enough air over the heating elements. When the thermostat is satisfied and the number of elements are reduced, the fan speed is also reduced (see figure **3-22**).

Virtually all of the electricity that enters the heating elements is turned into useful heat so we say that electric furnaces are 100% efficient. However, electric furnaces are often subject to large losses due to duct leakage. Duct leakage can be responsible for up to 30 % of the total home heating cost (see Section 3.4.1, Improving Supply and Return Air Systems).

Replacing air filters at regular intervals is vital to the efficient operation of electric furnaces. The electric heating elements should be dusted and vacuumed every few years to keep them clean. Cleaning the heating elements may not be necessary if the air filters are changed regularly.

Electric furnaces can be a problem for utility companies if they are using more 5-kw heating elements than are necessary to heat the home. The problem is that the utility must provide more expensive service than if only the minimum number of elements were used. During mild weather in most climates, only a couple elements are needed. As the temperature gets lower, other elements are needed. Some control systems allow fewer elements to be used during mild weather and more during cold weather. Either a two-stage heating thermostat or a standard heating thermostat with an outdoor thermostat can be used to accomplish the different levels of heat for different weather. This is not an energy-saving measure but a power-saving measure. Since staging elements benefit the utility company, they may be willing to pay for the savings to the utility power system.

Two-stage thermostats are actually just two thermostats in one enclosure. One of the thermostats brings on the first stage of heating, usually two 5-kw elements. The second thermostat brings on the other elements. The other option is an outdoor thermostat which connects the last series of 5-kw elements at an outdoor temperature at which all the elements are needed to heat the home.

Caution: Electric furnaces use 240 volts which can injure or kill a person who comes in contact with it. Only qualified technicians should work on mobile home heating equipment.

3-22 Operation of an Electric Furnace - Electric elements are engaged in a sequence and the furnace fan changes speed during each furnace cycle.

HEATING SYSTEMS

3.6 Heat Pumps

Electric heat pumps are the most efficient type of heating system for much of the southern and south central United States. There is always heat available in outdoor air which can be captured and moved at low temperatures by special fluids called refrigerants. Heat pumps are actually two furnaces packaged in the same unit. The first furnace is a compressor system which moves heat from the outdoors to indoors during the heating season using a refrigerant. The second furnace is an elec-

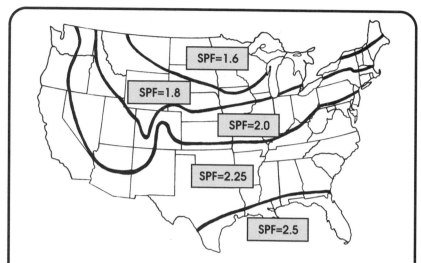

3-23 Heat Pump HSPF Map - The heating efficiency of a heat pump is called the "Heating Seasonal Performance Factor" or HSPF. Climate is the major determinant of the HSPF. (Courtesy of American Refrigeration Institute).

tric resistance heating unit like those found in electric furnaces (see Section 3.5 Electric Furnaces). Because the heat pump is primarily a heat mover and not just a heat producer, it can actually deliver more kilowatt-hours of heat to your home than the number of kilowatt-hours of electricity it uses. Therefore the heat pump can be more than 100% efficient in delivering heat energy.

In fact, the heat pump will give you 1.6 to 2.5 kilowatt-hours of heat for every kilowatt-hour of electricity it uses. This relationship of heat given to electricity used is called the Heating Seasonal Performance Factor (HSPF). The HSPF includes both the very efficient heating done by the compressor and the less efficient heating done by the electric resistance elements. An HSPF of 1.6 corresponds to 160% efficiency, and means that the heat pump delivers 1.6 kilowatt-hours of heat for every kilowatt-hour of electricity it uses. The HSPF is largely dependent on geographical location and the HSPF number generally gets larger as you go farther south as shown on the map in figure 3-23. In the more southern regions, the compressor part of the heat pump handles more of the heating responsibilities and the electric resistance elements handle less, accounting for the greater HSPFs found in the deep south.

Electric heat pumps work like mechanical air conditioning systems described in the Section 4.4, Air Conditioning. The difference between an air conditioner and a heat pump is that a heat pump is reversible. It moves heat into the home during the heating season and out of the home during the cooling season. The heat pump is almost identical to an air conditioner except for a few extra valves that allow the refrigerant to follow two different paths, one for heating and one for cooling. Heat pumps are either packaged units or split systems just like air conditioners. They are also available in small packaged units which are like room air conditioners. Follow the same maintenance procedures for heat pumps as for the air conditioners described in Section 4.4, Air Conditioning.

Heat pumps are controlled by two-stage thermostats. The first stage is the heat pump and then, if it's too cold for the compressor to keep up with the heat loss, electric resistance coils, which are the second stage of heat, come on. Most heat pumps have an outdoor thermostat that prevents the less efficient electric resistance heat from coming on until the outdoor temperature is below 40°F.

HEATING SYSTEMS

3.7 Zone Heating

Zone heating is a practical and effective way to reduce heating costs in homes. Zone heaters are more efficient than central heating systems because zone heaters do not have ducts which lose a portion of the heat that a heater produces. In cold climates, the zone heater can supplement the central heating system providing heat for areas where occupants spend most of their time. Tests conducted by the National Center for Appropriate Technology (NCAT) in Pennsylvania on mobile homes indicate that a coordinated effort at zone heating can save from 10% to 20% of heating costs. However, the success of zone heating depends on how the residents use the space heaters and the central heating system.

NCAT used wall-mounted electric space heaters in the "warm room" where the family spent most of their time while at home. Central heating was controlled by an automatic thermostat to provide a comfortable temperature throughout the house during the main activity periods, and then set back to a minimum temperature of 55° to 60°F for the remainder of the time. The bathroom was equipped with a 250 watt radiant heat lamp in an approved ceiling-mounted fixture to provide comfort there. And the residents slept under electric blankets at night. **This zone heating strategy is only effective if the residents understand the idea and cooperate.**

The problem with zone heating is that many common zone heaters are not safe for use in mobile homes. ***Caustion:*** *Never use open-combustion gas, propane, or kerosene space heaters in mobile homes.* Unvented space heaters can deplete oxygen and produce unsafe quantities of carbon monoxide, water vapor, and oxides of nitrogen. Oxygen depletion and carbon monoxide are serious health hazards which can be life-threatening. Because mobile homes are smaller than conventional homes, they have less air to lend to vented or unvented combustion space heaters.

Caution: *Many cheaper and older portable electric space heaters are not safe because red hot elements and lack of safety features can lead to fires.* Electric space heaters can be safe depending on the type you choose and the way you use them. Use the following guidelines when employing portable electric space heaters.

1. Make sure that you have a properly functioning smoke detector.
2. Never use electric space heaters in homes equipped with aluminum wiring.
3. Use a safe space heater.
4. Do not overload circuits.

Your best choice is a wall mounted space heater rated at between 1.5 and 3 kilowatts, installed by a qualified electrician. Or you can use a gas or propane space heater, designed for mobile homes, as shown in figure **3-24**. If you decide to use a portable space heater, select one that has the safety features described below.

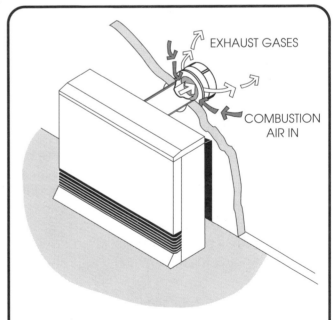

3-24 Gas/Propane Space Heater - Combustion space heaters must be rated for use in mobile homes. Like furnaces, these heaters must take combustion air from outdoors, and the burners must be sealed from indoors.

HEATING SYSTEMS

1. Tipover Switch - Tipover switches shut the portable electric heater off automatically if the heater falls over.

2. Protective grill - All electric elements that glow must be protected by a sturdy guard. A wire grill or other protection is essential to keep fingers and fabrics from touching the hot element.

3. Sealed heating elements - The heating elements must be sealed or otherwise inaccessible. Young children might push objects through the protective grill so having sealed heating elements reduces the risk of electric shock.

4. Temperature controller - An adjustable thermostat, variable wattage selector, or other energy control is necessary to regulate room temperature and to avoid overheating.

5. Signal light - An indicator light that stays on when the heater is working.

6. Handle for portable heaters - A handle is necessary for ease in carrying the heater from one location to another.

7. Electrical cord - A three-prong grounded power cord or two-prong polarized cord is necessary for safe operation. Do not use a heater with a frayed cord.

8. Use of extension cords - If an extension cord is to be used, it must be a heavy duty cord marked with a power rating at least as high as the rating on the heater itself. An incorrectly sized cord may create a fire hazard. If the heater has a three-prong plug, then the extension cord must be of the three-prong variety. Do not run extension cords under rugs or carpeting.

9. High-limit or fusible link - This important safety device protects against overheating if the fan of a forced-air electric heater stops working.

10. Clearances around heater - A minimum clearance of 36 inches above and 12 inches around is required by the National Fire Protection Association code.

Some mobile homes are equipped with built-in electric resistance heaters. These zone heaters, such as electric baseboard heaters, should have their heating elements gently dusted periodically to remove dust. You should leave adequate clearance around the heater to allow the heat to circulate into the room.

Combustion space heaters should be sealed-combustion units which are specifically rated for use in mobile homes (see figure **3-24**).

3.8 Wood Heat Safety

Safety is the main consideration when using wood heat because wood stoves have caused many fires in homes. Most house fires caused

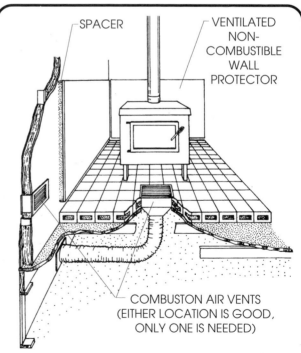

3-25 Wood Heating - Existing wood stoves should have combustion air delivered to the area of the wood stove. Walls and floors should be adequately protected from the high temperatures of the wood stove. New wood stoves must have combustion air connected directly to the firebox.

83

HEATING SYSTEMS

by wood stoves result from sparks thrown out of the firebox or inadequate clearances between the wood stove and surrounding combustible materials. Many home insurance companies now inspect wood stove installations for compliance with safety regulations. **Caution:** *If your wood stove installation does not meet the minimum requirements described here, you should not light another fire in the stove until you make the necessary improvements.*

The sheetrock or wood panel near the stove should never be uncomfortably warm to the touch. It is best to cover floors and walls adjacent to wood stoves with a non-combustible material. However, even if adequate clearances are met, the non-combustible material can still conduct heat to nearby wood (or other combustibles) drying the wood, reducing its ignition temperature, or even charring it. So, the National Fire Protection Association (NFPA) and other experts have created guidelines for protective materials and clearances between wood stoves and their surroundings.

The wood stove should be at least 36 inches away from wood or other unprotected combustible materials. Most people however don't want their wood stoves extending into the room the required 36 inches from a combustible wall. Wood stove wall clearances can be reduced if the wall is protected by an approved, ventilated, non-combustible wall protector (see figure **3-25**). You can use 28-gauge sheet metal or an approved manufactured wall protector. The wall protector must be spaced out from the wall with screws and spacers (made of porcelain or other materials that do not conduct heat well). The spacers should be kept as far away as possible from the hottest parts of the stove so that they do not conduct heat directly to the wood stud where they are embedded.

Single-wall steel stovepipe should be no closer than 18 inches from a combustible wall. The stovepipe can be 9 inches away from a ventilated protector or from a combustible wall if it is shielded by another piece of stovepipe two inches larger in diameter than the single wall chimney pipe. If an existing installation does not meet the clearance guidelines described above, then proper floor protection, ventilated protectors for walls and ceilings, and/or shielding for stoves and stovepipes should be added before another fire is lit in the stove. The recommendations presented here are minimum safety guidelines. Do not hesitate to exceed these recommendations by providing ad-

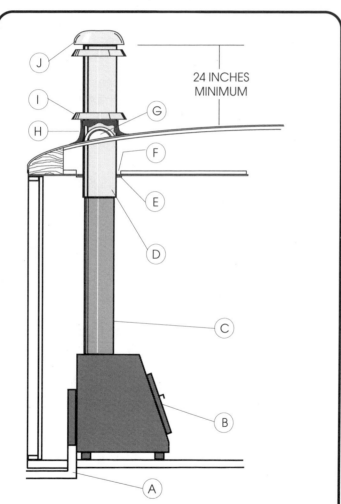

3-26 Typical New Wood Stove Installation - A. Combustion air directly to air tight wood stove, B. double-wall wood stove approved for mobile home, C. double-wall flue pipe directly to wood stove, D. triple-wall or insulated double-wall pipe through roof, E. trim collar, F. two-inch clearance from combustibles in roof assembly, G. roof support bracket, H. flashing, I. storm collar, J. rain cap.

HEATING SYSTEMS

ditional shielding for the wood stove, chimney, and the surrounding wall, floor, and ceiling surfaces. Shielding has the additional advantage of directing more heat into the room which is better than heating the combustible building materials.

Existing wood stoves without a combustion air inlet into the firebox should at least have an inlet on the floor near the stove (see figure **3-25**). The opening should use a medium-sized register (2 inches by 14 inches or 4 inches by 6 inches) and a sheet metal boot which goes all the way through the floor protector and floor or through a nearby wall. The inlet of the vent should be screened to exclude pests. The register should be the closable type so it can be closed when the wood stove is idle. If the mobile home has tight skirting with no vents, then a square-to-round sheet metal boot should be used to go through the floor and a piece of flexible duct run to an outlet in the skirting as shown in figure **3-25**. Be sure to locate the outlet vent in the skirting on a side of the house that is sheltered from the prevailing winds. This will prevent gusts of air from being forced into or pulled out of the combustion air inlet. If the crawl space is vented, then the combustion air inlet need not go through the skirting but may terminate in the crawl space.

Wood stoves can leak dangerous pollutants into the home if they do not draft properly. This means that there must be adequate suction in the flue pipe. If you can smell woodsmoke in a home, that is usually a sign of inadequate draft, inadequate ventilation, and/or dangerous levels of pollutants. Wood stove chimneys may need to be extended considerably higher than other combustion flues on the roof to provide adequate draft. Locate a smoke detector in the room where the wood stove is installed. Wood stove chimneys should be cleaned once each heating season or as often as needed to avoid chimney fires. Contact your local stove dealer or chimney sweep for advice on cleaning chimneys.

HUD requires that all heat producing appliances, including wood stoves that are installed as original equipment, must be approved for use in mobile homes. New installations of woodstoves should follow the guidelines summarized in figure **3-26**. **Wood stoves approved for mobile homes have metal heat shielding on the back and sides and they bring all combustion air into the firebox from outdoors.** Double-wall pipe must be used between the stove and about 8 inches from the ceiling. Insulated double-wall or triple-wall pipe must be used to take the chimney through the roof. The section of pipe that goes through the roof is usually supported by a support bracket which sits on top of the roof. Installers of wood stoves must comply with any local building or fire codes that apply to wood stoves. All new wood stove installations should be inspected by a local building or fire official to ensure that they meet all relevant fire codes and safety conventions. Be sure to contact a knowledgeable official or wood stove expert before buying or installing a wood stove to ensure that you understand all the requirements.

HEATING SYSTEMS

NOTES:

SUMMER COOLING

4.1 Summer Cooling

Feeling comfortable is a combination of several factors that affect heat loss, heat gain, and heat production by our bodies. Air temperature and humidity are the most important factors but air movement, sunshine, clothing, activity level, and the temperature of the surfaces around us also influence comfort (see figure **4-1**). If you pay attention to what makes you comfortable and change the environment in your home to use natural cooling methods, you won't pay as much to run mechanical air conditioning.

Shading is the most effective strategy for controlling cooling costs. Solar heat falling on your home comprises more than half of the heat you need to remove with a cooling system. Using fans to increase outside air ventilation during moderate weather and to circulate air when the air conditioner is operating are also very effective ways to improve comfort and reduce cooling costs.

4-1 What Determines Comfort? - Comfort is determined by four interrelated factors: air temperature, humidity, radiant temperature, and air movement.

The choice of cooling systems between an air conditioner and an evaporative cooler depends on how moist or dry your climate is. Air conditioners are necessary to provide a high degree of comfort in more humid climates. Evaporative coolers are effective for dry climates and much less expensive to buy and to operate than air conditioners.

4.2 Shading

Heat from the sun shining through windows and on the roof is a major reason for needing a mechanical cooling system. The most effective way to reduce this heat gain is to stop the solar heat before it enters the building with shade trees, vines and trellises, metalized window films, awnings, sun screens, and a bright roof coating. Shade trees and trellised vines provide the most effective shading because they stop the sun's rays before they touch the home. Shade trees and trellised vines also create cool areas near the home that act as cool buffer

PERCENT OF SOLAR HEAT BLOCKED BY COMMON WINDOW SHADING METHODS

Glass	
Clear Single-Pane Glass	10-15%
Clear Double-Pane Glass	25-30%
Heat Absorbing Glass	30-50%
Reflecting Glass	50-70%
Treatments for Single-Pane Glass (Includes a single pane of clear glass)	
Sun Screen (indoors)	20-30%
Colored Venetian Blind	25-40%
Draperies (light colored)	40-55%
Opaque Rolling Shade (dark)	45-50%
White Venetian Blind	45-50%
Window Films	40-75%
Light-Transmitting Rolling Shade	60-70%
Sun Screen (outdoors)	65-75%
Opaque Rolling Shade (white)	75-80%
Aluminum Louvered Sun Screen	80-85%
Awnings	50-90%

4-2 Window Shading - The table above shows the approximate percentage of solar heat blocked by different types of glass and shading devices.

SUMMER COOLING

zones (see Section 1.5.3, How Plants Affect Microclimate and Energy). Trellised vines (see figure **4-3**), like the fast-growing Chinese flame and the morning glory, can provide effective and inexpensive shade within a year in some regions.

4.2.1 Window Films, Reflecting Glass, and Interior Window Treatments

Metalized plastic window films, like the kind used to tint automotive windows, can save substantial amounts of cooling energy. Metalized films reflect 40% to 75% of the solar heat hitting a window (see figure **4-2**). Reflective window films, installed on the interior side of the glass, repel solar heat and reduce glare and fading through south, east, and west facing windows. Special all-season metalized films, sometimes called Low-E films, also reflect heat energy from inside the home back inside during the heating season. For all but the hottest climates, these films are more cost-effective than films that merely reflect solar heat. Window films (both all-season and reflective) come in different types for different climates. For sunny southern climates you want a film that stops most of the solar heat and glare, but for more northern climates you would want a film that lets more light and heat into the home. *Caution: Do not use reflective metalized window films on the inside of double-paned glass because it may lead to glass breakage.*

Installing window films is a moderately difficult do-it-yourself project. The films designed for do-it-yourself installation have a protective paper covering which is removed during installation. It's important to follow the manufacturer's installation instructions exactly.

Modern window films have a scratch resistant coating and they can be cleaned with soapy water and a soft cloth. Lower-quality window films may become cloudy or deteriorate because of intense sunlight, harsh cleaning fluids, or abrasion from rough towels.

4-3 Trellis for Shading - A trellis covered with climbing vines is a very effective shading device because it stops solar heat before it reaches the home.

Window films are probably the best shading method for sliding glass doors in exposed areas without patio covers. Window films also work well on outwardly opening windows which wouldn't open if you installed an exterior sun screen.

If you are purchasing new windows, consider ordering heat reflecting glass instead of clear glass. Reflective glass is the best choice for very sunny and hot climates because it reflects 50% or more of the solar heat away from the building.

Interior shades, blinds, and draperies are effective at shading if they have a reflective white surface facing the outdoors. The white surface of the window covering reflects direct sunlight and also reflects heat radiating from the warm glass. Room-darkening rolling shades with a white outer surface are the best, blocking up to 80% of the solar heat entering the window. White venetian blinds and draperies with white linings are also good at reflecting heat (see figure **4-2**). The disadvantage to shades and draperies is that they must be closed to be effective, blocking the view. Blinds still give most of their heat-blocking benefit when partially open.

SUMMER COOLING

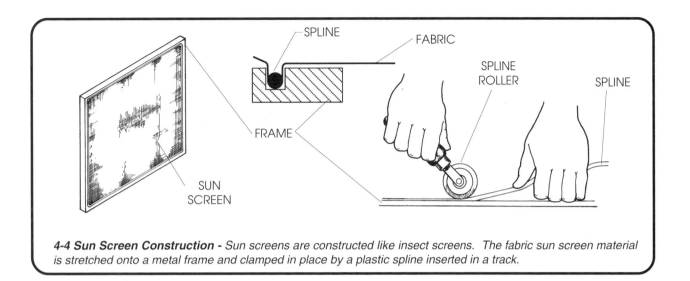

4-4 Sun Screen Construction - Sun screens are constructed like insect screens. The fabric sun screen material is stretched onto a metal frame and clamped in place by a plastic spline inserted in a track.

4.2.2 Sun Screens

Sun screens are made like insect screens with aluminum frames which have a channel and retaining spline (see figure **4-4**). **Sun screens are an effective and inexpensive window shading option which still allows a view through the window.** If you want solar heating during the winter through south-facing glass, removable sun screens are a better choice than window films. Sun screens, like window films, are good substitutes for awnings when headroom or price prevents the use of awnings. They don't work very well on awning, jalousie, and casement windows which open out, because putting the screen inside allows the solar heat to penetrate the home (see figure **4-2**). Sun screen walls, installed outdoors, are also used to shade patios from the sun in hot climates (see figure **4-5**).

The fabric used on sun screens is designed to absorb and/or reflect 65% to 70% of the solar heat before it enters the home. Sun screen fabric is available in a variety of colors. A different type of sun screen made of aluminum with tiny louvers blocks out about 85% of the solar heat. The aluminum, louvered sun screens are more expensive than standard sun screens. Sun screens are similar to window films in that they are not easy do-it-yourself projects. Kits are available for homemade screens and you can save 50% or more, but your final product probably won't last as long as a professionally-built sun screen.

4.2.3 Awnings

Awnings are usually more expensive than window films and sun screens. However, they are very effective at shading because they intercept the solar heat before it gets to the window. Awnings are popular in hot sunny climates. Custom-made canvas and aluminum awnings can be fairly expensive and are not as cost-effective as other shading methods. However, some awning companies sell do-it-your-

4-5 Shaded Patio- An aluminum patio cover and a wall of large sun screens shades this patio area from the strong desert sun.

89

SUMMER COOLING

self awnings that are only slightly more expensive than sun screens and window films (see figure **4-6**).

Lightweight patio covers and carport covers are nearly essential in very hot climates to shade these important outdoor areas from the sun (see figure **4-5**). These large outdoor awnings are required in some mobile home communities. Patio and carport covers should be self-supporting and should be securely anchored to the ground.

The three most important considerations in selecting and designing awnings are: 1) the amount of shade desired; 2) the importance of maintaining the view out of the window; and 3) the appearance of the awning. The amount of shade that an awning will produce is most closely related to the distance that the awning drops down over the window. Awnings on the east and west should drop down lower than awnings on the south to block solar radiation coming from lower in the sky. Making the awning wider than the window or buying a prefabricated awning with side panels will make it more effective at blocking the sun.

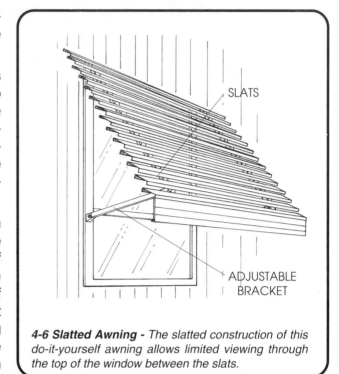

4-6 Slatted Awning - *The slatted construction of this do-it-yourself awning allows limited viewing through the top of the window between the slats.*

4.3 Air Circulation and Ventilation

Ceiling fans are probably the most effective air circulation devices you can buy, but many homes have ceilings that are too low for ceiling fans. Homes with adequate headroom should have ceiling fans in every room, ideally, if air conditioning costs are high. Oscillating fans do a very good job of circulating air within the home, too (see figure **4-7**). Box fans can be used in windows for ventilation, or for air circulation while the air conditioner or evaporative cooler are operating. The cooling wind produced by circulation fans allows about a 4°F increase in the thermostat setting with no decrease in comfort, and can save 15% to 40% on cooling costs. If you pay for air conditioning, this is an easy measure that you won't want to neglect.

Windows facing into the prevailing wind or away from it are the best for cross ventilation. Window fans can increase any breeze or they can create a breeze when the air outdoors is still. Use window fans to pull air in from the windward side of the home and push air out of the leeward side. Experiment with positioning the fans in different windows to see

4-7 Oscillating Fan - *The most popular and cost-effective cooling device available.*

SUMMER COOLING

which arrangement works best. It is worth the effort you spend to ventilate instead of air conditioning because it could save you up to 50% on cooling costs if you can ventilate during mild weather and at night. Channeling breezes with landscaping and creating cool zones around the home with shade trees and plants will enhance the opportunity to use more ventilation and less air conditioning (see Section 1.5.3, How Plants Affect Microclimate and Energy).

Humidity is a major concern when using ventilation to substitute for air conditioning. Removing moisture from humid air is an important part of the function of an air conditioning system. In the humid climates of the southeastern and southcentral United States, ventilation may introduce excessive moisture into the home causing the air conditioner to run longer in order to remove the moisture. If the air is very humid (70% relative humidity or above), you would want the air temperature to be less than 68°F before shutting down the air conditioner and ventilating in the evening.

4.4 Air Conditioning

Air conditioners gather heat from the home and move it outdoors. An air conditioner works like a refrigerator which cools one area (the refrigerator cabinet) while releasing that heat into another (the kitchen). The air conditioner cools the home with a cooling coil, called an evaporator, and dumps the heat outdoors using another coil called a condenser. Heat pumps work the same way as air conditioners and all of the measures discussed here under air conditioning apply to heat pump systems, too.

Heat is collected from indoors, by the evaporator and carried outdoors by a special fluid called a refrigerant. The refrigerant is pumped by the compressor between the evaporator and condenser to move the heat (see figure **4-8**). The refrigerant absorbs large amounts of heat from the indoor air when it changes from a liquid to a gas in the evaporator. You've felt this evaporator effect if you've had your index finger numbed with cold while using a can of spray paint. The liquid paint in the can is mixed with a refrigerant which is vaporized at the spray nozzle of the paint can. When the liquid refrigerant evaporates, that is, changes from liquid to gas, it absorbs heat from the surrounding air, numbing your finger. In the air conditioner, the refrigerant evaporates in the evaporator coil which cools the indoor air blowing through it. The hot gaseous refrigerant, laden with the heat it collected from the indoor air, condenses inside the condenser, releasing that heat into the outdoor air.

The evaporator removes water vapor from the air as the air passes over the evaporator coil. The evaporator is cold and the water in the indoor air condenses because as the air cools it loses its capacity to hold water vapor. This condensation on the evaporator coil dries the air and makes the home more comfortable. The amount of water that the evaporator must remove to provide comfort is part of the design and selection of an air conditioning system.

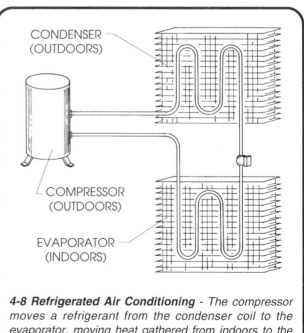

4-8 Refrigerated Air Conditioning - The compressor moves a refrigerant from the condenser coil to the evaporator, moving heat gathered from indoors to the outdoor air where the heat is released.

SUMMER COOLING

4.4.1 Introduction to Air Conditioners

Expecting too much from an air conditioner leads to high energy costs. To avoid high energy costs, keep the thermostat set to 75°F or higher and when you leave turn the thermostat up to 85°F or higher. The air conditioner will run longer than usual when you return, but you will save energy and money because the unit ran very little or not at all while you were gone.

The three most common problems with home air conditioners are oversizing, low air flow, and improper refrigerant charge. Selecting the proper size air conditioning equipment is very important for both efficiency and comfort. The evaporator, the condenser, and the compressor, along with the fan and the fan speed, should be matched to each particular installation for that particular home's cooling needs. There isn't much you can do if you have an oversized air conditioner but if you are buying a new one, have the cooling contractor calculate the proper size for your climate, size of home, solar load, and the amount of heat generated indoors. The air conditioner should have a ton of cooling capacity for every 500 to 1000 square feet, according to your home's energy efficiency and the sizing factors mentioned above.

All evaporators in home air conditioning systems should be protected by filters. These filters should be changed or cleaned regularly, as often as once a month. Evaporators can be difficult to clean. Clean filters will keep the evaporator clean for as long as several years and allow the proper level of air flow necessary for good cooling efficiency. Condensers (always outdoors) must be cleaned as often as they become dirty, and it's easy to see the dirt on the outside of the coil (see figure **4-14**).

Incorrect refrigerant charge is a common problem in all types of air conditioning systems. There is an ideal amount of refrigerant specific to each air conditioner and installation. **Either too much or too little refrigerant in the air conditioner reduces its efficiency, lowers its cooling capacity, and shortens the life of the compressor.** Many air conditioning technicians do not regularly check refrigerant charge. You should insist that your air conditioning contractor check refrigerant charge and make corrections, if necessary, during a maintenance call.

More is not better for refrigerant in an air conditioner. Overcharging is extremely harmful to your air conditioner and increases your cooling costs. Never add refrigerant or let a service technician add refrigerant without determining if the system needs refrigerant and, if so, how much. Checking refrigerant charge requires the measurement of indoor temperature, humidity, outdoor temperature, suction pressure, and system head pressure. Only

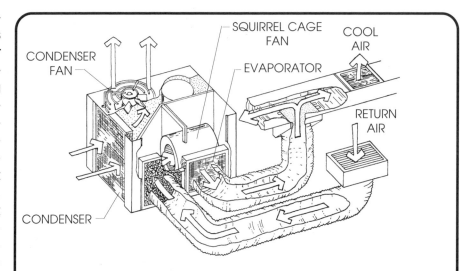

4-9 Packaged Air Conditioner - The packaged air conditioner has the evaporator, the condenser, and the compressor in a cabinet located outdoors. Indoor air is circulated through the unit by a fan, which is inclosed in the same metal cabinet.

SUMMER COOLING

trained air conditioning technicians are qualified to measure refrigerant and to charge an air conditioning system.

Refrigerants do not wear out and so they do not need to be replaced unless the system has a leak or unless the system needs major repairs. If your air conditioning system has needed refrigerant any time since you installed it, there is probably a leak. Refrigerant leaks should be repaired during the professional service call because refrigerant is expensive and its release damages the atmosphere.

The whole system will work better if the components are kept clean. Besides cleaning the coils and filters, you should clean fan blades, grilles, motors, compressors, and controls from time to time. Oil motor and fan bearings with a few drops of 20 weight electric motor oil once a year. *Caution: Remember to disconnect the electricity to the air conditioning unit at the main switch or breaker before beginning any maintenance work.*

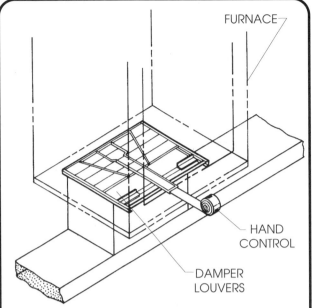

4-10 Manual Damper - *This manual damper is open during the heating season and closed during the cooling season. It is used with packaged air conditioners and ground-mounted evaporative coolers (see Section 4.5, Evaporative Coolers).*

4.4.2 Packaged Air Conditioners

Packaged air conditioning systems (also called unitary air conditioners and self-contained air conditioners) have the compressor, the condenser, and the evaporator all in a single cabinet located outside the home (see figure **4-9**). Packaged air conditioning systems may also contain a gas furnace or some electric resistance heating coils enclosed in the same cabinet with the cooling unit. Return air from the home is pulled into the cabinet through an insulated duct and a filter. Then the air is forced through the evaporator and into the main duct system of the mobile home through another flexduct by a blower fan in the air conditioner. Double-section homes have a Y-shaped duct fitting which splits a 12 or 14 inch diameter main cool air supply duct into two 10 or 12 inch branches. The branches connect to the main ducts on each half of the double-wide. The supply connections to the main duct are similar to those shown for evaporative coolers in figure **4-21**, page 101.

Some packaged air conditioners have no heating elements and instead work in cooperation with a standard mobile home furnace. These systems require dampers at the base of the furnace indoors and at the supply outlet of the air conditioner outdoors. The connection between the furnace and the main duct has a damper that is positioned either automatically or manually for heating or cooling. The automatic dampers are available only for furnaces that have a cooling coil compartment at the bottom of the furnace (see figure **4-11**). These dampers prevent cool air from blowing into the furnace closet and wasting energy or causing condensation and corrosion in the furnace heat exchanger. The automatic damper, installed in the cooling coil compartment, closes under pressure from the fan in the air conditioner and opens under pressure from the furnace fan. Furnaces that don't have a cooling coil compartment need a louvered manual damper installed right at the base of the furnace that is positioned for either heating or cooling by a hand control located at

93

SUMMER COOLING

the base of the furnace (see figure **4-10**). These two types of furnace dampers prevent cool air from filling the furnace compartment but don't prevent heated air from entering the packaged air conditioner outdoors during the heating season.

Preventing the heated air from circulating through the air conditioner requires another automatic damper inside the packaged air conditioner (see figure **4-12**). Inspect the air conditioner by removing an access panel near the evaporator on a cold day when the furnace is operating and see if warm air from the furnace is flowing into the evaporator cabinet of the packaged air conditioner. These one-way air flow dampers are forced open by the air conditioner fan and close by gravity. You can watch this damper operate to see if it works by disconnecting the duct from the supply side of the packaged air conditioner. If the damper does not open and close as the air conditioner fan is turned on and off, then it should be repaired. If you cannot repair the damper, then you should at least plug the flexduct during the heating season to prevent the loss of this heated air. The return air register in the home should also be plugged in the winter. **The absence or malfunction of these dampers can cause severe energy waste.**

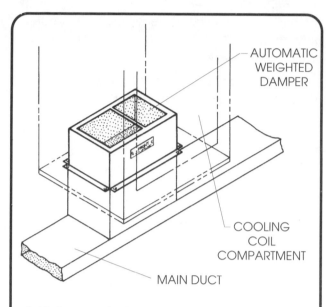

4-11 Automatic Damper - This damper prevents cooled air from entering the furnace. It is used with packaged air conditioners and ground-mounted evaporative coolers (See Section 4.5.1, Installation).

In very wet climates, the cabinets of packaged air conditioners may rust out. Rust holes can create excessive air leakage in the supply or return air. If the metal divider between the evaporator and condenser should rust from water in the evaporator pan, there can be a direct mixing of warm outdoor air with cool indoor air circulating through the evaporator. Rusting out often means that the air conditioner must be replaced, although you may be able to salvage it by fastening airtight patches to the holes and sealing them with duct mastic (see Section 3.4.1, Improving Supply and Return Air Systems). The formation of rust is accelerated if the air conditioner cabinet is placed directly on the concrete slab without spacers to provide a dry air space underneath the bottom of the cabinet. If you notice that an air conditioner sits directly on the slab, you can buy rubber spacers to put under the corners of the cabinet to hold the unit up off the slab.

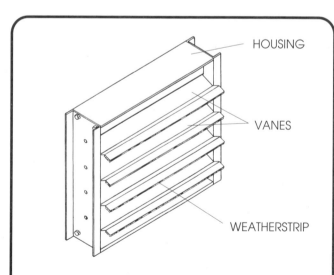

4-12 Damper for Outdoor Air Handlers - When a packaged air conditioner or evaporative cooler shares ductwork with an indoor furnace it must have a damper like this one to prevent hot air from flowing into the cooling unit during the winter. The blades of this damper are pushed open by the force of the fan in the evaporative cooler or packaged air conditioner, and they fall closed by gravity.

SUMMER COOLING

Evaporators and condensers in packaged air conditioners are usually easy to clean with a spray bottle of soapy water, a soft brush, and a garden hose with an adjustable spray nozzle. Open the access panel on the unit and spray the soapy water into both sides of the coils. Brush the coils gently, if necessary, to remove stubborn dirt or lint. Then rinse them with very light spray from a garden hose. *Caution: When cleaning any air conditioning coil, be careful not to bend the delicate metal fins with high-pressure water or vigorous scrubbing.*

4.4.3 Split-System Air Conditioners

Split-system air conditioners have the evaporator coil in the furnace cabinet to cool the indoor air and a condenser outdoors to get rid of heat that is collected by the evaporator (see figure **4-13**). The condenser and the evaporator are connected by refrigerant pipes that carry the refrigerant back and forth. The compressor, located outdoors, compresses the gaseous refrigerant and pushes it into the condenser where it is condensed back to a liquid. The liquid refrigerant flows to the evaporator (see figure **4-15**) where it evaporates and absorbs heat from the indoor air. The furnace blower pulls return air from the rooms into the furnace cabinet and forces the air through the evaporator coil, then into the main duct for distribution to the registers.

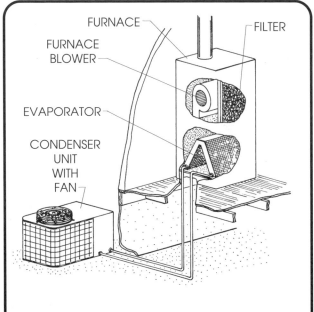

4-13 Split-System Air Conditioner - *The evaporator is placed in the cooling coil compartment of the furnace and the condenser, compressor, and condenser fan are installed outside on a concrete slab.*

The condenser outdoors has its own cabinet and fan (see figure **4-14**). The condenser fan moves outdoor air through the condenser coils, cooling the coils and releasing the heat outdoors. The entire process removes heat from inside the home and releases it into the outdoor air.

The filters in split-system air conditioners are located in the furnace compartment. The filter should be changed or cleaned each month that the air conditioner is in use. A clean filter will keep the evaporator coil clean longer. If your furnace doesn't have a filter, you can order a filter rack and filter from a local mobile home parts distributor or service company. Filters are important to keeping the evaporator clean be-

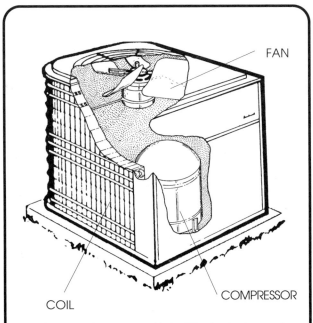

4-14 Outdoor Condenser Unit - *The fan in the outdoor unit pulls outdoor air through the condenser coil, cooling the coil and releasing the heat collected from the indoors. The refrigerant charge of the air conditioning system is measured at the compressor. (Courtesy of Lennox Industries)*

SUMMER COOLING

cause cleaning it is a messy job. The evaporator should be inspected at least every other year and cleaned if necessary. Here's how to clean the evaporator:

Step 1: Remove the access panel near the bottom of the furnace. Put some warm soapy water in a spray bottle and fill another spray bottle with rinse water. Get a shop vacuum that will suck up water and put a fitting, designed for getting into tight spots, on the end of the hose.

Step 2: Spray the soapy water on the coil from both sides and wait for the soap to soften the dirt. Spray some more soapy water on the coil and scrub the coil gently with a soft brush, if necessary, to remove stubborn dirt or lint.

Step 3: Spray the rinse water on the coil. Vacuum the duct underneath the coil to remove the dirt and water that has collected in the metal trough directly underneath the coil and in the ductwork below. Then put the access panel back on the cooling coil compartment.

4-15 A-Coil - *The evaporator coil of split-system air conditioners is an A-shaped panel of tubes and fins. A U-shaped pan under the bottom collects and removes water that condenses on the coil.*

You can use special foaming cleaners that push dirt out of the recesses of the coil if the dirt is lodged deeply in the coil. Caustic or basic cleaners are used by professionals to remove greasy deposits from evaporator coils. The caustic or basic cleaners are a last resort because they may corrode the metal in the coil. **Caution:** *Use rubber gloves to protect your hands from these strong cleaners.*

4.4.4 Central Air Conditioning Controls

Central air conditioning systems in mobile homes are controlled by either two-wire or four-wire thermostats. The two-wire thermostat is actually a heating thermostat which is used together with a reversing relay to turn the cooling system on and off. The reversing relay makes the heating thermostat work in reverse, turning the cooling system on when the temperature rises in the home and off when the temperature falls. Cooling systems using two-wire thermostats also have a system switch that locks out cooling during the heating season and vice versa. This switch is usually located at the furnace.

Four-wire thermostats do not need reversing relays because they accomplish the switching from heating to cooling themselves. The system switch on a four-wire thermostat is a lever on the thermostat that you move from the heating to the cooling position when the seasons change. **Residents who have regular schedules of occupancy and vacancy can save money and increase the comfort and convenience of both heating and cooling by using automatic setback heating/cooling thermostats.**

Thermostat location can be as big a problem with cooling systems as it is with heating systems.

SUMMER COOLING

If the thermostat is located on a warm outside wall, it could cause the air conditioner to operate erratically and, in that case, the thermostat should be moved.

4.4.5 Distribution Systems

Obstructions in the distribution system like a dirty evaporator coil, dents in ducts, debris inside ducts, and bent and dirty registers are even more of a problem with cooling than with heating. That is because cooling efficiency is even more sensitive to air flow than heating efficiency.

There should be about 400 cubic feet of air flow per minute in the system for each ton of air conditioning capacity. The cooling capacity and the efficiency of the system depend on adequate air flow. **Experts in the air conditioning field say that there is nothing you can do to a system that will compensate for low air flow except to increase the air flow.** Service technicians can measure the air flow in the air conditioning system to see if it is adequate in a variety of ways including: using an air speed meter, measuring air pressure in the ducts, and measuring temperature differences between the supply and return air. The temperature difference between supply and return air should be 15° to 21°F during cooling. A reading outside this range could indicate a problem with air flow or refrigerant charge.

If the air flow falls short of the manufacturer's recommendations, the technician may increase the air flow by: cleaning the evaporator coil, increasing fan speed, enlarging registers, adding more ducts, or even enlarging the ducts to increase the air flow. Adding or enlarging ducts may seem drastic, but in some cases it might be the only remedy to poor cooling efficiency and high cooling costs.

4-16 Leak Locations - Mobile homes with transverse joists have boots that connect the main duct to the floor. This illustration shows the common air leakage points in connections between the boot and the duct, and between the boot and the floor.

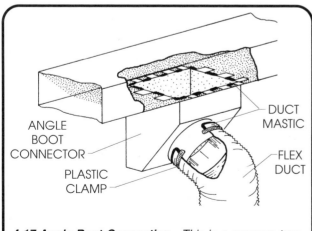

4-17 Angle Boot Connection - This is a common type of fitting used to connect ductwork from external packaged air conditioners and ground-mounted evaporative coolers to the main duct.

It is essential that air flowing out of every supply register have a constant and unobstructed path back to the furnace or air conditioner. Blockage in supply or return air ducts can cause portions of the home to be pressurized or depressurized and will greatly increase your energy use. Typical methods of improving free air return to a central return air register are cutting off the bottom of doors or installing louvered openings in doors. If you purchase a thicker carpet, be sure to maintain an inch or more clearance under interior doors.

Duct leaks are also very important and should be located and sealed as described in Section 3.4.1, Improving Supply and Return Air Systems. Pay particular attention to sealing the boots that connect the registers with the

SUMMER COOLING

main duct, because these are usually the areas with the most air leaks (see figure **4-16**). Check the connections between flexducts and packaged air conditioners for leaks while the fan is operating so you can feel the air leaks. Figure **4-17** shows a good way to seal the joint between the flexduct and a metal collar or boot. Before slipping the inner polyethylene lining over the collar, coat the collar with 1/4 inch of duct mastic. Clamp the flexduct to the collar with a plastic cable tie, available at most hardware stores. Many mobile homes in southern climates have ducted return air. Check these return air ducts as you would the supply air ducts.

4.4.6 Room Air Conditioners

Room air conditioners are small packaged air conditioning units that are installed in sliding windows or through the exterior wall. All room air conditioners manufactured after January 1, 1990, must have an energy efficiency rating (EER) of at least 8 but the most efficient units have an EER of 12. However, you can still buy room air conditioners with EERs as low as 5.3 unless you shop carefully.

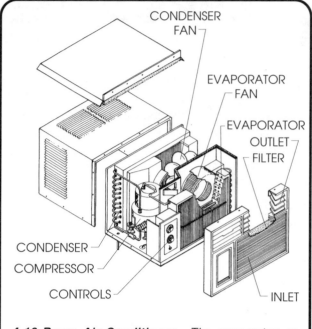

4-18 Room Air Conditioner - The evaporator, or cooling coil, faces indoors and the condenser coil faces the outdoors in this type of packaged unit.

The energy efficiency rating is computed by dividing cooling capacity, measured in British thermal units per hour (Btus/hour), by the watts of power used (see Section 4.4.7, Energy Ratings of Air Conditioners). The federal government requires all air conditioners to carry a yellow energy label listing the estimated cost of operation, including the EER. The higher the EER, the more efficient the air conditioner and the lower its operating cost. So a model with a higher EER may cost more, but will save money in the long run in lower electricity bills.

The cabinet of the room air conditioner contains the evaporator, the condenser, the compressor, controls, and all other parts (see figure **4-18**). The evaporator and its fan face the indoors, and the condenser and its fan face the outdoors. Warm air from the room enters through a filtered section of grille in the front cover of the unit, moves through the cooling evaporator coil, and back out through an unfiltered section of grille, also in the front cover. The heat, collected from indoors, is released into the outdoor air by the condenser and its fan. **Ceiling fans, oscillating fans, and box fans should be used to circulate air while room air conditioners are operating.**

The most important maintenance task for the home owner is to keep the filter and the coils clean. The filter is visible and easily removable from the front of the unit. Most filters are made of foam rubber which are designed for cleaning with soap and water. In some models, the mechanical components slide out of the cabinet for cleaning and servicing. With others, you have to remove the unit from the window to clean the coils. You clean the coils by spraying the coils, first with soap or coil cleaner, and then with clean rinse water. Be careful to keep the water off electrical components and let the unit air dry completely before using it again or storing it.

There are three other energy conservation measures specifically for room air conditioners besides the general recommendations discussed above.

SUMMER COOLING

1. Seal thoroughly around the perimeter of the room air conditioner's cabinet to prevent the infiltration of warm air in summer and cold air in winter (if you leave it in place).

2. During the heating season, remove the room air conditioner or cover it on the inside with plastic sheeting or an insulated removable box to prevent air leakage. Do not cover the unit on the outside, unless you also have an inside cover, because this can lead to condensation from warm moist indoor air infiltrating the unit.

3. If possible, shade the room air conditioner from direct sunlight with an awning to prevent the buildup of heat in the cabinet. Shading allows the condenser and its fan to operate more effectively. Mount the awning with at least 18 inches of clearance over the room air conditioner so that it does not restrict air flow.

4-19 Split-System Room Air Conditioner - These cooling systems use an outdoor condenser and one or more indoor evaporators mounted to the wall or ceiling. The advantages are individual room temperature control and no ductwork.

Room air conditioners do not have ducts and so, they don't have the inefficiencies associated with ducts. **Room air conditioners can save substantial energy and money over central units by cooling a specific comfort area where the occupants spend most of their time, instead of cooling the whole house.** There is a wide variety of small packaged heat pumps which are almost identical to room air conditioners except for their ability to both heat and cool (see Section 3.6, Heat Pumps).

Several manufacturers make split-system room air conditioners and heat pumps which have two main parts like the split-system central air conditioner illustrated in figure **4-13** on page 95. The evaporator or indoor unit attaches to a wall or ceiling indoors (see figure **4-19**). The condenser is located outdoors and is a smaller version of the unit shown in figure **4-14** on page 95. You can install two or more room units connected to the same condenser unit with refrigerant lines running from each indoor unit to the condenser outside. The advantage of these split-system room units is that they eliminate duct losses (because they have no ducts), they allow zone cooling and heating, and they can be attached to an interior wall or ceiling instead of through the wall.

Caution: The National Electrical Code allows a room air conditioner drawing less than 7.5 amps to be plugged into any 15 amp household circuit. However, you should not have any other major appliance on the same circuit. Room air conditioners should be powered by their own dedicated electric circuit if they draw more than 7.5 amps. A dedicated circuit means that you do not power anything other electrical devices with that circuit except for the room air conditioner.

Several manufacturers make portable room air conditioners that sit completely inside the room and do not remove heat from the home. Instead, they cool one part of a room while heating another. These models are **not** recommended.

SUMMER COOLING

4.4.7 Energy Ratings of Air Conditioners

Central air conditioners are rated by how much heat they remove for each watt of electric power they draw. Before January 1, 1979, the rating was called the Energy Efficiency Ratio (EER). This rating doesn't take into account the energy the air conditioner wastes getting started. In 1979, all manufacturers of central air conditioners were required to rate central air conditioners by their Seasonal Energy Efficiency Ratio (SEER). The SEER predicts seasonal performance better than the EER because it accounts for the energy that is wasted every time the air conditioner starts up. The SEER ratings of air conditioners are included in the Air Conditioning and Refrigeration Institute (ARI) Directory which is published in April each year. Room air conditioners are still rated by EER and the ratings are listed by the Association of Home Appliance Manufacturers (AHAM). The American Council for an Energy Efficient Economy lists the most efficient central air conditioners and room air conditioners in their annual guide, *The Consumer Guide to Home Energy Savings* (see Bibliography).

The EER and SEER are ratios of cooling capacity in Btus per hour divided by watts of electric power (SEER or EER = Btus/hour ÷ watts). The higher the EER or SEER, the more efficient the air conditioner is. SEERs of central air conditioners sold today range from 7.5 to almost 17, meaning that the most efficient air conditioners produce twice as much cooling for the same cost as the least efficient models. Room air conditioners are generally less efficient and have a range of EERs starting at 5 and going up to 12.

4.5 Evaporative Coolers

In the warm, dry climates of the Western United States, evaporative coolers (also called swamp coolers) are a popular and energy efficient cooling strategy. **Evaporative coolers use about one quarter of the energy of air conditioners and cost about half as much to install.** They do not work effectively in humid climates where the relative humidity is greater than 40% during much of the cooling season. Evaporative coolers cool outdoor air and blow the cooled air into the home from the roof, from a window, or from the duct system of the home. Water reduces the temperature of outdoor air when the water evaporates into the air as it moves through the evaporative cooler and into the home (see figure **4-20**). The cooled and humid air is forced into the house by the fan in the evaporative cooler. The cooler incoming air pushes warmer air out through the windows which are kept partially open. Evaporative coolers are rated by the number of cubic feet per minute that they deliver to the home. The evaporative cooler pressurizes the home with cooled air. Windows on the leeward side of the home should be partially opened to provide 1 to 2 square feet of window opening for each 1000 cubic feet per minute of cooler capacity.

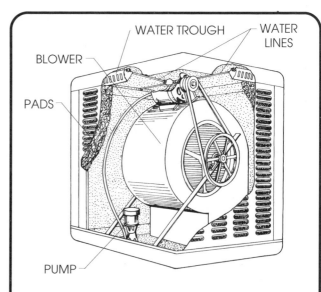

4-20 Evaporative Cooler - Most evaporative coolers, used in mobile homes, are downflow units that are mounted on the roof. Many manufacturers now encourage homeowners to install ground-mounted units because they are easier to service and give better comfort.

SUMMER COOLING

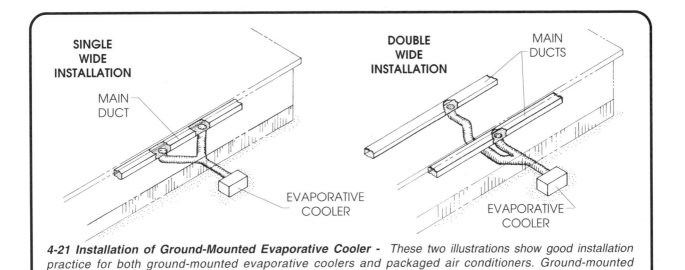

4-21 Installation of Ground-Mounted Evaporative Cooler - These two illustrations show good installation practice for both ground-mounted evaporative coolers and packaged air conditioners. Ground-mounted evaporative coolers discharge air out of the side of the unit horizontally.

The evaporative cooler pulls outdoor air into its cabinet through absorbent pads that are kept wet by water which is pumped through distribution tubes. The water distribution tubes are connected to a water pump that recirculates water from the bottom of the cabinet which serves as a water storage tank. A float valve, connected to the home's water supply, keeps the tank supplied with fresh water to replace the water evaporating from the pads.

4.5.1 Installation

Most evaporative coolers are installed on the roofs of mobile homes. However, many experts on evaporative cooling prefer window and ground-mounted units because rooftop units can contribute to roof leaks and because the rooftop location encourages the neglect of maintenance. An alternative is to install the cooler in a window which locates it closer to the ground and makes regular maintenance easier. The best place for an evaporative cooler is in the shade on the windward side of the home because the wind aids the circulation of cooled air through the unit and into the home, and because the windward location discourages the recirculation of exhaust air from the house. Horizontal flow evaporative coolers may be installed on a concrete pad like packaged air conditioners with a supply duct that connects to the main duct of the mobile home as shown in figure **4-21**. The evaporative cooler cools outdoor air and circulates it through the home so there is no return air duct. Evaporative coolers require the same types of dampers used with packaged air conditioners (see Section 4.4.2, Packaged Air Conditioners) so that heated air from the furnace is not delivered to the outdoors and moist cool air is not delivered to the furnace.

4.5.2 Maintenance

The more an evaporative cooler runs, the more maintenance it needs. **An evaporative cooler may need routine maintenance several times during the cooling season and it will definitely need a major cleaning every season.** Most problems with evaporative coolers are caused by neglect of maintenance. In very hot climates where the cooler is operating much of the time, you should look at the pads, filters, reservoir, and pump as often as once a week. The pads should be replaced at least once every cooling season and as often as once every six weeks during continuous operation. Some paper and synthetic cooler pads can be cleaned with soap and water or a weak acid according to manufacturer's instructions. If your unit has filters, they should be cleaned

SUMMER COOLING

when the pads are changed or cleaned. **Caution:** *Be sure to disconnect the electricity to the unit at the breaker or main switch before servicing it.*

Water quality is the single most important maintenance consideration. You can save yourself a lot of work and money in the long run by draining your reservoir regularly. Draining the reservoir regularly keeps the water quality good. There is a drain fitting on all coolers at the bottom of the unit. This drain fitting is connected to an overflow tube that guards against too high a water level in the reservoir, much like the overflow devices in toilets and bathtubs (see figure **4-22**). After shutting off the water, you can connect a garden hose to the fitting on the outside of the cooler cabinet and then unscrew the overflow tube to drain the reservoir.

Check the fan blades and, if there is any significant amount of dirt on the blades, clean the fan thoroughly using the same techniques described in Section 3.4.2, Cleaning the Blower and Heat Exchanger. Scrape the scale off the louvers in the cooler cabinet and clean the holes in the water trough that distribute the water to the pads. The reservoir should be thoroughly cleaned each year to remove scum, scale, and dirt. Pay particular attention to the intake area of the recirculating pump. The pump and the float assembly are the source of many maintenance problems in evaporative coolers. Most manufacturers recommend painting the reservoir area with a water-resistant coating once a year. Annual maintenance should also include checking the blower belt for wear and tightness; the belt shouldn't move more than 3/4 inch when you press on it. You should also check for leaks in the float valve when you turn the water back on.

4-22 Drain Fitting and Overflow - The reservoirs of evaporative coolers are drained through fittings like this one. When you remove the overflow tube, the water drains from the reservoir through a garden hose attached to a fitting on the outside of the cooler.

4.6 Refrigerators

Refrigerators consume 3% to 5% of the energy used in homes. In the past ten years, the appliance industry has improved refrigerators so that the current energy-efficient models use about half of the energy that older models did. The more energy-efficient models are more expensive than less efficient models.

If you're thinking of buying a new refrigerator, it pays to select an energy-efficient one. An energy-efficient model will repay your extra investment in 5 to 15 years. New refrigerators are required to have the approximate yearly consumption of electricity listed on a tag that cannot be removed until the unit is sold. The American Council for an Energy Efficient Economy lists the most efficient refrigerators in their annual guide, *The Consumer Guide to Home Energy Savings* (see Bibliography).

Defrost your refrigerator regularly, and clean dust off the coil on the outside of the refrigerator cabinet to minimize energy consumption.

PLUMBING AND ELECTRICAL

5.1 Introduction

This chapter provides general information about water heating systems, plumbing systems, and electrical systems. The section on water heating stresses energy conservation and maintenance. The section on plumbing gives a general description of plumbing systems and suggests remedies to leaks and other problems. The section on electrical systems attempts to explain how the electrical system works, what the different parts of the electrical systems do, and how professionals test electrical systems.

5.2 Water Heating Systems

The water heater is usually located in a closet space with an exterior door adjoining the bathroom or kitchen, although some electric water heaters and gas sealed-combustion water heaters are located within the home. Water heater tanks hold between 30 to 50 gallons of water, and are most often 40 gallons.

Your water heater uses energy in two ways: demand and standby. Demand refers to the energy required to heat the incoming cold water to the desired set temperature. Standby refers to the heat that is lost through the walls of the storage tank and piping while the system is waiting to be used.

An electric water heater is usually wired for 240 volts and has one or two electric elements, each with its own thermostat (see figures **5-1** and **5-3**). In two-element water heaters, the element at the bottom of the tank is the standby element which maintains the minimum setting on its thermostat. When hot water is not being used, the tank loses heat through its shell. The standby element adds heat to maintain the minimum setting so a full tank of hot water is available on demand. The upper element is the demand element which heats water at the top of the tank, if necessary, to provide quick recovery of usable hot water during times when a lot of hot water is being used. If an electric heating element becomes too hot, an overload switch will trip and will have to be manually reset (see figure **5-3**). If this switch trips regularly, you need to find out why it is overheating.

Electric water heaters generally have lower standby losses than gas water heaters because they do not have a flue pipe running up the center of the tank like the gas units do. Air flow in the flues of gas water heaters carries away some of the heat stored in the tank. Electric water heaters do not require a chimney, so they are easier to install than gas water heaters. However, since electricity is more expensive than gas and propane, many people choose gas and propane water heaters over electric.

In gas and propane water heaters, the water is

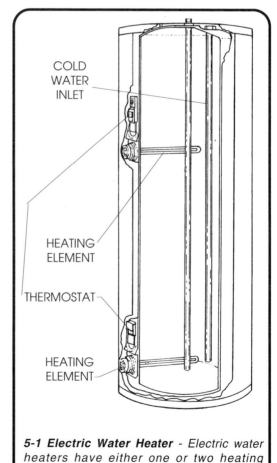

5-1 Electric Water Heater - *Electric water heaters have either one or two heating elements each having a thermostat.*

PLUMBING AND ELECTRICAL

heated by a gas burner (see figure **5-4**) located under the tank. A heat-activated control opens and closes the gas valve as the water temperature in the tank changes. Gas and propane water heaters designed for mobile homes are set up for either gas or propane and are equipped with a conversion kit for switching fuels. The kit contains a burner orifice, a pilot orifice, and a regulator screw. Check the water heater for the conversion kit, read the instructions, and make sure that the water heater is equipped for the proper fuel. When replacing a gas water heater or the gas valve on a water heater, use a convertible gas/propane water heater or gas valve unless you are absolutely sure that the home will never move or switch fuels in the future.

Caution: *Burning propane in a water heater equipped for gas or vice versa is very dangerous and may result in a fire or serious malfunction.*

Open-combustion gas water heaters are located in closets which are supposed to be isolated from the indoors, and should have a supply of combustion air from a vent in the floor or exterior door of the closet. In these units, the firebox and the draft diverter in the flue draw air from the surrounding area in the closet. The air is replaced through a combustion air hole or vent in the closet.

Sealed-combustion water heaters do not have draft diverters which let indoor air into the flue. Their burners draw air directly from the crawl space through a pipe that connects to the bottom of the water heater (see figure **5-2**). These safer water heaters, designed specifically for mobile homes, can be installed anywhere in the home.

Electric, gas, and propane water heaters must have pressure and temperature relief valves that will open and expel hot water or steam if the pressure or temperature in the tank becomes dangerously high. The relief valve is connected to a pipe that drains beneath the home. If the relief valve is expelling water, you should find out what is wrong. Usually the temperature is set too high.

5.2.1 Water Heating - What to Look For

1. Examine the condition of the water heater. How old is it? When was it last serviced or drained? Are there leaks at the water heater tank? How much insulation is between the shell and the tank? Are the pipes in the water heater closet insulated?

2. Measure the flow rate in gallons per minute in the shower using a 2-quart container and the second hand on your watch. The flow rate should be 3 gallons per minute or less. A 2-quart container should fill in 10 to 12 seconds. If the container fills sooner than 10 seconds, then consider replacing the shower head with a low-flow model.

3. Check for any evidence of pipe leaks. Be careful not to confuse dripping from condensation with actual pipe leaks. Check faucets, especially hot water faucets, for complete shut-off.

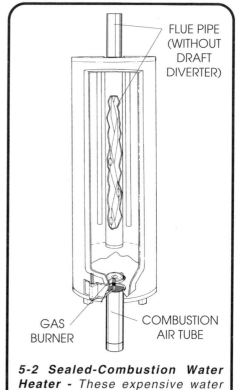

5-2 Sealed-Combustion Water Heater - *These expensive water heaters are necessary when a water heater must be installed within the living space.*

PLUMBING AND ELECTRICAL

4. Measure the hot water temperature at the farthest fixture from the tank location, and note the thermostat setting at the tank. The temperature should be about 120°F.

5. Is the floor in the water heater closet sagging and water damaged? If so, you should drain the tank, disconnect the utility service, remove the tank, and repair the floor.

Caution: Turn off the power to an electric water heater before cleaning it or replacing elements. Turn the knob on top of automatic gas valves on gas and propane water heaters to "off" or "pilot" before servicing.

5.2.2 Setting Hot Water Temperature

Electric water heaters have a thermostat which is adjusted by a set-screw or knob (see figure **5-3**). Gas and propane water heaters have a temperature dial that is located near the bottom of the tank on the gas valve (see figure **5-4**). Set the water temperature at 120°F using a thermometer to measure water temperature at the taps. You may need to make several adjustments until you get 120°F because the temperature may not be marked on the thermostat and even if it is, it may not indicate the actual temperature. If the home has a dishwasher, set the thermostat at 130°F unless the dishwasher has its own built-in water heating booster for this purpose. If additional insulation is wrapped around the outside of the tank, do not set the thermostat above 130°F. Check the temperature at the farthest tap to confirm the water heater setting and adjust the thermostat accordingly.

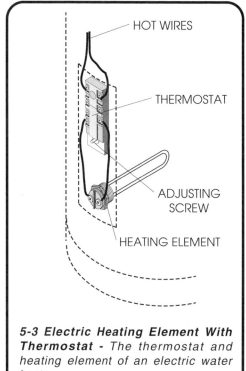

5-3 Electric Heating Element With Thermostat - The thermostat and heating element of an electric water heater.

5.2.3 Maintenance

The most common water heater maintenance problems are the result of the buildup of dirt and mineral deposits. Hard water may damage the tank elements as well as increase energy use. Water hardness is the concentration of calcium and magnesium and is measured in grains per gallon. You can expect problems from mineral buildup in the hot water system with a hardness level greater than 10 grains per gallon. Water temperatures above 140°F speed the buildup of calcium and magnesium deposits in the tank and pipes. Reducing the hot water temperature to 120°F helps to control mineral buildup and will decrease the energy required to heat water. Mineral deposits (also called scale) are most commonly found on the electric elements and in the bottom of the tank. Mineral buildup reduces the tank's storage capacity and can shorten electric element life.

5-4 Gas Valve, Burner, and Thermostat - Pictured here is the gas-burning system of a gas water heater.

PLUMBING AND ELECTRICAL

Draining water from the tank regularly will reduce sediment and scale in the tank. Sediment and scale are not as big an energy problem in electric water heaters as with gas water heaters because the heating elements in an electric water heater are surrounded by water inside the tank, while the gas burner is on the bottom of the tank where the sediment and scale accumulate. The biggest problem with scale and sediment in electric water heaters is that the volume of the tank is reduced and the ability of the water heater to provide hot water during periods of heavy use is also reduced. The biggest problem with scale and sediment in gas water heaters is that it insulates the water from the burner.

If the water heater tank leaks, then it needs to be replaced. If the tank has leaked, the floor under the tank may need to be replaced. Repair a moisture-damaged floor at the same time you replace a leaky tank and don't install a new tank on a damaged floor. If just the drain valve leaks, you can replace it with another drain valve which has the same size thread as the existing valve.

Hot water leaks in plumbing fixtures should be fixed immediately by replacing the rubber washer that plugs the valve seat before the leak ruins the valve seat. Repair leaks in fixtures or pipes before doing any other hot water energy conservation measures (see Section 5.3.3, Plumbing Leaks). Some repairs may have to be made by a qualified plumber.

To relight a pilot light that you have extinguished to perform maintenance, first hold a match above the pilot orifice, and then push and hold the red button on top of the gas valve (see figure **5-4**). Hold the button down for 30 seconds to a minute after the pilot flame ignites until the millivolt circuit, which holds the main gas supply open, is established (see Section 3.3.1, Burner Controls). If you have replaced the water heater or are reconnecting it, you may need to hold the button down for several minutes to purge air out of the gas lines before gas arrives at the pilot orifice.

5.2.4 Cleaning a Water Heater

Cleaning dirt and scale out of a water heater is not a difficult job. If you can't get 40 gallons of hot water out of your 40-gallon heater, or if the recovery of hot water is slow after periods of heavy use, or if you hear gurgling, your water heater may be filling up with sediment or scale. Consult a local plumber to determine the condition of the water in your area and what type of deposit might be building up in the bottom of your water heater. Depending on whether the deposit is loose dirt or a hard mass of scale, the procedure is slightly different for cleaning the tank.

If dirt is the problem, you will see brown liquid or runny sludge come out of the drain valve on the water heater when you open the valve under pressure. To clean the tank of dirt deposits, first drain the tank by closing the cold water supply and opening the drain valve at the bottom of the tank. You'll have to open a hot water tap to let air into the pipes so the water can run out. You may have to snake a wire up through the drain valve to clear some dirt aside and allow the water through. When the tank is empty, close the drain valve and open the cold water supply letting a

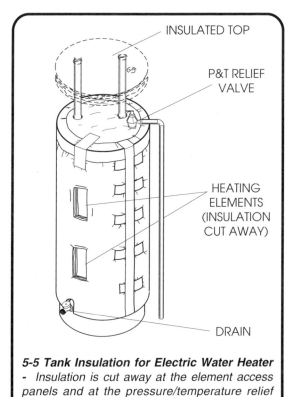

5-5 Tank Insulation for Electric Water Heater
- Insulation is cut away at the element access panels and at the pressure/temperature relief valve.

PLUMBING AND ELECTRICAL

blast of water shoot out of the cold water tube onto the pile of sediment in the tank, breaking it up and stirring it. Let the water run for thirty seconds, then shut it off and open the drain valve again, draining the water and dirt out. Repeat the process until the drain water runs clean. A small pump attached to a hose, which is connected to the drain valve, speeds up the process of draining the tank.

Removing scale in water heaters is a different process. You have to mix a solution of weak acid and pour it into the tank to dissolve the scale which is a hard, solid mass. You should use a mild acid solution, either vinegar or acidic solutions designed for cleaning water heaters or ice machines. Follow the directions on the acid container carefully. You can pour the solution of acid and water into the tank through the cold water inlet or the hot water outlet whichever is most convenient to disconnect. The solution sits in the tank for a few hours and then is drained out. Then, when the tank is empty, close the drain valve and open the cold water inlet to refill the tank. A hot water tap should be open during the cleaning process to allow air flow as the tank fills and drains.

You can remove the elements of electric water heaters and soak them in the same mild acidic solution to remove scale. While the tank is empty, you can inspect the bottom of the tank through the lower element hole and chip and scoop at the sediment or scale through that opening.

5.2.5 Tank/Closet Insulation

Water heater blankets can be purchased in most hardware stores. They typically are fiberglass insulation with a vinyl facing that wraps around the water heater and fastens at a lengthwise seam with vinyl tape 3 to 6 inches wide (see figures **5-5** and **5-6**). Mechanical fastening like wire or cord will provide a more permanent installation by taking some of the responsibility for holding the insulation in place away from the tape.

Most facings on water heater insulation blankets are combustible. Cut the facing away from the burner of a gas water heater and around the elements of an electric water heater to keep the facing away from potentially hot areas. Electric water heaters can be covered completely on the top of the tank. However it's a good idea to cut the insulation away from the access doors to the elements (see figure **5-5**). Gas water heaters may not be insulated on top because of the high temperature of the flue on top of the water heater, and the possibility that the insulation would interfere with the functioning of the draft diverter (see figure **5-6**).

The Bonneville Power Administration's Hood River Conservation Study found average savings of 730 Kwh per year from wrapping electric water heaters in 220 homes. This represents dollar savings of about $40 per year at $0.06 per kilowatt-hour. **Water heater insulation is one of the surest and best conservation measures, if there is room around your water heater to install insulation.** If there is not room to insulate the tank inside the closet, you can insulate the walls of the closet and the door with unfaced fiberglass insulation held in place by wire.

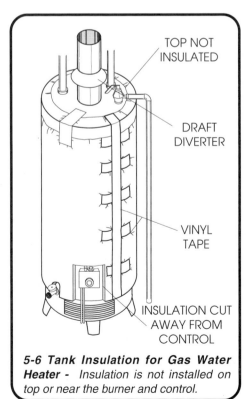

5-6 Tank Insulation for Gas Water Heater - Insulation is not installed on top or near the burner and control.

107

PLUMBING AND ELECTRICAL

5.2.6 Pipe Insulation

Insulate all uninsulated water pipes near the water heater. It is especially important to insulate the water heater pipes if the tank and pipes are located in an exterior closet. Pipes can be insulated with dense foam pipe coverings sized to fit the pipes or with fiberglass pipe insulation which wraps around the pipes.

5.2.7 Low-Flow Showerheads

Low-flow showerheads save energy by limiting hot water use. **Low-flow showerheads are one of the most cost-effective energy conservation projects for mobile homes.** There are two general types of low-flow showerheads, the laminar-flow models and the aerating models (see figure **5-7**). The aerating models mix air with the water coming out of the small holes in the showerhead forming a misty spray. Laminar-flow showerheads do not mix water and air at the nozzle, and instead, form distinct individual streams of water. The laminar-flow models are recommended for damp climates because aerating showerheads create too much steam and put too much moisture in the air. Many bathrooms have moisture problems already and don't need any additional moisture.

5-7 Types of Low-Flow Showerheads - Laminar-flow showerheads produce smooth streams of water, while aerating shower heads produce a mist of drops.

Install showerheads with a maximum flow rate of from 2.5 to 3 gallons per minute if existing flow rate exceeds 4 gallons per minute (see Section 5.1.2, Water Heating - What to Look For). Low-flow showerheads are not difficult to install. Use cloth or rubber grips in the jaws of pliers and pipe wrenches to avoid scoring chrome fittings. Seal the threads of the chrome fitting with pipe-joint compound or teflon tape to prevent leaks.

5.2.8 Purchasing a Water Heater

Since May of 1980, all new water heaters sold in the U.S. must have an Energy Guide Label which cannot be removed before they are sold (see figure **5-8**). The Energy Guide Label is intended for comparison shopping and not as a table for actual operating cost and performance. It features an estimated yearly operating cost, a bar scale comparing operating costs for similar models, and a table to allow you to estimate the operating costs for your area.

You should check the insulation level around the various models of tanks that you consider buying. Conventional tanks have a thermal resistance (R-Value) of

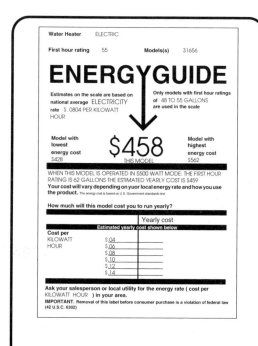

5-8 Water Heater Energy Label - It is wise to buy the most energy-efficient water heater available.

PLUMBING AND ELECTRICAL

R-3 to R-5 while heavily insulated tanks have an R-12 to R-16. The extra cost of the better insulated water heaters will be returned to the buyer in energy savings in a year or less. The American Council for an Energy Efficient Economy lists the most efficient water heaters in their annual guide, *The Consumer Guide to Home Energy Savings* (see Bibliography).

5.3 Plumbing Systems

Plumbing supply and drain piping in mobile homes is usually made of plastic. Mobile home drain piping and some supply piping is plastic pipe which cements together at fittings. Some other homes have flexible copper tubing with flared compression fittings. Older homes had galvanized iron pipe with threaded fittings. Parts for plastic, galvanized iron, and flexible copper are available at most hardware stores. Polybutylene plastic pipe and fittings make up the most common supply piping system for manufactured housing.

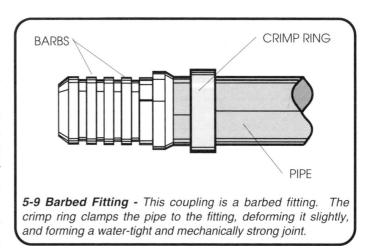

5-9 Barbed Fitting - This coupling is a barbed fitting. The crimp ring clamps the pipe to the fitting, deforming it slightly, and forming a water-tight and mechanically strong joint.

The fittings that join any type of pipe together are all classified by what they do. An ell turns the pipe at a 45° or 90° angle; a coupling joins two pipes in a straight line; a tee joins three pieces of pipe together; and a shutoff joins pipe in a straight line or at 90° and provides a way to shut the water off to a part of the system. Some types of fitting joints are described as male or female depending on whether they slip into (male) or over the top of (female) the joint. Adapters are fittings that change from one size or type of pipe to another. Adapters come in a large selection and are described by the type of pipe and size that the fitting adapts to and from.

5.3.1 Supply Piping

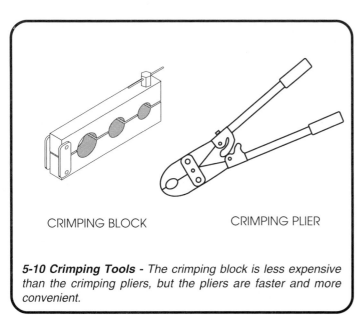

5-10 Crimping Tools - The crimping block is less expensive than the crimping pliers, but the pliers are faster and more convenient.

Polybutylene is the most common type of supply pipe and fittings for manufactured housing. The polybutylene supply pipe is easy to repair and easy to install. The common pipe diameters are 3/8 inch, 1/2 inch, and 3/4 inch inside diameters. The outside diameter is 1/8 inch larger than the inside diameter. The majority of the fittings used with polybutylene pipe are made of polybutylene, too. However, these fittings have cracked in regions with highly chlorinated water. The failing of these fittings has prompted some manufacturers to begin using copper and nylon fittings with the polybutylene pipe. Polybutlyene pipe and fittings are available at some hardware stores and most mobile home suppliers.

PLUMBING AND ELECTRICAL

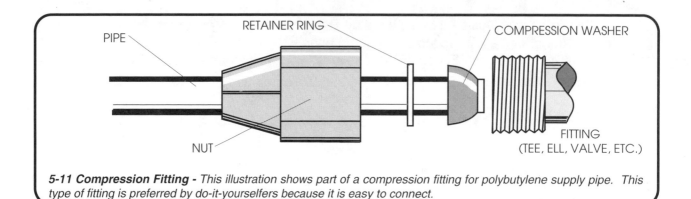

5-11 Compression Fitting - This illustration shows part of a compression fitting for polybutylene supply pipe. This type of fitting is preferred by do-it-yourselfers because it is easy to connect.

There are two distinct designs of fittings used with polybutylene pipe: the barbed fitting and the compression fitting (see figures **5-9** and **5-10**). The barbed fitting slips inside the pipe and a copper or aluminum crimp ring slips over the end of the pipe and fitting. A special tool crimps the ring tightly clamping the pipe to the barbed fitting. The barbed fittings are used by professional repairmen, who own a special tool required for crimping (see figure **5-10**), because the barbed fittings are slightly less expensive than compression fittings and they are a little more reliable. A stainless steel hose clamp may be used for emergency repairs on barbed fittings, but the clamp and the pipe need to be gently heated so that the clamp will deform the pipe onto the barbed fitting.

Most do-it-yourselfers use the compression fittings because all you need to install them is a knife or hacksaw to cut the pipe, and an adjustable wrench to tighten the nuts on the fittings. The compression fitting has four major parts as shown in figure **5-11**. The pipe, with the nut, retainer ring and compression washer already in place, slips into the fitting, and the nut is tightened to the male threads on the fitting. As the nut is tightened, the compression washer is squeezed into the space between the fitting and the pipe forming a tight seal. The retainer ring bites into the pipe and prevents it from slipping out of the fitting. For either the barbed or the compression fittings, you need to know the pipe size to buy the correct fitting.

5.3.2 Drains, Traps, and Vents

Drain fittings and pipe rarely fail and they are easy to repair with standard plastic fittings from any hardware store. Drain piping is 1-1/4 to 4 inches in diameter and is cemented together at fittings. The plastic drain pipe and fittings are joined by a special cement. Cleaning compound may be required, also. Follow the directions on the cement and cleaner containers carefully.

There are a few drain problems that are unique to mobile homes. Plumbing fixtures in mobile homes, like sinks and bathtubs, must have traps. Traps are U-shaped pipes that must remain filled with water to perform their function of preventing sewer gases from entering the home. If the plumbing system weren't vented, water flowing in the drain pipes could create a suction that would pull the wa-

5-12 Drain Vent - These plumbing vents are often used in manufactured housing to avoid having to vent the drain piping through the roof.

PLUMBING AND ELECTRICAL

ter out of the traps. If this happens, you hear a gurgling noise coming from the drain. When a trap is dry, sewer gases can come into the home. To prevent suction, plumbing vents attached to the drain let air into the drain pipes. The air comes from the vent's opening on the roof or under a sink. The vents installed under sinks are one-way air valves that let air into the pipes but not out (see figure **5-12**). If these vents fail, you may smell sewer gases in the home. Replacing the vent will usually cure the problem.

Another possibility for the origin of a sewer gas smell is plumbing vents on the roof. In some cases, the vent pipe can spill sewer gas into the home from the hole in the roof through which it passes. The hole in the roof is sometimes considerably larger than the pipe, and this gap doesn't leak water because of the rain cap used on metal roofs to cover the vent. But, if the roof cavity has air leaks into the furnace closet, the furnace blower can create a suction that will pull some sewer gas from the vent into the roof cavity and then into the home (see figure **5-13**). Remove the rain cap on the roof and seal between the roofing and the pipe to solve this problem. Then replace the rain cap. It's also a good idea to seal the air leaks in the furnace closet (see Section 2.2, Air Leakage Control).

5-13 Drain Vent Backdrafting - If the furnace fan creates a vacuum in the roof cavity because of air leaks in the furnace closet, sewer gases can be drawn into the home.

5.3.3 Plumbing Leaks

Sometimes the anti-siphon valve on a built-in dishwashers will leak. This valve is located on the drain hose running from the dishwasher to the drain. If you see wetness or leakage in this area you can remove the valve and replace it with tubing and hose clamps. If this temporary procedure stops the leak, then replace the anti-siphon valve with one of a larger capacity than the one you took out, if possible.

The spigots on bathtubs are sometimes a source of water damage problems. Water flow or leakage through the spigot can cling to the bottom of the spigot and flow back toward the wall of the tub enclosure if there is no drip edge. These spigots may be replaced with a new spigot that has a drip edge of at least 1/4 inch. Joints in the tub enclosure, especially around the spigot, and valves should be sealed with silicone caulking as often as necessary. Faucet washers should be replaced whenever the faucet is leaking. Any book on home plumbing will give details about repairing faucets.

The supply and drain plumbing should be checked for leaks whenever a new home is installed or when a used home is moved. Manufacturers recommend testing the supply water system with 100 psi (pounds per square inch) air pressure. The water heater must be isolated during such a test or the high pressure could permanently damage it. The system should hold 100 psi of air for 15 minutes after being disconnected from the compressor by an air shut-off valve.

The drain system can be leak-tested by filling the sinks, bathtubs, and toilets, and then marking the level after plugging the main sewer. The fixtures should maintain that water level for 15 minutes to a half hour.

PLUMBING AND ELECTRICAL

5.4 Electrical Systems

The electrical system of a mobile home consists of: service wires; an electric meter; feeder wires; one or two main switches; a main service panel box with breakers or fuses; and the wires, receptacles, and fixtures in the home. This section provides some general information and is not intended as a code or instructional manual.

Caution: *Electricity is one of the most dangerous hazards of modern life. Flaws in the home electrical system could cause a fire or serious injury. A qualified electrician should make all necessary inspections, connections, and repairs.*

5-14 50-Amp Receptacle and Plug - Older homes often use a 50-amp plug from the house and a matching receptacle from the meter to feed power to the home.

The most authoritative book to consult for specific electrical information on a home is its factory installation manual. If the installation manual is not available, the Manufactured Housing Institute's Model Manufactured Home Installation Manual (see Bibliography) is a very good reference. The National Electrical Code (see Bibliography), Article 550 is the accepted standard on mobile home electrical systems but it is more difficult to understand than the installation manuals.

5.4.1 Service Equipment and Feeder Wires

The main service wires come through the ground or overhead from the utility company's transformer. These three wires, two hot wires and a neutral wire, attach to the utility side of the electric meter. Attached to the house side of the electric meter are the feeder wires. The feeder wires are two hot wires (red and black), a neutral wire (white), and an equipment grounding wire (green). These wires are either part of a cable or are carried in a metal conduit (pipe).

The meter and a main switch are usually located on a utility pole or a pedestal on the ground, but the meter is sometimes attached to the outside of the home. Older homes had service equipment rated at only 50 amps. Modern manufactured homes have at least 100 amps of service capacity. The main switch should be marked with the service capacity of the system in amps.

The feeder wires run from the meter and main switch into the home's service panel box. In modern homes these wires are continuous, but in older homes, the feeder wires may be terminated in a plug or a junction box that connects the service panel box inside the home to the electric meter

5-15 Junction Box - In older homes, the feeder cable is sometimes spliced under the home in a junction box. Junction boxes, like this one, are often used as a crossover connection between the sections of multi-section homes.

112

PLUMBING AND ELECTRICAL

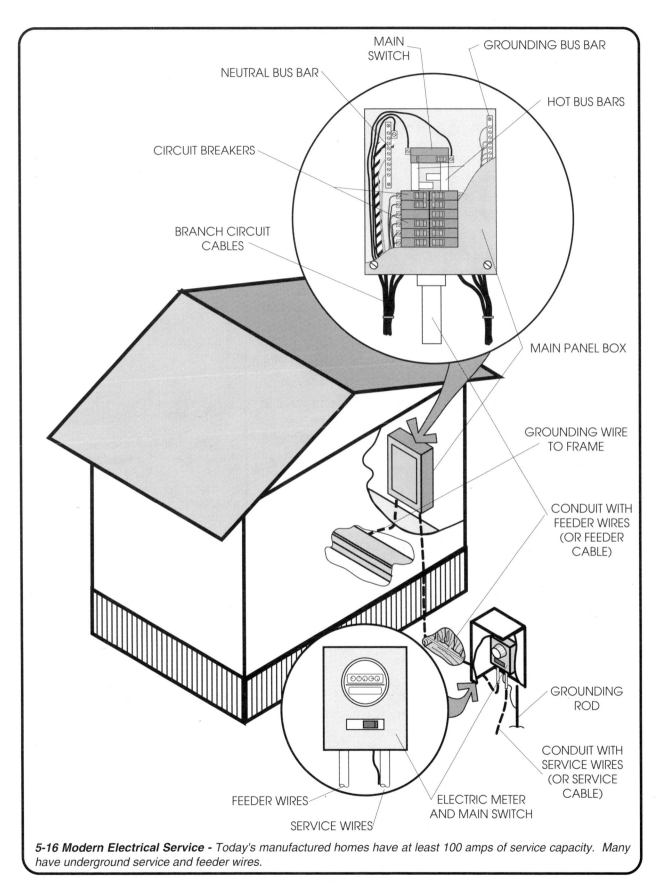

5-16 Modern Electrical Service - Today's manufactured homes have at least 100 amps of service capacity. Many have underground service and feeder wires.

PLUMBING AND ELECTRICAL

(see figures **5-14** and **5-15**). The black and red feeder wires are connected to bus bars which hold the breakers or fuses in the panel box (see figure **5-16**). The white feeder wire is the neutral and is connected to the neutral bus bar, which is electrically insulated from the panel box. A bus bar is a large electrical terminal where many wires may be connected. In multi-section homes, there are crossover wires that connect by special plugs or at a junction box (see figure **5-15**).

5.4.2 Branch and Appliance Circuits

Branch circuits are systems of wire, outlets, and built-in fixtures for lighting, heating, and other purposes. Appliance circuits are circuits which serve a single appliance like a furnace, air conditioner, electric range, or electric dryer (see figure **5-17**).

The breakers or fuses protect the wire in branch circuits from carrying too much electrical current. When a breaker trips or a fuse blows, the home owner should try to understand what caused the circuit to be overloaded. If a breaker on a circuit fails, or if the fuse blows, it should be replaced with another having the proper amp rating to match the wire used in the home (15 amps for older homes, 20 amps for newer homes in branch circuits).

Short circuits in appliances are particularly dangerous in the kitchen and bathroom because of the presence of water in those areas. In newer homes, circuits in the kitchen and bathroom are protected by special breakers known as ground fault circuit interrupters (GFCI). These GFCIs will trip if they detect electricity flowing in the grounding wires. Electricity should not flow in the grounding wires unless there is a short circuit.

5-17 Branch and Appliance Circuit Receptacles - The most common types of receptacles, found in homes, are for outlets, ranges and dryers. Older dryer receptacles had only 3 wires but 4-wire receptacles have been standard since the 1970s.

It's very important that all the neutral wires in the branch circuits be connected to the neutral bus bar in the panel box (see figure **5-16**). Sometimes the neutral is accidently connected to a hot wire somewhere in the system. This can happen at an outlet if the hot and neutral wires are reversed. When the wires are reversed, the white wire is connected to the dark colored terminal and the black wire is connected to the light colored terminal of the outlet. This reversal is dangerous and inefficient; it can be detected using a circuit tester.

5.4.3 Grounding

Home electrical systems use the earth or the ground in two ways. The first way is to ground the neutral feeder wire. The earth is electrically neutral and provides a kind of vacuum that draws electricity from the hot wires towards the earth through the electrical devices in the home by way of the grounded neutral wires.

The second way electrical systems use the ground is for equipment grounding. The equipment grounding wire is the bare wire connected to: each grounding terminal of a receptacle; each metal electrical box (including the main panel box); the chassis; ducts; metal roofing; metal siding; and metal plumbing. Multi-section homes should have a jumper wire or other means of connecting the steel frames together electrically. The usually bare copper wires, which connect the metal parts of the home together electrically, are clamped to the grounding bus bar in the main panel box. This

PLUMBING AND ELECTRICAL

grounding bus bar is itself electrically connected to the metal panel box. The purpose of this network of equipment grounding connections is to give stray electricity an easy and safe path to flow into the ground rather than flowing through some unlucky person in the event of a short circuit.

A bare or insulated grounding wire is fastened to a copper grounding rod with an approved mechanical clamp. The grounding rod is driven into the ground or buried in the ground near the meter. The grounding wire (connected to the grounding rod), the neutral wire, and the equipment grounding wire (from the home) all connect to a bus bar in the service box that contains the electric meter and main switch (see figure **5-16**).

5.4.4 Testing

Professional electricians perform the following tests to ensure the safety of the electrical system in a mobile home before power is connected, or to troubleshoot the electrical system.

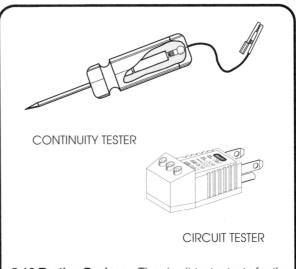

5-18 Testing Devices - *The circuit tester tests for the correct connection of the hot and neutral wires with the power on. The continuity tester tests whether or not a complete circuit exists. Continuity tests are performed with the power off.*

1. With the main switch off, test for continuity between each hot and neutral wire in the service box with the grounding bus bar. There should be no continuity between hot or neutral wires and grounding bus bar. The continuity tester is a small battery-powered flashlight that lights up when its terminals are attached to two metal surfaces that are connected together electrically (see figure **5-18**).

2. Using the continuity tester, check metal electrical boxes, metal ducts, the metal chassis, metal siding, roofing, and pipes for continuity to ground. The metal parts are connected together electrically at the factory and should be grounded through the grounding bus bar in the service panel box.

3. Insert a circuit tester (see figure **5-18**) into each outlet to check for the proper connection of the hot wire and neutral. The same tester will indicate whether the grounding plug is connected to ground. This test is performed with the power on.

4. Make sure that ground fault circuit interrupters (GFCIs) are connected to all bathroom and outdoor circuits. Test the GFCIs by pushing a button on the device. The breaker should trip when the button is pressed. (Older homes may not have GFCIs).

5. Check for power at all outlets and fixtures. This test can be performed with the power on using a circuit tester and a 120 volt test light or a light bulb. Or the test can be performed with the power off, using a continuity tester. During this test, all switches are tested for operation.

5.4.5 Special Safety Precautions

Heat tape, used to prevent pipe freezing, has caused many fires in mobile homes. Do not use lightweight, thermostatically-controlled heat tape. Use only shielded heat tape rated specifically for

PLUMBING AND ELECTRICAL

manufactured housing. Follow the installation instructions carefully.

Do not plug electric space heaters, irons, or other heating devices into lightweight extension cords designed for lamps (lamp cord). Electric space heaters and room air conditioners use most of the capacity of the circuits that they are plugged into. You might be able to plug a lamp or radio into the same circuit, but electric space heaters and room air conditioners should not share a circuit with appliances like toasters and refrigerators.

Some older mobile homes are equipped with aluminum wiring. Aluminum wiring may corrode and may also expand and contract enough to loosen connections. Old aluminum wiring may reach dangerously high temperatures when connected to large loads like space heaters. Avoid buying an older mobile home with aluminum wiring.

The panel box should be clearly marked with the areas of the home that each breaker or fuse protects. Adults and older children should know the location of the main electrical switch and the location of breakers or fuses for the various branch circuits so they can disconnect power in the event of an emergency.

GLOSSARY

Air changes at 50 pascals (ACH50) - The number of times that the complete volume of a home is exchanged for outside air when a blower door depressurizes the home to 50 pascals

Air infiltration barrier - A woven plastic sheet that stops almost all the air traveling through a building cavity, while allowing moisture to pass through the cavity.

Amp - A unit of measurement of the flow of electrical current.

Backdraft damper - A damper, installed near a fan, that allows air to flow in only one direction.

Belly - The bottom of the floor of a mobile home which is covered by the rodent barrier.

Beltrail - A piece of 3/4-inch thick lumber fastened to wall, floor, or ceiling framing at right angles across the framing members to provide extra strength and a fastening surface for siding, roofing, or flooring.

Bimetal element - A metal spring, lever, or disc made of two dissimilar metals that expand and contract at different rates as the temperature around them changes. This movement operates a switch in the control circuit of a heating or cooling device.

Blower door - A device composed of a fan, a removable panel, and gauges used to measure and locate air leaks.

Blowing wool - Insulation packaged in bags and intended to be blown into attics, walls, and floors.

Blowing machine - A machine with a powerful fan used to blow insulation through a tube into a building. It also has an agitator to break up the insulation which is compressed in bags.

Boot - A duct section that connects between a duct and a register or between round and square ducts.

Bowstring truss - A truss shaped like a bow, made of lightweight wood framing, used to support the weight of a mobile home roof.

Branch circuit - An electrical circuit used to power outlets and lights within a home.

Building cavities - The spaces inside walls, floors, and ceilings between the interior and exterior sheeting.

Cellulose insulation - Insulation made from newspaper or wood waste and treated with a fire retardant packaged in bags for blowing.

CFM50 - The number of cubic feet per minute of air flowing through the fan housing of a blower door when the house pressure is 50 pascals (0.2 inches of water). This figure is the most common and accurate way of comparing the airtightness of buildings that are tested using a blower door.

CFMn - The number of cubic feet of air flowing through a house from indoors to outdoors during typical, natural conditions. This figure can be roughly estimated using a blower door.

Chassis - The steel trailer that carries the weight of the mobile home.

Circuit breaker - A device that disconnects an electrical circuit from electricity when it senses an overload of current in the circuit.

Cladding - The covering over a building framework like siding, roofing, or flooring.

Combustion air - Air that chemically combines with a fuel during combustion to produce heat and flue gases, mainly carbon dioxide and water vapor.

GLOSSARY

Condenser - The outdoor, heat-transfer coil of an air conditioner that heats outdoor air when the refrigerant, inside it, condenses and releases heat.

Conduction - Heat flow through a solid object by vibration from molecule to molecule.

Countersink - A cone-shaped hole drilled by a special bit to allow a flat-head wood screw head to sit at or below the surface of the material where it is installed.

Crossmember - A structural steel piece that connects the main beams of a mobile home.

Crossover duct - A duct connecting the plenums and duct systems of the two halves of a double-section mobile home.

Density - The weight of a material divided by its volume, usually measured in pounds per cubic foot.

DOE - The United States Department of Energy

Draft booster - A small fan that helps to move combustion air into the firebox and combustion products out.

Envelope - The exterior walls, floor, and roof assembly of a mobile home. The building parts that actually separate the indoors from the outdoors.

Environmentally sensitive - A person who is highly sensitive to pollutants, often because of overexposure, is said to be environmentally sensitive.

Evaporative cooler - A device for cooling homes in dry climates that cools the incoming air by humidifying it.

Evaporator - The indoor, heat-transfer coil of an air conditioner that cools the surrounding air as the refrigerant inside the coil evaporates and absorbs heat.

Fan control - A bimetal thermostat that turns the furnace blower on and off as it senses the presence of heat.

Feeder wires - The wires connecting the electric meter and main switch with the main panel box indoors.

Fender washer - A large washer with a small hole that prevents a screw head from pulling through a soft material through which the screw is attached.

Foamboard - Plastic foam insulation manufactured most commonly in 4x8 foot sheets in thicknesses of 1/4 inch to 3 inches.

Footing - The part of a foundation system that actually transfers the weight of the building to the ground.

Footing base - The piece of ground underneath the footing which is compacted to provide adequate support and is designed to drain water away.

Frost line - The maximum depth of the soil where water will freeze during the coldest weather

Gypsum board - A common interior sheeting material for walls and ceilings made of gypsum rock powder packaged between two sheets of heavy building paper. Also called sheetrock, gyprock, or gypboard.

Heat anticipator - A very small electric heater in a thermostat that causes the thermostat to turn off before room temperature reaches the thermostat setting so that the house does not overheat from heat remaining in the furnace and ducts after the burner shuts off.

Heat rise - The number of degrees of temperature increase that air is heated as it is blown over the heat exchanger. Heat rise equals supply temperature minus return temperature.

GLOSSARY

High limit - A bimetal thermostat that turns the heating element of a furnace off if it senses a dangerously high temperature.

House pressure - The difference in pressure between the indoors and outdoors as measured by a gauge on the blower door when the blower door is operating.

HUD Code - The U.S. Department of Housing and Urban Development's standards for new mobile homes.

Humidistat - An automatic control that switches a fan, humidifier, or dehumidifier on and off.

I-beam - One of two steel beams shaped like 'I's that provide the main support for the mobile home and which are the main structural parts of the chassis or trailer.

Infiltration - The inflow of outdoor air into the indoors which is accompanied by an equal outflow of air from indoors to the outdoors.

J-rail - The metal strip that clamps a metal, mobile home roof down to the siding around the perimeter of the roof and also acts as a miniature rain gutter.

Jalousie windows - Windows that have multiple horizontal panes that allow the whole area of the window to be used for ventilation.

Jamb - The finished side or top piece of a window or door opening.

Joist - A horizontal wood framing member that supports a floor or ceiling.

Main beam - One of two steel beams shaped like 'I's that provide the main support for the mobile home and which are the main structural parts of the chassis or trailer.

Main panel box - The service box containing a main switch, and the fuses or circuit breakers located inside the home.

Manifold - A section of pipe with multiple openings.

Marriage wall - The joint between two sections of a double-section or triple-section home.

Mastic - A thick creamy substance used to seal seams and cracks in building materials.

Microclimate - A very localized climatic area, usually of a small site or habitat.

Mil - One one-thousandth of an inch.

Moisture diffusion - The flow of water vapor through materials going from a wetter area to a drier area.

Open-combustion heater - A heating device that takes its combustion air from the surrounding room air is called an open-combustion heater.

Orifice - A hole in a gas pipe where gas exits the pipe to be mixed with air in a burner before combustion in a heating device.

Outrigger - A triangular piece of structural steel that connects to the main beam and stretches to the outside edge of the wood floor for support.

Outward clinching staple - A staple driven by a special staple gun that will stitch belly paper together without wood backing (also called "stitch stapler").

Packaged air conditioner - An air conditioner, installed outdoors, that contains both the evaporator and the condenser and often heating equipment. It is connected to the home by supply and return air ducts.

Pascal - A unit of measurement of air pressure. (See Inch of water)

Perm - A measurement of how much water vapor a material will let pass through it per unit of time.

GLOSSARY

Pier - A short column of masonry or steel that provides support between the footing and the main beam.

Plate - A piece of lumber installed horizontally to which vertical studs in a wall frame are attached.

Plenum - The piece of ductwork that connects the furnace to the main supply duct.

Plumb - At a right angle to the earth's surface. Absolutely vertical.

Polybutylene - A plastic used for supply pipes in many mobile homes.

Polyvinyl chloride - A plastic used for moisture resistant flexible film and drain piping.

Polystyrene insulation - A rigid plastic foam insulation, usually white or blue in color.

Prime window - The main window installed on the outside wall. Not to be confused with a storm window.

R-value - A measurement of resistance to conduction heat flow. Single-pane windows have an R-value of about 1 and insulation materials have R-values of 2-6 per inch of thickness.

Radiant barrier - A foil or coating designed to reflect heat rays. Radiant barriers are not insulating materials.

Refrigerant - A special fluid used in air conditioners and heat pumps that heats air when it condenses from a gas to a liquid and cools air when it evaporates from a liquid to a gas.

Relay - An automatic, electrically-operated switch.

Retrofit - An energy conservation measure that is applied to an existing building. Also means the action of improving the thermal performance or maintenance of a building.

Return air - Air circulating back to the furnace from the house to be heated by the furnace and supplied to the rooms.

Rim joist - The outermost joist around the perimeter of the floor framing.

Rodent barrier - A rigid or flexible material that protects the bottom of the floor from animals at the home site and road dirt during transport. Same as underbelly material.

Roof cap - Insulation and roofing installed directly over the existing roof of the mobile home.

Room air conditioner - A unitary air conditioner installed through a wall or window which cools the room by removing heat from the room and releasing the heat outdoors.

Sash - A movable or stationary part of a window that frames a piece of glass.

Sealed-combustion heater - A heater that draws combustion air from outdoors and has a sealed exhaust system is called a sealed-combustion heater.

SERI - The Solar Energy Research Institute of Golden, Colorado, a national laboratory (now called the National Renewable Energy Laboratory or NREL).

Service wires - The wires coming from the utility transformer to the service equipment at the home.

Sequencer - A bimetal switch that turns on the elements of an electric furnace in sequence.

Service equipment - The electric meter and main switch usually located outside the home.

Service wires - The wires coming from the utility transformer to the service equipment at the home site.

GLOSSARY

Shading coefficient - A decimal describing how much solar energy is transmitted through a window opening. Clear glass is 1 and shaded glass is a decimal number less than 1.

Sheathing - A structural cladding, attached to the framing underneath siding and roofing of a building, that strengthens or insulates the walls or roof.

Sheetrock - Gypsum interior wallboard used to produce a smooth and level interior wall surface and to resist fire. *See also* Gypsum board.

Short circuit - A dangerous malfunction in an electrical circuit where electricity is flowing through conductors and into the ground without going through an electric load like a light or motor.

Sill - The bottom of a window or door frame.

Site - A location for setting up a mobile home.

Spline - A strip that, when inserted into a groove, holds a screen or plastic film in place on a frame.

Split-system air conditioner - An air conditioner that has the evaporator coil in the furnace and the condenser outdoors.

Stitch stapler - An outward clinch stapler used for fastening paper and cloth underbelly material to cloth or paper patches.

Strongback - A beam used as a stiffener usually in a roof or floor.

Stuffer - A flat flexible plate used to stuff insulation into wall cavities.

Supply air - Air that has been heated or cooled and is then moved through the ductwork and out the supply registers of a home.

Termination bar - A metal strip that clamps the rubber roof membrane at the edge of the roof and wall in a rubber roof installation.

Trim - Decorative wood that covers cracks around window and door openings and at the corners where walls meet floors and ceilings. Sometimes called molding.

Truss - A lightweight, rigid framework designed to be stronger than a solid beam of the same weight.

Underbelly - The bottom part of the mobile home floor as viewed from underneath the floor in the crawl space.

Vapor barrier - A material that blocks the passage of water vapor.

Ventilated walls - Wall systems in mobile homes that were intentionally vented to the outdoors to remove moisture.

Weatherization - The process of reducing energy consumption and increasing comfort in buildings by improving energy efficiency of the building.

Webbing - A reinforcing fabric used with mastics and coatings to prevent patches from cracking.

Weep holes - Holes drilled for the purpose of allowing water to drain out of an area in a building where it has accumulated.

APPENDIX A

BUSINESSES AND ORGANIZATIONS

MANUFACTURERS OF HEATING AND COOLING EQUIPMENT:

Coleman/Evcon Industries
310 North Mead
Wichita, Kansas 67219   316-832-6450

Nordyne Corporation
1801 Park 270 Drive
PO Box 46911
St. Louis, Missouri 63146-6911   314-878-6200

ORGANIZATIONS:

Florida Solar Energy Center
300 State Line Road
Cape Canaveral, Florida 32920   407-783-0300

Manufactured Housing Institute
1745 Jefferson Davis Highway
Arlington, VA 22202   703-979-6620

National Appropriate Technology Assistance Service (NATAS)
National Center for Appropriate Technology (NCAT)
PO Box 2525
Butte, Montana 59702   800-428-2525
                                   800-428-1718 (Montana)

National Council of States on Building Codes & Standards, Inc.
505 Hunter Park Drive, Suite 210
Herndon, VA 22076   703-437-0100

National Fire Protection Association
Batterymarch Park
Quincy, MA 02269   617-770-3000

National Foundation of Manufactured Home Owners
PO Box 33
Redmond, WA 98073   206-885-4650

Solar Energy Research Institute (SERI)
(now calledThe National Renewable Energy Laboratory, NREL
1617 Cole Boulevard
Golden, Colorado 80401   303-231-1000

U.S. Department of Housing and Urban Development
Manufactured Housing Division
451 Seventh St, SW
Washington, DC 20410   202-755-6920

APPENDIX B

FIRE SAFETY

Mobile home occupants suffer from many tragic fires every year. Fire prevention and safety should be a major concern of every household. The major causes of fires are:

1. Careless cooking,
2. Careless smoking,
3. Improper installation of heat tape on pipes,
4. Unsafe use of extension cords,
5. Improper installation of wood stoves,
6. Unsafe use of electric space heaters, and
7. Problems with electrical wiring

Since cooking fires are so common, every kitchen should have a container of baking soda clearly marked and accessible to use extinguish fires. To put out fires outside the kitchen, a pressurized 2.5-gallon fire extinguisher is probably best for fires involving wood and other building materials. A 5-pound ABC fire extinguisher is a good choice for an all purpose fire extinguisher for grease, wood and electrical fires. Locate the fire extinguisher near an outside door so the person using the fire extinguisher will not be caught between the fire and an exit.

Smoke alarms are designed to wake sleeping occupants in the event of a fire. Mobile homes should have at least one smoke detector in a common area adjacent to the bedrooms. If the bedrooms are not close together then there should be smoke detectors near each bedroom or group of bedrooms. Keep the smoke detector as far away from the kitchen as possible so that residents do not tamper with it to prevent the alarm from sounding during routine cooking. Test smoke detectors once a year to ensure that they are working.

Families should discuss and practice a fire escape plan. Each bedroom should have two exit routes, one through the bedroom door and one through a window. Some mobile home window units are hinged in their frames to facilitate fire escape. Others have enough area, when opened, to let a person out during a fire. Do not block a window exit and make sure that the window opens easily. Teach all family members how to operate the exit window. It is also important to discuss and practice opening and escaping through the windows to ensure escape during a fire. Some windows, like awning windows, may not provide a large enough opening to escape without breaking the window out. In this case the occupants should identify some large heavy object to break the window out for escape. Objects like wooden chairs and baseball bats will work well to break out windows.

Another important element for a fire escape plan is to establish a meeting place outside the home for occupants after escape. The meeting place will assure that everyone is accounted for and unnecessary panic will be avoided.

If you ever have to travel through a fire to escape, remember that it's cooler and safer to crawl along the floor away from the smoke which concentrates higher in the room. The smoke from most home fires is so toxic that several breaths are all it takes to produce serious injury or death.

APPENDIX C

SUGGESTIONS FOR MOVING MOBILE HOMES

1. Mobile homes are not designed to be moving vans. All major furniture and appliances should be removed from the home and shipped separately. Appliances like water heaters, furnaces, and built-in kitchen ranges, that were shipped with the home originally need not be removed.

2. Heavy items like books and dishes should be packed in boxes and moved separately. Any light-weight furnishings that are moved with the mobile home should be located near the hitch or axle.

3. Your home have the same number of axles as were originally present. Moving the home with fewer axles could bend the frame or cause tires to blow out.

4. Check tire pressure and condition. Make sure that the bearings in the axle are packed with grease. Ship at least two spare tires in good condition with the home.

5. Drain the water heater and make sure that it will not move. Strap it to the wall of its compartment, if necessary.

6. Remove swamp coolers and other unsecured roof protrusions and check roof fittings to ensure that they won't blow off in transit.

7. Remove top of toilet tank and place it in a safe location where it will not break.

8. Install a furring strip along the first row of asphalt shingles on the roof.

9. Repair the belly as described in Section 2.4.4, Repairs to the Floor Area, to prevent wind from tearing the underbelly.

10. Remove the skirting, tie the panels together, and ship them separately.

11. Disconnect anchors and secure loose strapping.

12. Close, lock, and wire doors shut so they don't pop open in transit.

13. Tape all drawers and cabinet doors shut.

14. Place wedges under both sides of interior doors to prevent them from swinging back and forth during transport.

15. Have gas lines, oil lines, electrical service, and air conditioning ducts disconnected by a qualified service person.

16. Cover halves of double-section homes with reinforced polyethylene sheeting. Carefully fasten the sheeting inside and outside. Bridge large gaps with lumber so that the sheeting will not flap excessively and tear.

17. If you are a home owner preparing for the move have all the preparation work you can do completed before the mover arrives.

18. Arrange for trip insurance either through the mover or through a local insurance agent.

19. Make sure that all necessary site work and foundation construction work is completed before delivery at the new site.

APPENDIX D

MAINTENANCE TIPS

1. Interior wood finishes can be restored by cleaning them with soap and water, drying the walls, and then treating the paneling and trim with an oil that protects and polishes the wood. Lemon oil or linseed oil work well for this purpose. Products, designed for furniture, that both clean and polish work well too.

2. Scratches and gouges in paneled walls can be filled and disguised by using colored putties or crayons available in lumber yards or hardware stores.

3. Waxing tile and linoleum floors protects them from water and makes them easier to clean.

4. Water condensation and odors can be reduced by opening windows and doors during mild weather and thoroughly ventilating the home.

5. Metal roofs should be coated with a reflective coating to prevent solar heat from degrading the waterproofing on the roof and overheating the home in the summer months. Clean your metal roof with a water hose once a year to remove dirt and enhance reflectivity.

6. If you remove exterior fixtures, like roof vents and windows, be sure to have the appropriate sealants like: putty tape, caulking, or roof cement ready when you reinstall or replace them. Apply caulking to the edge of all seams to prevent water penetration. Exterior seams around penetrations in the building envelope are a main area of water leakage.

7. Metal sidings should be washed and waxed like automotive finishes to preserve their finish and appearance. Most dirt can be removed by spraying the siding with water on a warm day, especially if the siding is waxed. Don't spray cold water on hot siding in the summer. If the home has been recently moved or if the wind drives dirt into the walls of the home, then you may have to use a mild soap and a soft brush to remove the dirt. Oil and grease can be removed with an automotive polishing compound but be careful not to remove too much paint.

8. Bare aluminum must be treated with a special primer before painting. Rust, on steel siding, must be sanded down to bare metal and primed with an automotive primer before painting.

9. Gouges and scratches in white fiberboard ceilings can be covered with chalk or white acrylic latex caulk. Holes and cracks in ceilings should be filled and sealed to prevent heated or cooled air from the living space from escaping into the attic. Smudges can be removed with an art gum eraser.

10. Water stains in white fiberboard or sheetrock can be repainted after you're sure that the source of the water damage is repaired. First paint the area with a mild bleach solution (1:4, bleach to water) to kill mold and other microbes and to whiten the area. You can paint after the area dries.

11. Dark surfaces or dirty surfaces on walls and roofs absorb more solar heat than light and shiny surfaces. If you want to stay cool in the summer, paint, wax, and wash your walls and roof. If you need sunglasses to be near your home on a sunny day — that's a good sign.

12. Avoid stirring up dirt around condensers and unitary air conditioners to minimize the dirt that is deposited on the condenser coil.

APPENDIX E

ENERGY COST INDEX CHART

Choosing Fuels

People decide to switch fuels or heating systems usually for economic reasons. They feel that their current heating system is costing too much money. Sometimes people feel that their existing system is insufficient and should be replaced. Or they are choosing a heating system for a new building. At the same time they wonder, "What fuel should I choose for my new heating system."

Useful Heat

Useful heat is the heat that reaches the living space providing comfort to the occupants of the space. Useful heat is always less than the potential heating value of the fuel because heat is wasted in the combustion process, in the heat transfer process, and in the delivery process. As the efficiency becomes less, the cost of useful heat becomes greater.

The energy cost index chart will help you to estimate the comparative cost of various fuels.

* The fuels are listed at the top of each column on the chart and an assumed seasonal heating efficiency is listed at the bottom of each column.
* The left side of the chart gives costs per one million Btus (A Btu or British thermal unit is roughly the amount of heat contained in a kitchen match).
* Each column contains a yardstick marked off in dollars or cents. Above each column is a ratio like $/MCF or ¢/KWH that will inform you of the units used on the yardstick.
* Natural gas, propane, and oil are assumed to have seasonal heating efficiencies of 70% which is characteristic of central heating systems which use ducts to distribute the heat. All the other fuels are assumed to be space heating systems without the distribution losses.

ENERGY COST INDEX ($/MMBTU)	Hardwood $/CORD	Softwood $/CORD	Wood Pellets $/TON	Electricity Heat Pump ¢/KWH	Electricity Resistance ¢/KWH	Natural Gas $/MCF	Propane $/GAL	Oil $/GAL
$30					10¢			$30
$28								$28
$26					9¢			$26
$24					8¢			$24
$22								$22
$20				10¢	7¢			$20
$18				9¢	6¢		$1.20	$18
$16				8¢			1.00	$1.60 / $16
$14				7¢	5¢			1.40 / $14
$12	$160	$120		6¢	4¢	$9 / 8	0.80	1.20 / $12
$10	140	100	$140	5¢		7		1.00 / $10
$8	120	80	120	4¢	3¢	6	0.60	0.80 / $8
$6	100 / 80	60	100 / 80	3¢		5 / 4	0.40	0.60 / $6
$4	60 / 40	40				3		$4
$2								$2
Efficiency	60%	60%	80%	150%	100%	70%	70%	70%

How to use this chart.

1. Find the columns for the fuels you wish to compare by looking at the tops of the columns where the fuel type is marked.
2. Locate the cost per unit of fuel on the yardstick in the columns and mark the yardsticks with an X to mark your local cost.
3. Draw lines parallel to the horizontal lines on the chart starting at the X on the yardstick and extending to the left until you intersect the left vertical axis of the chart.
4. Read the cost per million Btus where the lines you've drawn intersect the axis of the chart.

APPENDIX F

MOBILE HOME ENERGY RATING

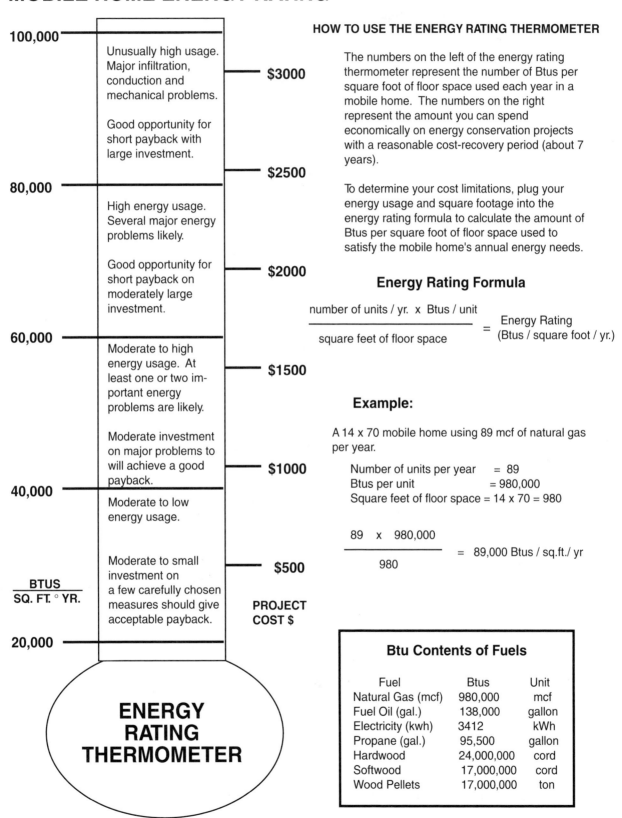

HOW TO USE THE ENERGY RATING THERMOMETER

The numbers on the left of the energy rating thermometer represent the number of Btus per square foot of floor space used each year in a mobile home. The numbers on the right represent the amount you can spend economically on energy conservation projects with a reasonable cost-recovery period (about 7 years).

To determine your cost limitations, plug your energy usage and square footage into the energy rating formula to calculate the amount of Btus per square foot of floor space used to satisfy the mobile home's annual energy needs.

Energy Rating Formula

$$\frac{\text{number of units / yr.} \times \text{Btus / unit}}{\text{square feet of floor space}} = \text{Energy Rating (Btus / square foot / yr.)}$$

Example:

A 14 x 70 mobile home using 89 mcf of natural gas per year.

Number of units per year = 89
Btus per unit = 980,000
Square feet of floor space = 14 x 70 = 980

$$\frac{89 \times 980{,}000}{980} = 89{,}000 \text{ Btus / sq.ft./ yr}$$

Btu Contents of Fuels

Fuel	Btus	Unit
Natural Gas (mcf)	980,000	mcf
Fuel Oil (gal.)	138,000	gallon
Electricity (kwh)	3412	kWh
Propane (gal.)	95,500	gallon
Hardwood	24,000,000	cord
Softwood	17,000,000	cord
Wood Pellets	17,000,000	ton

APPENDIX G

ESTIMATED COSTS OF MATERIALS AND LABOR FOR IMPROVEMENTS

The following prices are rough estimates made by the author in December of 1991. The prices are based on contacts with manufacturers, distributors and service companies and on the author's experience. When making purchases, especially major ones, always ask for a discount or try to negotiate a better price.

DESCRIPTION OF MATERIAL / IMPROVEMENT	MATERIAL COST	LABOR COST	TOTAL COST
Concrete/cu.yd. (27 cu.ft.)	$50-$70		
Crushed Gravel/cu.yd. (27 cu.ft.)	$7-$25		
Hollow-Core Concrete Block @ each	$1-$1.5		
Solid Concrete Block @ each	$1.25-$1.75		
Anchor @ each	$15-$45		
Earthquake Stabilization System			$2000-$5000
Polyethylene film 6 mil moisture barrier /sq.ft.	$0.03		
Vinyl or metal skirting/lin.ft.			$1.25-$2.00
R-11 fiberglass batts/sq.ft.	$0.14		
R-19 fiberglass batts/sq.ft.	$0.25		
Urethane foamboard .5 inch /sq.ft	$0.21		
Fabric or paper underbelly /sq.ft	$0.25-$0.35		
Insulate floor with blown fiberglass /sq.ft.	$0.30	$0.45	$0.75
Insulate sidewall with blown fiberglass /sq.ft.	$0.20	$0.65	$0.85
Add 5 inches of fiberglass to attic/sq.ft.	$0.25	$0.40	$0.65
Add 5 inches of beads to attic/sq.ft.	$0.30	$0.35	$0.65
Insulated rubber roof cap /sq.ft.	$1.50	$1.25	$2.75
Urethane roof cap /sq.ft.			$2.50
Metal roof cap /sq.ft.			$3-$4.50
Roof coating premium asphalt /5 gal.	$40		
Roof coating latex rubber /5 gal.	$140		
Replace mobile home door	$75	$40-$70	
Install house-type door w/ storm door	$235	$50-$90	
Repair and weatherize leaky difficult door	$25	$60	$85
Install window film on windows / sq.ft.			$3-$4

APPENDIX G

ESTIMATED COSTS OF MATERIALS AND LABOR FOR IMPROVEMENTS

DESCRIPTION OF MATERIAL / IMPROVEMENT	MATERIAL COST	LABOR COST	TOTAL COST
Install sun screen on windows /sq.ft.			$2-$4
Install glass interior storm window /sq.ft.			$3-$7
Install new vinyl or metal window @ each	$200	$75	$275
Awning - medium window @ each			$150-$300
Shade tree - 8 foot tall (depending on species)	$45-$100	$40	$85-$145
Automatic thermostat / electronic	$110	$35	$145
Install flame retention burner on oil furnace	$275	$200	$475
Replace gas 80+% efficient furnace	$950	$350	$1300
Service oil heating system (yearly)			$40-$100
Clean gas furnace fan and heat exchanger			$50-$100
Safe portable electric space heater	$55		
Wood Stove (mobile home approved)	$1000+		
Quality smoke alarm	$50		
Fire extinguisher (5 lb. ABC)	$55		
Energy-efficient room air conditioner	$400		
Evaporative cooler	$500	$125	$625
Energy-efficient central air conditioner	$1100	$600	$1700
Low-flow showerhead	$8		
Wrap water tank R-7-11 @ each	$12	$10	$22
Install new energy efficient water heater	$150	$100	$250
Sealed-combustion water heater	$300	$125	$425
Polybutylene pipe /lin.ft.	$0.80-$1.20		
Barbed polybutylene fitting @ each	$3		
Compression polybutylene fitting @ each	$3.50		
Coleman Blend-Air™ (fan powered ventilator)	$350	$200	$550
Intertherm VentilAire™ (fan powered ventilator)	$140	$160	$300
Intertherm VentilAire™ (no fan)	$50	$60	$110
Standard exhaust fan for bath or kitchen	$40	$70	$110
Energy-efficient medium-sized refrigerator	$600-$1200		

APPENDIX H

FOUNDATION DESIGN REFERENCE

H-1 APPROXIMATE WEIGHT OF THE COMPONENTS OF AN INSTALLED HOME

Component	Weight (lbs)	lbs/sq-ft
Home (Each Section)	14,000-28,000	13-25
Contents (Single-Section)	5,000-8,000	5-10
Contents (Double-Section)	10,000-14,000	3-8
Snow Load (Each Section)	12,000-50,000	20-40

H-1 The maximum weight of the home, which the foundation must support, is the sum of the home's weight, the weight of its contents, and the snow load prescribed for the region where it is located.

H-2 APPROXIMATE WEIGHT-BEARING CAPACITY OF SOILS

Soil Type	Weight-Bearing Capacity (PSF)
Massive Crystalline Bedrock	4000
Sedimentary and Foliated Rock	3000
Sandy Gravel and/or Gravel	2000
Silt or Clay Mixed with Sand or Gravel	1500
Mixtures of Sand, Silt, and Clay	1000

H-2 A pocket penetrometer, sold at engineering supply outlets, is the best tool for measuring the weight-bearing capacity of soil. However, you can estimate the weight-bearing capacity of the soil in pounds per square foot (psf) using this table, if you know the type of soil.

H-3 MINIMUM SIZES FOR SQAURE FOOTINGS

Footing Capacity	Soil Capacity			
	1000 PSF	1500 PSF	2000 PSF	4000 PSF
1000	12 x 12	10 x 10	8 x 8	6 x 6
2000	17 x 17	14 x 14	12 x 12	8 x 8
3000	21 x 21	17 x 17	15 x 15	10 x 10
4000	24 x 24	20 x 20	17 x 17	12 x 12
5000	27 x 27	22 x 22	19 x 19	13 x 13
6000	29 x 29	24 x 24	21 x 21	15 x 15
7000	32 x 32	26 x 26	22 x 22	16 x 16
8000	34 x 34	28 x 28	24 x 24	17 x 17
9000	36 x 36	29 x 29	25 x 25	18 x 18
10000	38 x 38	31 x 31	27 x 27	19 x 19
12000	42 x 42	34 x 34	29 x 29	21 x 21
14000	45 x 45	37 x 37	32 x 32	22 x 22
16000	48 x 48	39 x 39	34 x 34	24 x 24
18000	51 x 51	43 x 43	37 x 37	26 x 26

H-3 This table gives the dimensions of the minimum square-shaped footing for the weight it needs to support. The weight that a footing must support is specified by the manufacturer. See also H-4, next page.

APPENDIX H

FOUNDATION DESIGN REFERENCE

H-4 PIER/FOOTING TYPES AND CHARACTERISTICS

Type of Pier/Footing	Spacing	Capacity Range Per Pier/Footing	Applicability
Frame Without Perimeter	8'	3000-6000	Single and double-section homes in central and southern regions
Frame and Perimeter	8'	1500-4000	Usually required in northern and mountain regions. Often required by manufacturer for multi-section homes
Marriage Wall	10' 20'	2000-5000 3500-10000	Required on all multi-section homes
Roof Support Column	As needed	7000-18000	Required under marriage wall at specific locations on ends of large spans in open rooms

H-4 The weight that a footing and pier must support is specified by the manufacturer for the 4 different kinds of pier/footing combinations (see figure *1-7*, page 9). The amount of weight each footing must carry depends on the weight of the home, its contents, the snow load in the region, and the location of the pier/footing. Home furnishings like pianos and water beds require extra pier/footings directly beneath them.

H-5 MAXIMUM FROST PENETRATION MAP

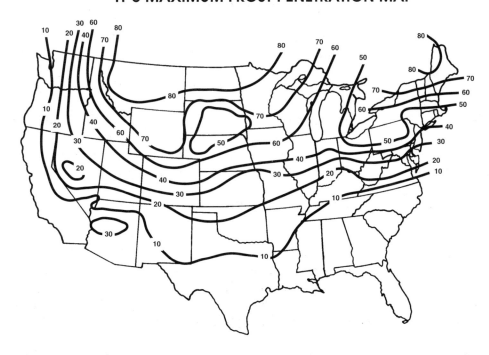

H-5 The above map shows the maximum frost penetration in the continental U. S. In unsupportive or wet soil where frost heaving is likely, the footing or its gravel base may need to extend all the way to the frost line. Footings underneath the home at the main beam and marriage line may only need to be 40% to 60% as deep as perimeter footings because the footings underneath the home are sheltered. Where the ground remains dry, footings may rest on undisturbed ground.

APPENDIX I

ENERGY PROJECT SUMMARY

The tables on these two pages summarize and list the energy projects discussed in this book. The energy projects are listed in order of priority, payback period, and level of difficulty. Labor is assumed to cost $20 per hour.

Level of Difficulty
1. Expert Technician
2. Skilled Technician
3. Skilled Homeowner
4. Average Homeowner

Equipment
A. Unique equipment
B. Rental Equipment
C. Specialiazed tools
D. Ordinary tools

Climate	PROJECT	METHOD / MATERIAL	SECTION	DIFF. EQUIP.	PAYBACK PERIOD
COLD CLIMATE	Sealing air leaks	Blower door guided air sealing	2.2.1	2A	0.5-1 yr.
	Domestic hot water	Wrap hot water tank	5.2.5	4D	0.5-1 yr.
		Low-flow showerhead	5.2.7	4D	0.5-1 yr.
	Heating system	Seal duct leaks	3.4.1	3D	0.5-1 yr.
		Change/clean filters/clean fan	3.4.2	4D	0.5-1 yr.
		Remove obstructions	3.4.1	4D	0.5-1 yr.
		Tune oil heater	3.2.2	2A	0.5-1 yr.
		Furnace operating temperatures	3.3.2	2D	0.5-1 yr.
	Setback Thermostat	Electronic	3.3.3	2D	1-2 yrs.
	Insulate roof	Roof cavity blown insulation	2.6.5	3B	3-6 yrs.
		Roof top insulation	2.6.4	2D	10-15 yrs.
	Insulate floor	Blow fiberglass or beads	2.4.5	3B	3-6 yrs.
	Insulate walls	Blow fiberglass and/or stuff batts	2.5.5.1	3BC	4-8 yrs.
		Remove siding and install batts	2.5.5.3	3D	6-10 yrs.
	Storm Windows	Interior, movable or fixed	2.8.3	2D	4-10 yrs.
	Landscaping	Siting changes	1.6.2	2D	4-10 yrs.
		Windbreaks	1.6.3	4D	7-10 yrs.
TEMPERATE CLIMATE	Sealing air leaks	Blower door guided air sealing	2.2.1	2A	0.5-1 yr.
	Domestic hot water	Wrap hot water tank	5.2.5	4D	0.5-1 yr.
		Low-flow showerhead	5.2.7	4D	0.5-1 yr.
	Heating system	Seal duct leaks	3.4.1	3D	0.5-1 yr.
		Change/clean filters/clean fan	3.4.2	4D	0.5-1 yr.
		Remove obstructions	3.4.1	4D	0.5-1 yr.
		Tune oil heater	3.2.2	1A	0.5-1 yr.
		Furnace operating temperatures	3.3.2	2D	0.5-1 yr.
	Cooling system	Seal duct leaks	3.4.1	3D	0.5-1 yr.
		Filters/obstructions	3.4.1	4D	0.5-1 yr.
		Adjust freon charge	4.4.1	1A	0.5-1 yr.
		Increase air flow	4.4.5	1A	0.5-1 yr.

APPENDIX I

PROJECT	METHOD / MATERIAL	SECTION	DIFF. EQUIP.	PAYBACK PERIOD	
Passive cooling	Ventilation and air circulation	4.3	4D	0.5-1 yr.	**TEMPERATE CLIMATE**
Setback thermostat	Electronic	3.3.3	2D	1-2 yrs.	
Insulate roof	Roof cavity blown insulation Roof top insulation	2.6.5 2.6.4	3B 2D	5-10 yrs. 15-30 yrs.	
Insulate floor	Blow fiberglass or beads	2.4.5	3B	6-12 yrs.	
Insulate walls	Blow fiberglass and/or stuff batts Remove siding and install batts	2.5.5 2.5.5.3	3BC 3D	6-12 yrs. 7-14 yrs.	
Landscaping	Vines and shade trees	1.6.3	4D	6-10 yrs.	
Storm windows	Interior, movable or fixed	2.8.3	2D	6-12 yrs.	
Shading	Shade screens, films and awnings	4.2	2D	5-20 yrs.	
Sealing air leaks	Blower door guided air sealing	2.2.1	2A	0.5-1 yr.	**HOT CLIMATE**
Domestic hot water	Wrap hot water tank Low-flow shower head	5.2.5 5.2.7	4D 4D	0.5-1 yr. 0.5-1 yr.	
Passive cooling	Ventilation and air circulation	4.3	4D	0.5-1 yr.	
Cooling system	Seal duct leaks Filters/obstructions Adjust freon charge Increase air flow	3.4.1 3.4.1 4.4.1 4.4.5	3D 4D 1A 1A	0.5-1yrs. 0.5-1 yr. 0.5-1 yr. 1-4 yrs.	
Setback thermostat	Electronic	3.3.3	2D	1-3 yrs.	
Heating system	Seal duct leaks Change/clean filters/clean fan Remove obstructions Tune oil heater Furnace operating temperatures	3.4.1 3.4.2 3.4.1 3.2.2 3.3.2	3D 4D 4D 1A 2D	0.5-1 yr. 0.5-1 yr. 0.5-1 yr. 1-3 yrs. 1-3 yrs.	
Landscaping	Vines and shade trees Site changes	1.5.3 1.6.2	4D 2D	0.5-1 yr. 2-8 yrs.	
Shading	Shade screens Window films Awnings	4.2.2 4.2.1 4.2.3	2D 2D 2D	3-6 yrs. 5-8 yrs. 8-12 yrs.	
Roof insulation	Roof cavity blown insulation Roof top insulation	2.6.5 2.6.4	3B 2D	5-10 yrs. 8-20 yrs.	

BIBLIOGRAPHY

Abrams, Donald. *Natural Cooling*. Knoxville, TN: Tennessee Valley Authority, n.d.

Chandra, Subrato, Philip W. Fairey III, and Michael M. Houston. *Cooling with Ventilation*. Golden, CO: Solar Energy Research Institute, December 1986.

Electric Space Heaters, Product Safety Fact Sheet No. 98. Washington, DC: Consumer Product Safety Commission, , 1984.

Fox, Jill and Rick Bond, eds. *Creative Home Landscaping*. San Ramon, CA: Ortho Books, 1987.

Home Owner's Manual. Atlanta, GA: Compliance Systems Publications, Inc., 1990.

Judkoff, R. et al. *Mobile Home Weatherization Measures: A Study of Their Effectiveness*. Golden, CO: Solar Energy Research Institute, 1988.

Judkoff, R. *Mobile Home Retrofits: CMFERT Phase II*: Golden, CO: Solar Energy Research Institute, 1990.

Knight, Paul and Larissa Rangelov. *Mobile Home Retrofit Handbook*. Chicago: University of Illinois at Chicago, Energy Resource Center, May 1985.

Manufactured Home Construction and Safety Standards. Washington, DC: U.S. Department of Housing and Urban Development, 1987.

Manufactured Housing Installation. Herndon, VA: National Council of States on Building Codes & Standards, 1987.

McKie, Clint A. *The Do's and Don'ts of Mobile Home Repairing*. Carlsbad, NM: Manufactured Housing Services, 1990.

Model Manufactured Home Installation Manual. Arlington, VA: Manufactured Housing Institute, 1990.

Moffat, A. Simon and Marc Schiler. *Landscape Design that Saves Energy*. New York: William Morrow & Co. Inc., 1981.

National Electrical Code - 1990. Quincy, MA: National Fire Protection Association, 1990.

1991 Garden Annual; Oxmoor House; Birmingham AL; 1991.

Permanent Foundations Guide for Manufactured Housing. Washington, DC: U.S. Department of Housing and Urban Development, 1989.

Porter, George N. *Installation Course*. Nasua, DE: Manufactured Housing Resources, 1990.

Shelton, Jay. *Jay Shelton's Solid Fuel Encyclopedia*. Charlotte, VT: Garden Way Publishers, 1983.

Wallis, Allan D. *Wheel Estate: The Rise and Fall of Mobile Homes*. New York, NY: Oxford University Press, 1991.

Wilson, Alex. *Consumer Guide to Home Energy Savings*. Berkeley, CA: Home Energy Magazine, 1991.

Weatherwise Gardening: How Best to Manage Sun, Wind, Shade, and Rain (West edition). San Ramon, CA: Ortho Books Division, 1974.

INDEX

A

Air Changes, *See* Natural Air Change Rate
Air Infiltration, *See* Air Leakage
Air Conditioners, 91, *See Also* Cooling; Fans
    central, 96
    packaged, 92
    room, 98
Air Leakage, 23, 27, 36, 65, 75, 76, 98, 99
Air Quality, Indoor, 24
American National Standards Institute
    mobile home construction standards, 3
Anchors, 13
ANSI, *See* American National Standards Institute
Assembly, 7
Attics, ventilation, 23, 25
Awnings, 87, 89, 90, 99

B

Backdraft Damper, 23, 24, *See Also* Fans
Belly
    insulation, 36, 39, 40
    repairs, 36, 37, 40
    wrap, 5, 6
Blower Doors, 28
    testing, 28, 76
Building Codes, 3
Building Permits, 4

C

Caulking, 28
Climate
    HUD zones, 3, 4
    map, 17
    microclimates, 18
Combustion Air, 16, 67, 68, 69, 82, 83, 85
Combustion Efficiency, 68, 69, 70, 72, 73, 80, 87
Condensation, *See Also* Moisture; Ventilation
    insulation, 22, 23
    roof cavity, 23, 49
    walls, 23, 42, 43
    windows, 63
Condenser, 91, 94, 95, 98
Controls, 71, 72, 73, 80, 81, 96, *See Also* Thermostats
Cooling, *See Also* Air Conditioning; Fans
    air conditioning, 91
    landscaping, 17, 20, 21, 87, 88
    radiant barriers, 35
    shading, 87, 88
Costs, *See* Appendix E & G
Crank Gear Box, 63

D

Decking, 4
Dehumidifiers, 23
Doors
    design and construction, 56, 57
    installation, 58, 59
    weatherstripping, 57
Draft Booster, 68, 72
Drainage, 10
Ducts, 4
    air leakage, 36, 75, 76, 77, 97
    branch, 77
    crossover, 77
    flexduct, 77, 78, 97
    inspection, 76
    location, 36, 37, 75, 76
    mastic, 77, 94
    sealants, 76, 77

E

Earthquakes, protection against, 13
Electric Furnaces, 79
Electrical
    controls, 71, 72, 81, 96
    grounding, 112
    heating, 79
    safety, 72
    systems, 111
Energy Conservation, *See Also* Weatherization
    effectiveness, 6, 28
    cost-effectiveness, 6, 44, 59, 62, 65, 90, 108
    HUD standards, 4, 37
    mobile home research, 5
    landscaping, 17
Energy Cost Index, *See* Appendix E
Energy Efficiency Ratio (EER), 100
Envelopes, 27
Evaporative Coolers, 100
    maintenance, 101
Evaporators
    cleaning, 94, 95, 98
    packaged air conditioners, 94
    room air conditioners, 98
    split system, 95, 96

INDEX

F

Fan Controls, 72, 73
Fans, 23, 87, *See Also* Air Conditioning; Cooling
    attic, exhaust, 23
    backdraft damper, 24
    bathroom, exhaust, 23
    ceiling, 90
    installation, 23
Fire Safety, *See* Appendix B
Flame Retention Burner, 69
Flexduct, 77, 78, 97
Floating Slab, 12
Floors, 4, 7, 35
    design and construction, 37
    insulation, 4, 36, 39, 41
    leveling, 38
    repairs, 36, 38, 39, 40
Florida Solar Energy Center, 7
Formaldehyde, 4, 25
Foundations, 8, *See Also* Appendix H
    ANSI standards, 9
    design, 9
    floating slab, 12
    HUD standards, 3, 9
    pier locations, 9
FSEC, *See* Florida Solar Energy Center
Furnaces
    atmospheric, 67
    cleaning, 68
    downflow, 67, 74
    efficiency, 69
    electric, 79
    forced draft, 68
    natural gas, 68, 72
    oil burning, 69, 72
    propane, 68, 72
    service, 70
    tune-ups, 6

G

Gas Furnaces, 68, 72
Ground Covers, 15, 39

H

Heat Anticipator, 71
Heat Ducts, *See* Ducts
Heat Exchanger, 78
Heat Loss, 6, 59
Heat Tape, 114
Heat Pumps, 81

Heating Seasonal Performance Factor (HSPF), 81
Heating Systems, 67
    air circulation systems, 74
    cleaning, 78
    controls, 71, 72
    electric, 79
    forced air, 74
    safety switches, 72
    thermostats, 71
    zone, 82
HSPF, *See* Heating Season Performance Factor
HUD, *See* U.S. Dept. of Housing and Urban Development

I

Installation,
    anchors, 13
    home orientation, 17, 18
    leveling, 14
    procedures, 14
Insulation, 4, 30
    belly, 5, 6, 36, 39, 40
    blowing, 34, 40, 41, 44, 53, 54,
    cellulose blowing wool, 31, 33, 49
    chimney, 49, 50, 51
    density, 32
    fiberglass batts, 31, 32, 39, 44, 45, 46, 49, 50
    fiberglass blowing wool, 31, 32, 39
    floors, 4, 39
    HUD standards, 4, 37
    mineral (rock) blowing wool, 31
    pipe, 107
    polystyrene beads, 31, 33, 39, 49, 50, 54
    polystyrene beadboard, 31, 33, 39, 50
    R-values, 31
    roof cap, 5, 50
    roof cavity, 53
    roof insulation, 7, 48
    skirting, 5, 6, 15, 37
    stuffing fiberglass batts, 44, 46
    urethane foam board, 31, 33, 39
    walls, 5, 6, 42, 43
    water heater, 107

INDEX

L

Landscaping, 17
Leveling
    mobile homes, 14, 55
    floors, 38

M

Maintenance, *See* Appendix D
Manufactured Housing, 2, *See Also* Mobile Homes
Manufactured Housing Institute, 3, 9
Mastic, Duct, 77
Mobile Home Manufacturers Association, 2, 3
Mobile Homes
    assembly, 7
    construction, 4, 7, 8
    construction standards, 3
    energy conservation, 5
    history, 2
    installation guidelines, 3, 9, 14
    insulation, 5, 30
    leveling, 14, 55
    orientation, 17, 19
    sizes, 8
Moisture, 22
    air circulation, 31
    ceiling, 22
    foundations, 9
    reducing, 24
    roof cavities, 48, 49, 52
    walls, 22, 23, 42, 43
    windows, 63
Moving, *See* Appendix C

N

NCAT, *See* National Center for Appropriate Technology
National Center for Appropriate Technology, 6, 82
Natural Air Change Rate, 29, 30, 31

O

Oil Burning Furnaces, 69, 72

P

Perimeter Drain System, 10
Piers, 9
Pipes
    insulation, 107
    polybutylene, 109
Plants, 21, 88
Plumbing, 108
    repairs, 110, 111
Propane Furnaces, 68, 72

R

Radiant Barriers, 35
R-Values, 31, 32
Refrigerant, 92
Refrigerators, 102
Registers, 78, 97
Repairs, 1, 2
    belly, 36, 37
    floors, 36, 38
    foundation, 15
    plumbing, 110, 111
    roof, 54, 55
    walls, 43
    windows, 63, 64
Reset
    electric water heater, 106
    oil burner, 70
Return air, 74
    ceiling, 76
    floor, 76
Rodent Barrier, 4, 37, 40
Roof Caps
    insulated rubber, 50, 51
    metal, 53
    sprayed urethane, 52
Roof Coatings
    asphalt/aluminum, 35, 55
    latex rubber, 55
Roof Rumble, 56
Roofs
    chimneys, 49, 50, 51
    design and construction, 48, 49, 52
    fire safety, 49
    insulated rubber roof cap, 50, 51
    insulation, 48
    metal, 48, 49, 50, 52
    moisture, 48, 49, 52
    repairs, 54, 55
    urethane roof cap, 52
Rumble Washers, 56

S

Safety, *See Also* Fire Safety
    leveling a mobile home, 14
    manufactured home construction and safety standards, 3
    roof insulation, 49
    space heaters, 82, 114
    wiring, 114
    wood heat, 83

INDEX

SERI, *See* Solar Energy Research Institute
Set-up, *See* Installation
Shade and Shading, 20, 21, 87
Shading Devices, 87, 88
Showerheads, low-flow, 107
Siding, 4
Silicone
    caulk, 58, 65, 77
    tube weatherstrip, 56
Skirting, 5, 6, 15, 37
Site preparation, 10
    drainage, 10
    foundations, 8
    ground covers, 15
    moisture, 9
Solar Energy Research Institute, 5, 27
Space Heaters, 82, 114
Storm Windows, 60, 61, 633
Sunscreens, 21, 87, 89

T

Thermostats
    automatic, 73
    bimetal controls, 71
    location, 72
    mercury switch, 71
    snap-disc, 71, 73
    two-stage, 81, 96
Torsion Rod Holder, 63
Trees, Shade, 17, 20, 87
Trellis, 88
Trusses, Bowstring, 4, 48

U

Underbelly, 36, 37
Undercarriage, construction, 4
U.S. Dept. of Housing and Urban
  Development
    climate zone map, 3
    foundation design manual, 3, 9
    heating equipment standards, 67, 85
    insulation standards, 5
    mobile home construction code, 3, 4

V

Vapor Barriers, 4, 22, 47
Ventilation, 22
    active systems, 24, 25
    fans, 90
    natural, 20, 90
    passive systems, 24
    walls, 22

W

Walls
    blowing insulation, 44
    design and construction, 41
    inspection, wall cavity, 42
    insulation, 43
    repairs, 43
    stuffing insulation, 44, 45, 46
    ventilation, 22, 23
Water Heaters
    cleaning, 106
    electric, 105
    gas, 103
    insulation, 107
    maintenance, 105
    propane, 103
    sealed combustion, 104
Water Heating Systems, 103
Weatherization
    cost-effectiveness, 1, 6, 59, 62, 65
    costs, Appendix G
    effectiveness, 5, 6, 44
    when to weatherize, 1
Weatherstrip, 58
    compression, 66
    pile, 64
    vinyl, 58
    silicone, 56
    tube, 58
    v-strip, 57, 58
Weatherstripping, 28, 56, 57, 58, 64
Window Films, 62, 87, 88
    acrylic window film, 61, 62
Window Shades, 87
Windows, 59
    awning, 62, 63, 64
    condensation, 63
    installation, 65, 66
    jalousie, 60, 64
    prime, 60
    repairs, 63, 64
    sliding, 60, 61, 64
    storm, 60, 61, 63
    thermopane, 65
Wood Stoves, 84

Z

Zone Cooling, 98
Zone Heating, 82, 83

Saturn Resource Management Order Form

PUBLICATION TITLE: ☐ YOUR HOME COOLING ENERGY GUIDE $12.50
(please check)   ☐ YOUR MOBILE HOME ENERGY AND REPAIR GUIDE $15.95
                                   (second edition)

From: Name: _____
        Title: _____
        Company: _____
        Address: _____
        City: _____ State: _____ Zip: _____

Please send _____ copies YOUR MOBILE HOME ENERGY AND REPAIR GUIDE at $_____ for a total of $_____
Please send _____ copies YOUR HOME COOLING GUIDE at $_____ for a total of $_____

☐ **Check or money order enclosed**   We pay shipping on prepaid orders
☐ **Charge my VISA / Mastercard #** _____ **Expiration Date:** _____
   Signature: _____ Date: _____

ORDER BY FAX   (406) 442-1316

Fold this flap first   Fold this flap first

Staple Check Here

Fold this flap second   Fold this flap second

SATURN RESOURCE MANAGEMENT
Publishing, Training, Research
Full Service Technical Communications

BUSINESS REPLY MAIL
FIRST CLASS MAIL   PERMIT NO. 41   HELENA, MONTANA

POSTAGE WILL BE PAID FOR BY ADDRESSEE

NO POSTAGE
NECESSARY
IF MAILED
IN THE
UNITED STATES

SATURN RESOURCE MANAGEMENT
324 FULLER AVENUE, S-8
HELENA, MT 59601-9984